FIELD AND HEDGEROW

D0130210

Field and Hedgerow

The Last Essays of
RICHARD JEFFERIES

Collected by his Widow

Oxford New York
OXFORD UNIVERSITY PRESS
1982

Oxford University Press, Walton Street, Oxford OX2 6DP

London Glasgow New York Toronto
Delhi Bombay Calcutta Madras Karachi
Kuala Lumpur Singapore Hong Kong Tokyo
Nairobi Dar es Salaam Cape Town
Melbourne Auckland

and associates in
Beirut Berlin Ibadan Mexico City Nicosia

First published 1889
First issued as an Oxford University Press paperback 1982

All rights reserved. No part of this publication may be reproduced,
stored in a retrieval system, or transmitted, in any form or by any means,
electronic, mechanical, photocopying, recording, or otherwise, without
the prior permission of Oxford University Press

This book is sold subject to the condition that it shall not, by way
of trade or otherwise, be lent, re-sold, hired out or otherwise circulated
without the publisher's prior consent in any form of binding or cover
other than that in which it is published and without a similar condition
including this condition being imposed on the subsequent purchaser

British Library Cataloguing in Publication Data
Jefferies, Richard
Field and Hedgerow. — (Oxford paperbacks)
1. Natural history — Great Britain — 19th
century — Addresses, essays, lectures
I. Title
574.941 QH138.A1
ISBN 0-19-281355-2

Library of Congress Cataloging in Publication Data
Jefferies, Richard, 1848-1887.
Field and hedgerow.
Reprint. Originally published: London:
Longmans, Green, 1889.
1. Natural history — England — Addresses, essays,
lectures. 2. England — Description and travel —
1801–1900 — Addresses, essays, lectures.
I. Jefferies, J. Baden, Mrs. II. Title.
QH138. A1J43 1982 508.42 82-2262
ISBN 0-19-281355-2 (pbk.) AACR2

Printed in Great Britain by
Richard Clay (The Chaucer Press) Ltd
Bungay, Suffolk

CONTENTS.

	PAGE
HOURS OF SPRING	I
NATURE AND BOOKS	19
THE JULY GRASS	37
WINDS OF HEAVEN	41
THE COUNTRY SUNDAY	50
THE COUNTRY-SIDE: SUSSEX	76
SWALLOW-TIME	94
BUCKHURST PARK	102
HOUSE-MARTINS	110
AMONG THE NUTS	112
WALKS IN THE WHEAT-FIELDS	121
JUST BEFORE WINTER	157
LOCALITY AND NATURE	167
COUNTRY PLACES	173
FIELD WORDS AND WAYS	187
COTTAGE IDEAS	192
APRIL GOSSIP	200

	PAGE
SOME APRIL INSECTS	204
THE TIME OF YEAR	209
MIXED DAYS OF MAY AND DECEMBER	215
THE MAKERS OF SUMMER	220
STEAM ON COUNTRY ROADS	230
FIELD SPORTS IN ART: THE MAMMOTH HUNTER	240
BIRDS' NESTS	250
NATURE IN THE LOUVRE	255
SUMMER IN SOMERSET	267
AN ENGLISH DEER-PARK	287
MY OLD VILLAGE	311

FIELD AND HEDGEROW.

HOURS OF SPRING.

IT is sweet on awaking in the early morn to listen to the small bird singing on the tree. No sound of voice or flute is like to the bird's song; there is something in it distinct and separate from all other notes. The throat of woman gives forth a more perfect music, and the organ is the glory of man's soul. The bird upon the tree utters the meaning of the wind—a voice of the grass and wild flower, words of the green leaf; they speak through that slender tone. Sweetness of dew and rifts of sunshine, the dark hawthorn touched with breadths of open bud, the odour of the air, the colour of the daffodil—all that is delicious and beloved of spring-time are expressed in his song. Genius is nature, and his lay, like the sap in the bough from which he sings, rises without thought. Nor is it necessary that it should be a song; a few short notes in the sharp spring morning are sufficient to stir the heart. But yesterday the least of them all came to a bough by my window, and in his call I heard the sweet-briar wind rushing over the young grass. Refulgent fall the golden rays of the sun; a minute only, the clouds cover him and the hedge is dark. The bloom of the gorse is shut like a book ; but it is there—a few hours of warmth and the covers will fall open. The meadow is bare, but in a little while the heart-shaped celandine leaves will come in their accustomed place. On the pollard willows the long wands are yellow-ruddy in the passing gleam of sunshine, the first colour of spring appears in their bark. The delicious wind rushes among them and they bow and rise ; it touches the top of the dark pine that looks in the sun the same now as in summer ; it lifts and swings the arching trail of bramble ; it dries and crumbles the earth in its fingers ; the hedge-sparrow's feathers are fluttered as he sings on the bush.

I wonder to myself how they can all get on without me—how they manage, bird and flower, without me to keep the calendar for them. For I noted it so carefully and lovingly, day by day, the seed-leaves on the mounds in the sheltered places that come so early, the pushing up of the young grass, the succulent dandelion, the coltsfoot on the heavy, thick clods, the trodden chickweed despised at the foot of the gate-post, so common and small, and yet so dear to me. Every blade of grass was mine, as though I had planted it separately. They were all my pets, as the roses the lover of his garden tends so faithfully. All the grasses of the meadow were my pets, I loved them all ; and perhaps that was why I never had a 'pet,' never cultivated a flower, never kept a caged bird, or any creature. Why keep pets when every wild free hawk that passed overhead in the air was mine ? I joyed in his swift, careless flight, in the throw of his pinions, in his rush over the elms and miles of woodland ; it was happiness to see his unchecked life. What more beautiful than the sweep and curve of his going through the azure sky ? These were my pets, and all the grass. Under the wind it seemed to dry and become grey, and the starlings running to and fro on the surface that did not sink now stood high above it and were larger. The dust that drifted along blessed it and it grew. Day by day a change ; always a note to make. The moss drying on the tree trunks, dog's-mercury stirring under the ash-poles, bird's-claw buds of beech lengthening ; books upon books to be filled with these things. I cannot think how they manage without me.

To-day through the window-pane I see a lark high up against the grey cloud, and hear his song. I cannot walk about and arrange with the buds and gorse-bloom ; how does he know it is the time for him to sing ? Without my book and pencil and observing eye, how does he understand that the hour has come ? To sing high in the air, to chase his mate over the low stone wall of the ploughed field, to battle with his high-crested rival, to balance himself on his trembling wings outspread a few yards above the earth, and utter that sweet little loving kiss, as it were, of song—oh, happy, happy days ! So beautiful to watch as if he were my own, and I felt it all ! It is years since I went out amongst them in the old fields, and saw them in the green corn ; they must be dead, dear little things, by now. Without me to tell him, how does this lark to-day that I hear through the window know it is his hour ?

The green hawthorn buds prophesy on the hedge ; the reed pushes up in the moist earth like a spear thrust through a shield ; the eggs of the starling are laid in the knot-hole of the pollard elm—common eggs, but within each a speck that is not to be found in the cut diamond of two hundred carats—the dot of protoplasm, the atom of life. There was one row of pollards where they always began laying first. With a big stick in his beak

the rook is blown aside like a loose feather in the wind ;
he knows his building-time from the fathers of his house
—hereditary knowledge handed down in settled course :
but the stray things of the hedge, how do they know ?
The great blackbird has planted his nest by the ash-stole,
open to every one's view, without a bough to conceal it
and not a leaf on the ash—nothing but the moss on the
lower end of the branches. He does not seek cunningly
for concealment. I think of the drift of time, and I see
the apple bloom coming and the blue veronica in the
grass. A thousand thousand buds and leaves and
flowers and blades of grass, things to note day by day,
increasing so rapidly that no pencil can put them down
and no book hold them, not even to number them—and
how to write the thoughts they give ? All these without
me—how can they manage without me ?

For they were so much to me, I had come to feel that
I was as much in return to them. The old, old error :
I love the earth, therefore the earth loves me—I am her
child—I am Man, the favoured of all creatures. I am
the centre, and all for me was made.

In time past, strong of foot, I walked gaily up the
noble hill that leads to Beachy Head from Eastbourne,
joying greatly in the sun and the wind. Every step
crumbled up numbers of minute grey shells, empty and
dry, that crunched under foot like hoar-frost or fragile
beads. They were very pretty ; it was a shame to crush
them—such vases as no king's pottery could make.
They lay by millions in the depths of the sward, and I
thought as I broke them unwillingly that each of these
had once been a house of life. A living creature dwelt
in each and felt the joy of existence, and was to itself all
in all—as if the great sun over the hill shone for it, and
the width of the earth under was for it, and the grass

and plants put on purpose for it. They were dead, the whole race of them, and these their skeletons were as dust under my feet. Nature sets no value upon life neither of minute hill-snail nor of human being.

I thought myself so much to the earliest leaf and the first meadow orchis—so important that I should note the first zee-zee of the titlark—that I should pronounce it summer, because now the oaks were green ; I must not miss a day nor an hour in the fields lest something should escape me. How beautiful the droop of the great brome-grass by the wood ! But to-day I have to listen to the lark's song—not out of doors with him, but through the window-pane, and the bullfinch carries the rootlet fibre to his nest without me. They manage without me very well ; they know their times and seasons—not only the civilised rooks, with their libraries of knowledge in their old nests of reference, but the stray things of the hedge and the chiffchaff from over sea in the ash wood. They go on without me. Orchis flower and cowslip—I cannot number them all—I hear, as it were, the patter of their feet—flower and bud and the beautiful clouds that go over, with the sweet rush of rain and burst of sun glory among the leafy trees. They go on, and I am no more than the least of the empty shells that strewed the sward of the hill. Nature sets no value upon life, neither of mine nor of the larks that sang years ago. The earth is all in all to me, but I am nothing to the earth : it is bitter to know this before you are dead. These delicious violets are sweet for themselves ; they were not shaped and coloured and gifted with that exquisite proportion and adjustment of odour and hue for me. High up against the grey cloud I hear the lark through the window singing, and each note falls into my heart like a knife.

Now this to me speaks as the roll of thunder that cannot be denied—you must hear it ; and how can you shut your ears to what this lark sings, this violet tells, this little grey shell writes in the curl of its spire ? The bitter truth that human life is no more to the universe than that of the unnoticed hill-snail in the grass should make us think more and more highly of ourselves as human—as men—living things that think. We must look to ourselves to help ourselves. We must think ourselves into an earthly immortality. By day and by night, by years and by centuries, still striving, studying, searching to find that which shall enable us to live a fuller life upon the earth—to have a wider grasp upon its violets and loveliness, a deeper draught of the sweet-briar wind. Because my heart beats feebly to-day, my trickling pulse scarcely notating the passing of the time, so much the more do I hope that those to come in future years may see wider and enjoy fuller than I have done ; and so much the more gladly would I do all that I could to enlarge the life that shall be then. There is no hope on the old lines—they are dead, like the empty shells ; from the sweet delicious violets think out fresh petals of thought and colours, as it were, of soul.

Never was such a worshipper of earth. The commonest pebble, dusty and marked with the stain of the ground, seems to me so wonderful ; my mind works round it till it becomes the sun and centre of a system of thought and feeling. Sometimes moving aside the tufts of grass with careless fingers while resting on the sward, I found these little pebble-stones loose in the crumbly earth among the rootlets. Then, brought out from the shadow, the sunlight shone and glistened on the particles of sand that adhered to it. Particles adhered to my skin—thousands of years between finger and thumb, these atoms of quartz, and sunlight shining all that time, and flowers blooming and life glowing in all, myriads of living things, from the cold still limpet on the rock to the burning, throbbing heart of man. Sometimes I found them among the sand of the heath, the sea of golden brown surging up yellow billows six feet high about me, where the dry lizard hid, or basked, of kin, too, to old time. Or the rush of the sea wave brought them to me, wet and gleaming, up from the depths of what unknown Past? where they nestled in the root crevices of trees forgotten before Egypt. The living mind opposite the dead pebble—did you ever consider the strange and wonderful problem there? Only the thickness of the skin of the hand between them. The chief use of matter is to demonstrate to us the existence of the soul. The pebble-stone tells me I am a soul because I am not that that touches the nerves of my hand. We are distinctly two, utterly separate, and shall never come together. The little pebble and the great sun overhead—millions of miles away: yet is the great sun no more distinct and apart than this which I can touch. Dull-surfaced matter, like a polished mirror, reflects back thought to thought's self within.

I listened to the sweet-briar wind this morning; but for weeks and weeks the stark black oaks stood straight out of the snow as masts of ships with furled sails frozen and ice-bound in the haven of the deep valley. Each was visible to the foot, set in the white slope, made individual in the wood by the brilliance of the background. Never was such a long winter. For fully two months they stood in the snow in black armour of iron bark unshaken, the front rank of the forest army that would not yield to the northern invader. Snow in broad flakes, snow in semi-flakes, snow raining down in frozen specks, whirling and twisting in fury, ice raining in small shot of frost, howling, sleeting, groaning ; the ground like iron, the sky black and faintly yellow -- brutal colours of despotism—heaven striking with clenched fist. When at last the general surface cleared, still there remained the trenches and traverses of the enemy, his ramparts drifted high, and his roads marked with snow. The black firs on the ridge stood out against the frozen clouds, still and hard ; the slopes of leafless larches seemed withered and brown ; the distant plain far down gloomy with the same dull yellowish blackness. At a height of seven hundred feet the air was sharp as a scythe—a rude barbarian giant wind knocking at the walls of the house with a vast club, so that we crept sideways even to the windows to look out upon the world. There was everything to repel—the cold, the frost, the hardness, the snow, dark sky and ground, leaf-lessness ; the very furze chilled and all benumbed. Yet the forest was still beautiful. There was no day that we did not, all of us, glance out at it and admire it, and say something about it. Harder and harder grew the frost, yet still the forest-clad hills possessed a something that drew the mind open to their largeness and grandeur. Earth is always beautiful—always. Without colour, or leaf, or sunshine, or song of bird and flutter of butterfly's wing ; without anything sensuous, without advantage or gilding of summer—the power is ever there. Or shall we not say that the desire of the mind is ever there, and *will* satisfy itself, in a measure at least, even with the barren wild ? The heart from the moment of its first beat instinctively longs for the beautiful ; the means we possess to gratify it are limited—we are always trying to find the statue in the rude block. Out of the vast block of the earth the mind endeavours to carve itself loveliness, nobility, and grandeur. We strive for the right and the true: it is circumstance that thrusts wrong upon us.

One morning a labouring man came to the door with a spade, and asked if he could dig the garden, or try to, at the risk of breaking the tool in the ground. He was starving; he had had no work for two months; it was just six months, he said, since the first frost started the winter. Nature and the earth and the gods did not trouble about *him*, you see; he might grub the rock-frost ground with his hands if he chose—the yellowish black sky did not care. Nothing for man! The only good he found was in his fellow-men; they fed him after a fashion—still they fed him. There was no good in anything else. Another aged man came once a week regularly; white as the snow through which he walked. In summer he worked; since the winter began he had had no employment, but supported himself by going round to the farms in rotation. They all gave him a trifle—bread and cheese, a penny, a slice of meat—something; and so he lived, and slept the whole of that time in outhouses wherever he could. He had no home of any kind. Why did he not go into the workhouse? ' I be afeared if I goes in there they'll put me with the rough uns, and very likely I should get some of my clothes stole.' Rather than go into the workhouse he would totter round in the face of the blasts that might cover his weak old limbs with drift. There was a sense of dignity and manhood left still; his clothes were worn, but clean and decent; he was no companion of rogues; the snow and frost, the straw of the outhouses, was better than that. He was struggling against age, against nature, against circumstance; the entire weight of society, law, and order pressed upon him to force him to lose his self-respect and liberty. He would rather risk his life in the snowdrift. Nature, earth, and the gods did not help him; sun and stars, where were they? He knocked at the doors of the farms and found good in man only—not in Law or Order, but in individual man alone.

The bitter north wind drives even the wild fieldfare to the berries in the garden hedge; so it drives stray human creatures to the door. A third came—an old gipsy woman—still stout and hearty, with green fresh brooms to sell. We bought some brooms—one of them was left on the kitchen floor, and the tame rabbit nibbled it; it proved to be heather. The true broom is as green and succulent in appearance in January as June. She would see the 'missis.' 'Bless you, my good lady, it be weather, bean't it? I hopes you'll never know what it be to want, my good lady. Ah, well, you looks good-tempered if you don't want to buy nothing. Do you see if you can't find me an old body, now, for my girl—now do'ee try; she's confined in a tent on the common—nothing but one of our tents, my good lady—that's true—and she's doing jest about well' (with briskness and an air of triumph), 'that she is! She's got twins, you see, my lady, but she's all right, and as well as can be. She wants to get up; and she says to me, "Mother, do'ee try and get me a body; 'tis hard to lie here abed and be well enough to get up, and be obliged to stay here because I've got nothing but a bedgown." For you see, my good lady, we managed pretty well with the first baby; but the second bothered us, and we cut up all the bits of things we could find, and there she ain't got nothing to put on. Do'ee see if 'ee can't find her an old body.' The common is an open piece of furze and heath at the verge of the forest; and here, in a tent just large enough to creep in, the gipsy woman had borne twins in the midst of the snow and frost. They could not make a fire of the heath and gorse even if they cut it, the snow and whirling winds would not permit. The old gipsy said if they had little food they could not do without fire, and they were compelled to get coke and coal somehow—apologising for such a luxury. There was no whining—not a bit of it; they were evidently quite contented and happy, and the old woman proud of her daughter's hardihood. By-and-by the husband came round with straw beehives to sell, and cane to mend chairs—a strong, respectable-looking man. Of all the north wind drove to the door, the outcasts were the best off—much better off than the cottager who was willing to break his spade to earn a shilling; much better off than the white-haired labourer, whose strength was spent, and who had not even a friend to watch with him in the dark hours of the winter evening—not even a fire to rest by. The gipsy nearest to the earth was the best off in every way; yet not even for primitive man and woman did the winds cease. Broad flakes of snow drifted up against the low tent, beneath which the babes were nestling to the breast. Not even for the babes did the snow cease or the keen wind rest; the very fire could scarcely struggle against it. Snow-rain and ice-rain; frost-formed snow-granules, driven along like shot, sting-ing and rattling against the tent-cloth, hissing in the fire; roar and groan of the great wind among the oaks of the forest. No kindness to man, from birth-hour to ending; neither earth, sky, nor gods care for him, innocent at the mother's breast. Nothing good to man but man. Let man, then, leave his gods and lift up his ideal beyond them.

Something grey and spotted and puffy, not unlike a

toad, moved about under the gorse of the garden hedge one morning, half hidden by the stalks of old grasses. By-and-by it hopped out—the last thrush, so distended with puffed feathers against the frost as to be almost shapeless. He searched about hopelessly round the stones and in the nooks, all hard and frostbound ; there was the shell of a snail, dry and whitened and empty, as was apparent enough even at a distance. His keen eye must have told him that it was empty ; yet such was his hunger and despair that he took it and dashed it to pieces against a stone. Like a human being, his imagination was stronger than his experience ; he tried to persuade himself that there might be something there ; hoping against hope. Mind, you see, working in the bird's brain, and overlooking facts. A mere mechanism would have left the empty and useless shell untouched— would have accepted facts at once, however bitter, just as the balance on the heaviest side declines immediately, obeying the fact of an extra grain of weight. The bird's brain was not mechanical, and therefore he was not wholly mastered by experience. It was a purely human action—just what we do ourselves. Next he came across to the door to see if a stray berry still remained on a creeper. He saw me at the window, and he came to the window—right to it—and stopped and looked full at me some minutes, within touch almost, saying as plainly as could be said, ' I am starving—help me.' I never before knew a thrush make so unmistakable an appeal for assistance, or deliberately approach so near (unless previously encouraged). We tried to feed him, but we fear little of the food reached him. The wonder of the incident was that a thrush should still be left—there had not been one in the garden for two months. Berries all gone, ground hard and foodless, streams frozen, snow lying for weeks, frost stealing away the vital heat—ingenuity could not devise a more terrible scene of torture to the birds. Neither for the thrushes nor for the new-born infants in the tent did the onslaught of the winter slacken. No pity in earth or heaven. This one thrush did, indeed, by some exceptional fortune, survive ; but where were the family of thrushes that had sung so sweetly in the rainy autumn ? Where were the blackbirds ?

Looking down from the stilts of seven hundred feet into the deep coombe of black oaks standing in the white snow, day by day, built round about with the rugged mound of the hills, doubly locked with the key of frost —it seemed to me to take on itself the actuality of the ancient faith of the Magi. How the seeds of all living things—the germs—of bird and animal, man and insect, tree and herb, of the whole earth—were gathered together into a four-square rampart, and there laid to sleep in safety, shielded by a spell-bound fortification against the coming flood, not of water, but of frost and snow ! With snow and frost and winter the earth was overcome, and the world perished, stricken dumb and dead, swept clean and utterly destroyed—a winter of the gods, the silence of snow and universal death. All that had been passed away, and the earth was depopulated. Death triumphed. But under the snow, behind the charmed rampart, slept the living germs. Down in the deep coombe, where the dark oaks stood out individually in the whiteness of the snow, fortified round about with immovable hills, there was the actual presentment of Zoroaster's sacred story. Locked in sleep lay bud and germ—the butterflies of next summer were there somewhere, under the snow. The earth was swept of its inhabitants, but the seeds of life were not dead. Near by were the tents of the gipsies —an Eastern race, whose forefathers perhaps had seen

that very Magian worship of the Light ; and in those
tents birth had already taken place.   Under the Night
of winter—under the power of dark Ahriman, the evil
spirit of Destruction—lay bud and germ in bondage,
waiting for the coming of Ormuzd, the Sun of Light and
Summer.   Beneath the snow, and in the frozen crevices
of the trees, in the chinks of the earth, sealed up by the
signet of frost, were the seeds of the life that would re-
plenish the air in time to come.   The buzzing crowds of
summer were still under the snow.

This forest land is marked by the myriads of insects
that roam about it in the days of sunshine.   Of all the
million million heathbells—multiply them again by a
million million more—that purple the acres of rolling
hills, mile upon mile, there is not one that is not daily
visited by these flying creatures.   Countless and incal-
culable hosts of the yellow-barred hover-flies come to
them ; the heath and common, the moor and forest, the
hedgerow and copse, are full of insects.   They rise under
foot, they rise from the spray brushed by your arm as
you pass, they settle down in front of you—a rain of insects, a coloured shower.   Legion is a little word for the
butterflies ; the dry pastures among the woods are brown
with meadow-brown ; blues and coppers float in endless
succession ; all the nations of Xerxes' army were but a
handful to these.   In their millions they have perished ;
but somewhere, coiled up, as it were, and sealed under
the snow, there must have been the mothers and germs
of the equally vast crowds that will fill the atmosphere
this year.   The great humble-bee that shall be mother
of hundreds, the yellow wasp that shall be mother of
thousands, were hidden there somewhere.   The food of
the migrant birds that are coming from over sea was
there dormant under the snow.   Many nations have a

tradition of a former world destroyed by a deluge of water, from the East to the West, from Greece to Mexico, where the tail of a comet was said to have caused the flood ; but in the strange characters of the Zend is the legend of an ark (as it were) prepared against the snow. It may be that it is the dim memory of a glacial epoch. In this deep coombe, amid the dark oaks and snow, was the fable of Zoroaster. For the coming of Ormuzd, the Light and Life Bringer, the leaf slept folded, the butter-fly was hidden, the germ concealed, while the sun swept upwards towards Aries.

There is nothing so wearying as a long frost—the endless monotony, which makes one think that the very fault we usually find with our climate—its changeableness —is in reality its best quality. Rain, mist, gales—any-thing ; give us anything but weary, weary frost. But having once fixed its mind, the weather will not listen to the usual signs of alteration.

The larks sang at last high up against the grey cloud over the frost-bound earth. They could not wait longer ; love was strong in their little hearts—stronger than the winter. After a while the hedge-sparrows, too, began to sing on the top of the gorse-hedge about the garden. By-and-by a chaffinch boldly raised his voice, ending with the old story, ' Sweet, will you, will you kiss—me —dear ? ' Then there came a hoar-frost, and the earth, which had been black, became white, as its evaporate 1 vapours began to gather and drops of rain to fall. Even then the obstinate weather refused to quite yield, wrap-ping its cloak, as it were, around it in bitter enmity. But in a day or two white clouds lit up with sunshine appeared drifting over from the southward, and that was the end. The old pensioner came to the door for his bread and cheese : ' The wind's in the south,' he said, 'and I hopes she'll stay there.' Five dull yellow spots on the hedge—gorse bloom—that had remained unchanged for so many weeks, took a fresh colour and became golden. By the constant passing of the waggons and carts along the road that had been so silent it was evident that the busy time of spring was here. There would be rough weather, doubtless, now and again, but it would not again be winter.

Dark patches of cloud—spots of ink on the sky, the 'messengers'—go drifting by ; and after them will follow the water-carriers, harnessed to the south and west winds, drilling the long rows of rain like seed into the earth. After a time there will be a rainbow. Through the bars of my prison I can see the catkins thick and sallow-grey on the willows across the field, visible even at that distance ; so great the change in a few days, the hand of spring grows firm and takes a strong grasp of the hedges. My prison bars are but a sixteenth of an inch thick ; I could snap them with a fillip—only the window-pane, to me as impenetrable as the twenty-foot wall of the Tower of London. A cart has just gone past bearing a strange load among the carts of spring ; they are talking of poling the hops. In it there sat an old man, with the fixed stare, the animal-like eye, of extreme age ; he is over ninety. About him there were some few chairs and articles of furniture, and he was propped against a bed. He was being moved—literally carted—to another house, not home, and he said he could not go without his bed ; he had slept on it for seventy-three years. Last Sunday his son—himself old—was carted to the churchyard, as is the country custom, in an open van ; to-day the father, still living, goes to what will be to him a strange land. His home is broken up—he will potter no more with maize for the chicken ; the gorse hedges will become solid walls of golden bloom, but there will never again be a spring for him. It is very hard, is it not, at ninety? It is not the tyranny of any one that has done it; it is the tyranny of circumstance, the lot of man. The song of the Greeks is full of sorrow; man was to them the creature of grief, yet theirs was the land of violets and pellucid air. This has been a land of frost and snow, and here too, it is the same. A stranger, I see, is already digging the old man's garden.

How happy the trees must be to hear the song of birds again in their branches! After the silence and the leaflessness, to have the birds back once more and to feel them busy at the nest-building; how glad to give them the moss and fibres and the crutch of the boughs to build in! Pleasant it is now to watch the sunlit clouds sailing onwards; it is like sitting by the sea. There is voyaging to and fro of birds; the strong wood-pigeon goes over—a long course in the air, from hill to distant copse; a blackbird starts from an ash, and, now inclining this way and now that, traverses the meadows to the thick corner hedge; finches go by, and the air is full of larks that sing without ceasing. The touch of the wind, the moisture of the dew, the sun-stained raindrop, have in them the magic force of life—a marvellous some-thing that was not there before. Under it the narrow blade of grass comes up freshly green between the old white fibres the rook pulled; the sycamore bud swells and opens, and takes the eye instantly in the still dark wood; the starlings go to the hollow pollards; the lambs leap in the mead. You never know what a day may bring forth—what new thing will come next. Yes-terday I saw the ploughman and his team, and the earth gleam smoothed behind the share; to-day a butterfly has gone past; the farm-folk are bringing home the fagots from the hedgerows ; to-morrow there will be a merry, merry note in the ash copse, the chiffchaffs' ringing call to arms, to arms, ye leaves ! By-and-by a bennet, a bloom of the grass ; in time to come the furrow, as it were, shall open, and the great buttercup of the waters will show a broad palm of gold. You never know what will come to the net of the eye next—a bud, a flower, a nest, a curled fern, or whether it will be in the woodland or by the meadow path, at the water's side or on the dead dry heap of fagots. There is no settled succession, no fixed and formal order—always the unexpected ; and you cannot say, ' I will go and find this or that.' The sowing of life in the spring time is not in the set straight line of the drill, nor shall you find wild flowers by a foot measure. There are great woods without a lily of the valley ; the nightingale does not sing everywhere. Nature has no arrangement, no plan, nothing judicious even ; the walnut trees bring forth their tender buds, and the frost burns them—they have no mosaic of time to fit in, like a Roman tesselated pavement ; nature is like a child, who will sing and shout though you may be never so deeply pondering in the study, and does not wait for the hour that suits your mind. You do not know what you may find each day ; perhaps you may only pick up a fallen feather, but it is beautiful, every filament. Always beautiful ! everything beautiful ! And are these things new—the ploughman and his team, the lark's song the green leaf ? Can they be new ? Surely they have been of old time ! They are, indeed, new—the only things that are so ; the rest is old and grey, and a weariness.

NATURE AND BOOKS.

WHAT is the colour of the dandelion? There are
many dandelions: that which I mean flowers in May,
when the meadow-grass has started and the hares are
busy by daylight. That which flowers very early in the
year has a thickness of hue, and is not interesting; in
autumn the dandelions quite change their colour and are
pale. The right dandelion for this question is the one
that comes about May with a very broad disc, and in
such quantities as often to cover a whole meadow. I
used to admire them very much in the fields by Surbiton
(strong clay soil), and also on the towing-path of the
Thames where the sward is very broad, opposite Long
Ditton; indeed, I have often walked up that towing-path
on a beautiful sunny morning, when all was quiet except
the nightingales in the Palace hedge, on purpose to
admire them. I dare say they are all gone now for evermore; still, it is a pleasure to look back on anything
beautiful. What colour is this dandelion? It is not
yellow, nor orange, nor gold; put a sovereign on it and
see the difference. They say the gipsies call it the
Queen's great hairy dog-flower—a number of words to
one stalk; and so, to get a colour to it, you may call it
the yellow-gold-orange plant. In the winter, on the
black mud under a dark, dripping tree, I found a piece
of orange peel, lately dropped—a bright red orange

speck in the middle of the blackness. It looked very beautiful, and instantly recalled to my mind the great dandelion discs in the sunshine of summer. Yet certainly they are not red-orange. Perhaps, if ten people answered this question, they would each give different answers. Again, a bright day or a cloudy, the presence of a slight haze, or the juxtaposition of other colours, alters it very much ; for the dandelion is not a glazed colour, like the buttercup, but sensitive. It is like a sponge, and adds to its own hue that which is passing, sucking it up.

The shadows of the trees in the wood, why are they blue? Ought they not to be dark? Is it really blue, or an illusion? And what is their colour when you see the shadow of a tall trunk aslant in the air like a leaning pillar? The fallen brown leaves wet with dew have a different brown from those that are dry, and the upper surface of the green growing leaf is different from the under surface. The yellow butterfly, if you meet one in October, has so toned down his spring yellow that you might fancy him a pale green leaf floating along the road. There is a shining, quivering, gleaming ; there is a changing, fluttering, shifting ; there is a mixing, weaving—varnished wings, translucent wings, wings with dots and veins, all playing over the purple heath ; a very tangle of many-toned lights and hues. Then come the apples : if you look upon them from an upper window, so as to glance along the level plane of the fruit, delicate streaks of scarlet, like those that lie parallel to the eastern horizon before sunrise ; golden tints under bronze, and apple-green, and some that the wasps have hollowed, more glowingly beautiful than the rest ; sober leaves and black and white swallows : to see it you must be high up, as if the apples were strewn on a sward of foliage. So have I gone in three steps from May dandelion to September apple ; an immense space measured by things beautiful, so filled that ten folio volumes could not hold the description of them, and I have left out the meadows, the brooks, and hills. Often in writing about these things I have felt very earnestly my own incompetence to give the least idea of their brilliancy and many-sided colours. My gamut was so very limited in its terms, and would not give a note to one in a thousand of those I saw. At last I said, I will have more words ; I will have more terms ; I will have a book on colour, and I will find and use the right technical name for each one of these lovely tints. I was told that the very best book was by Chevreul, which had tinted illustrations, chromatic scales, and all that could be desired.

Quite true, all of it ; but for me it contained nothing. There was a good deal about assorted wools, but nothing about leaves ; nothing by which I could tell you the difference between the light scarlet of one poppy and the deep purple-scarlet of another species. The dandelion remained unexplained ; as for the innumerable other flowers, and wings, and sky-colours, they were not even approached. The book, in short, dealt with the artificial and not with nature. Next I went to science—works on optics, such a mass of them. Some I had read in old time, and turned to again ; some I read for the first time, some translated from the German, and so on. It appeared that, experimenting with physical colour, tangible paint, they had found out that red, yellow, and blue were the three primary colours ; and then, experimenting with light itself, with colours not tangible, they found out that red, green, and violet were the three primary colours ; but neither of these would do for the dandelion. Once upon a time I had taken an interest in spectrum analysis, and the theory of the polarisation of light was fairly familiar; any number of books, but not what I wanted to know. Next the idea occurred to me of buying all the colours used in painting, and tinting as many pieces of paper a separate hue, and so comparing these with petals, and wings, and grass, and trifolium. This did not answer at all; my unskilful hands made a very poor wash, and the yellow paper set by a yellow petal did not agree, the scientific reason of which I cannot enter into now. Secondly, the names attached to many of these paints are unfamiliar to general readers; it is doubtful if bistre, Leitch's blue, oxide of chromium, and so on, would convey an idea. They might as well be Greek symbols : no use to attempt to describe hues of heath or hill in that way. These, too, are only distinct colours. What was to be done with all the shades and tones ? Still there remained the language of the studio ; without doubt a master of painting could be found who would quickly supply the technical term of anything I liked to show him ; but again no use, because it would be technical. And a still more insurmountable difficulty occurs : in so far as I have looked at pictures, it seems as if the artists had met with the same obstacle in paints as I have in words— that is to say, a deficiency. Either painting is incompetent to express the extreme beauty of nature, or in some way the canons of art forbid the attempt. Therefore I had to turn back, throw down my books with a bang, and get me to a bit of fallen timber in the open air to meditate.

Would it be possible to build up a fresh system of colour language by means of natural objects ? Could we say pine-wood green, larch green, spruce green, wasp yellow, humble-bee amber ? And there are fungi that have marked tints, but the Latin names of these agarics are not pleasant. Butterfly blue—but there are several varieties; and this plan is interfered with by two things : first, that almost every single item of nature, however minute, has got a distinctly different colour, so that the dictionary of tints would be immense ; and next, so very few would know the object itself that the colour attached to it would have no meaning. The power of language has been gradually enlarging for a great length of time, and I venture to say that the English language at the present time can express more, and is more subtle, flexible, and, at the same time, vigorous, than any of which we possess a record. When people talk to me about studying Sanscrit, or Greek, or Latin, or German, or, still more absurd, French, I feel as if I could fell them with a mallet happily. Study the English, and you will find everything there, I reply. With such a language I fully anticipate, in years to come, a great development in the power of expressing thoughts and feelings which are now thoughts and feelings only. How many have said of the sea, ' It makes me feel something I cannot say ' ! Hence it is clear there exists in the intellect a layer, if I may so call it, of thought yet dumb—chambers within the mind which require the key of new words to unlock. Whenever that is done a fresh impetus is given to human progress. There are a million books, and yet with all their aid I cannot tell you the colour of the May dandelion. There are three greens at this moment in my mind : that of the leaf of the flower-de-luce, that of the yellow iris leaf, and that of the bayonet-like leaf of the common flag. With admission to a million books, how am I to tell you the difference between these tints ? So many, many books, and such a very, very little bit of nature in them !

Though we have been so many thousand years upon the earth we do not seem to have done any more as yet than walk along beaten footpaths, and sometimes really it would seem as if there were something in the minds of many men quite artificial, quite distinct from the sun and trees and hills—altogether house people, whose gods must be set in four-cornered buildings. There is nothing in books that touches my dandelion.

It grows, ah yes, it grows! How does it grow? Builds itself up somehow of sugar and starch, and turns mud into bright colour and dead earth into food for bees, and some day perhaps for you, and knows when to shut its petals, and how to construct the brown seeds to float with the wind, and how to please the children, and how to puzzle me. Ingenious dandelion! If you find out that its correct botanical name is *Leontodon taraxacum*, or *Leontodon dens-leonis*, that will bring it into botany ; and there is a place called Dandelion Castle in Kent, and a bell with the inscription—

> John de Dandelion with his great dog
> Brought over this bell on a mill cog—

which is about as relevant as the mere words *Leontodon taraxacum*. Botany is the knowledge of plants according to the accepted definition ; naturally, therefore, when I began to think I would like to know a little more of flowers than could be learned by seeing them in the fields, I went to botany. Nothing could be more simple. You buy a book which first of all tells you how to recognise them, how to classify them ; next instructs you in their uses, medical or economical ; next tells you about the folk-lore and curious associations ; next enters into a lucid explanation of the physiology of the plant and its relation to other creatures ; and finally, and most important, supplies you with the ethical feeling, the ideal aspiration to be identified with each particular flower. One moderately thick volume would probably suffice for such a modest round as this.

Lo! now the labour of Hercules when he set about bringing up Cerberus from below, and all the work done by Apollo in the years when he ground corn, are but a little matter compared with the attempt to master botany. Great minds have been at it these two thousand years, and yet we are still only nibbling at the edge of the leaf, as the ploughboys bite the young hawthorn in spring. The mere classification—all plant-lore was a vast chaos till there came the man of Sweden, the great Linnæus, till the sexes were recognised, and everything was ruled out and set in place again. A wonderful man! I think it would be true to say it was Linnæus who set the world on its present twist of thinking, and levered our mental globe a little more perpendicular to the ecliptic. He actually gathered the dandelion and took it to bits like a scientific child ; he touched nature with his fingers instead of sitting looking out of window —perhaps the first man who had ever done so for seventeen hundred years or so, since superstition blighted the progress of pagan Rome. The work he did ! But no one reads Linnæus now ; the folios, indeed, might moulder to dust without loss, because his spirit has got into the minds of men, and the text is of little consequence. The best book he wrote to read now is the delightful 'Tour in Lapland,' with its quaint pen-and-ink sketches, so realistically vivid, as if the thing sketched had been banged on the paper and so left its impress. I have read it three times, and I still cherish the old yellow pages ; it is the best botanical book, written by the greatest of botanists, specially sent on a botanical expedition, and it contains nothing about botany. It tells you about the canoes, and the hard cheese, and the Laplander's warehouse on top of a pole, like a pigeon-house ; and the innocent way in which the maiden helped the traveller in his bath, and how the aged men ran so fast that the devil could not catch them ; and, best of all, because it gives a smack in the face to modern pseudo-scientific medical cant about hygiene, showing how the Laplanders break every ' law,' human and ' divine,' ventilation, bath, and diet—all the trash—and therefore enjoy the most excellent health, and live to a great old age. Still I have not succeeded in describing the immense labour there was in learning to distinguish plants on the Linnæan system. Then comes in order of time the natural system, the geographical distribution ; then there is the geological relationship, so to say, to Pliocene plants, natural selection and evolution. Of that let us say nothing ; let sleeping dogs lie, and evolution is a very weary dog. Most charming, however, will be found the later studies of naturalists on the interdependence of flowers and insects ; there is another work the dandelion has got to do—endless, endless botany ! Where did the plants come from at first ? Did they come creeping up out of the sea at the edge of the estuaries, and gradually run their roots into the ground, and so make green the earth ? Did Man come out of the sea, as the Greeks thought ? There are so many ideas in plants. Flora, with a full lap, scattering knowledge and flowers together ; everything good and sweet seems to come out of flowers, up to the very highest thoughts of the soul, and we carry them daily to the very threshold of the other world. Next you may try the microscope and its literature, and find the crystals in the rhubarb.

I remember taking sly glances when I was a very little boy at an old Culpepper's Herbal, heavily bound in leather and curiously illustrated. It was so deliciously wicked to read about the poisons ; and I thought perhaps it was a book like that, only in papyrus rolls, that was used by the sorceress who got ready the poisoned mushrooms in old Rome. Youth's ideas are so imaginative, and bring together things that are so widely separated. Conscience told me I had no business to read about poisons ; but there was a fearful fascination in hemlock, and I recollect tasting a little bit—it was very nasty. At this day, nevertheless, if any one wishes to begin a pleasant, interesting, unscientific acquaintance with English plants, he would do very well indeed to get a good copy of Culpepper. Grey hairs had insisted in showing themselves in my beard when, all those weary years afterwards, I thought I would like to buy the still older Englishman, Gerard, who had no Linnæus to guide him, who walked about our English lanes centuries ago. What wonderful scenes he must have viewed when they were all a tangle of wild flowers, and plants that are now scarce were common, and the old ploughs, and the curious customs, and the wild red-deer—it would make a good picture, it really would, Gerard studying English orchids ! Such a volume !—hundreds of pages, yellow of course, close type, and marvellously well printed. The minute care they must have taken in those early days of printing to get up such a book—a wonderful volume both in bodily shape and contents. Just then the only copy I could hear of was much damaged. The cunning old bookseller said he could make it up ; but I have no fancy for patched books, they are not genuine ; I would rather have them deficient ; and the price was rather long, and so I went Gerardless.

Of folk-lore and medicinal use and history and associations here you have hints. The bottom of the sack is not yet; there are the monographs, years of study expended upon one species of plant growing in one locality, perhaps; some made up into thick books and some into broad quarto pamphlets, with most beautiful plates, that, if you were to see them, would tempt you to cut them out and steal them, all sunk and lost like dead ships under the sand: piles of monographs. There are warehouses in London that are choked to the beams of the roof with them, and every fresh exploration furnishes another shelf-load. The source of the Nile was unknown a very few years ago, and now, I have no doubt, there are dozens of monographs on the flowers that flourish there. Indeed, there is not a thing that grows that may not furnish a monograph. The author spends perhaps twenty years in collecting his material, during which time he must of course come across a great variety of amusing information, and then he spends another ten years writing out a fair copy of his labours. Then he thinks it does not quite do in that form, so he snips a paragraph out of the beginning and puts it at the end; next he shifts some more matter from the middle to the preface; then he thinks it over. It seems to him that it is too big, it wants condensation. The scientific world will say he has made too much of it; it ought to read very slight, and present the facts while concealing the labour. So he sets about removing the superfluous — leaves out all the personal observations, and all the little adventures he has met with in his investigations; and so, having got it down to the dry bones and stones thereof, and omitted all the mortar that stuck them together, he sends for the engraver, and the next three years are occupied in working up the illustrations. About this

time some new discovery is made by a foreign observer,
which necessitates a complete revision of the subject;
and so having shifted the contents of the book about
hither and thither till he does not know which is the end
and which is the beginning, he pitches the much-muti-
lated copy into a drawer and turns the key. Farewell,
no more of this; his declining days shall be spent in
peace. A few months afterwards a work is announced
in Leipsic which ' really trenches on my favourite subject, and really after spending a lifetime I can't stand
it.' By this time his handwriting has become so shaky
he can hardly read it himself, so he sends in despair for
a lady who works a type-writer, and with infinite patience
she makes a clean manuscript of the muddled mass. To
the press at last, and the proofs come rapidly. Such a
relief! How joyfully easy a thing is when you set about
it! but by-and-by this won't do. Sub-section A ought
to be in a foot-note, family B is doubtful; and so the
corrections grow and run over the margin in a thin treble
hand, till they approach the bulk of the original book—
a good profit for the printer; and so after about forty
years the monograph is published—the work of a life is
accomplished. Fifty copies are sent round to as many
public libraries and learned societies, and the rest of the
impression lies on the shelves till dust and time and
spiders' webs have buried it. Splendid work in it too.
Looked back upon from to-day with the key of modern
thought, these monographs often contain a whole chest
of treasure. And still there are the periodicals, a century
of magazines and journals and reviews and notices that
have been coming out these hundred years and dropping
to the ground like dead leaves unnoticed. And then
there are the art works—books about shape and colour
and ornament, and a naturalist lately has been trying to

see how the leaves of one tree look fitted on the boughs
of another.   Boundless is the wealth of Flora's lap ; the
ingenuity of man has been weaving wreaths out of it for
ages, and still the bottom of the sack is not yet.   Nor
have we got much news of the dandelion.   For I sit on
the thrown timber under the trees and meditate, and I
want something more : I want the soul of the flowers.

The bee and the butterfly take their pollen and their
honey, and the strange moths so curiously coloured, like
the curious colouring of the owls, come to them by night,
and they turn towards the sun and live their little day,
and their petals fall, and where is the soul when the
body decays?   I want the inner meaning and the under-
standing of the wild flowers in the meadow.   Why are
they?   What end ?   What purpose?   The plant knows,
and sees, and feels ; where is its mind when the petal
falls?   Absorbed in the universal dynamic force, or
what?   They make no shadow of pretence, these beautiful flowers, of being beautiful for my sake, of bearing
honey for me ; in short, there does not seem to be any
kind of relationship between us, and yet—as I said just
now—language does not express the dumb feelings of
the mind any more than the flower can speak.   I want to
know the soul of the flowers, but the word soul does not
in the smallest degree convey the meaning of my wish.
It is quite inadequate ; I must hope that you will grasp
the drift of my meaning.   All these life-laboured monographs, these classifications, works of Linnæus, and our
own classic Darwin, microscope, physiology, and the
flower has not given us its message yet.   There are a
million books ; there are no books : all the books have
to be written.   What a field !   A whole million of books
have got to be written.   In this sense there are hardly
a dozen of them done, and these mere primers.   The

thoughts of man are like the foraminifera, those minute shells which build up the solid chalk hills and lay the level plain of endless sand ; so minute that, save with a powerful lens, you would never imagine the dust on your fingers to be more than dust. The thoughts of man are like these : each to him seems great in his day, but the ages roll, and they shrink till they become triturated dust, and you might, as it were, put a thousand on your thumb-nail. They are not shapeless dust for all that ; they are organic, and they build and weld and grow together, till in the passage of time they will make a new earth and a new life. So I think I may say there are no books ; the books are yet to be written.

Let us get a little alchemy out of the dandelions. They were not precise, the Arabian sages, with their flowing robes and handwriting ; there was a large margin to their manuscripts, much imagination. Therein they failed, judged by the monograph standard, but gave a subtle food for the mind. Some of this I would fain see now inspiring the works and words of our great men of science and thought—a little alchemy. A great change is slowly going forward all over the printing-press world, I mean wherever men print books and papers. The Chinese are perhaps outside that world at present, and the other Asian races ; the myriads, too, of the great southern islands and of Africa. The change is steadily, however, proceeding wherever the printing-press is used. Nor Pope, nor Kaiser, nor Czar, nor Sultan, nor fanatic monk, nor muezzin, shouting in vain from his minaret, nor, most fanatic of all, the fanatic shouting in vain in London, can keep it out—all power-less against a bit of printed paper. Bits of printed paper that listen to no command, to which none can say, ' Stand back ; thou shalt not enter.' They rise on the summer whirlwinds from the very dust of the road, and float over the highest walls ; they fall on the well-kept lawns — monastery, prison, palace — there is no fortress against a bit of printed paper. They penetrate where even Danaë's gold cannot go. Our Darwins, our Lyalls, Herschels, Faradays—all the immense army of those that go down to nature with considering eye—are steadfastly undermining and obliterating the superstitious past, literally burying it under endless loads of accumulated facts ; and the printing-presses, like so many Argos, take these facts on their voyage round the world. Over go temples, and minarets, and churches, or rather there they stay, the hollow shells, like the snail shells which thrushes have picked clean ; there they stay like Karnac, where there is no more incense, like the stone circles on our own hills, where there are no more human sacrifices. Thus men's minds all over the printing-press world are unlearning the falsehoods that have bound them down so long ; they are unlearning, the first step to learn. They are going down to nature and taking up the clods with their own hands, and so coming to have touch of that which is real. As yet we are in the fact stage ; by-and-by we shall come to the alchemy, and get the honey for the inner mind and soul. I found, therefore, from the dandelion that there were no books, and it came upon me, believe me, as a great surprise, for I had lived quite certain that I was surrounded with them. It is nothing but unlearning, I find now ; five thousand books to unlearn.

Then to unlearn the first ideas of history, of science, of social institutions, to unlearn one's own life and purpose ; to unlearn the old mode of thought and way of arriving at things ; to take off peel after peel, and so get by degrees slowly towards the truth—thus writing as it were, a sort of floating book in the mind, almost re-making the soul. It seems as if the chief value of books is to give us something to unlearn. Sometimes I feel indignant at the false views that were instilled into me in early days, and then again I see that that very indignation gives me a moral life. I hope in the days to come future thinkers will unlearn us, and find ideas infinitely better. How marvellous it seems that there should be found communities furnished with the printing-press and fully convinced they are more intelligent than ants, and yet deliberately refusing by a solid 'popular' vote to accept free libraries! They look with scorn on the mediæval times, when volumes were chained in the college library or to the desk at church. Ignorant times those! A good thing it would be if only three books were chained to a desk, open and free in every parish throughout the kingdom now. So might the wish to unlearn be at last started in the inert mind of the mass. Almost the only books left to me to read, and not to unlearn very much, are my first books—the graven classics of Greece and Rome, cut with a stylus so deeply into the tablet they cannot be erased. Little of the monograph or of classification, no bushel baskets full of facts, no minute dissection of nature, no attempt to find the soul under the scalpel. Thoughts which do not exactly deal with nature direct in a mechanical way, as the chemist labels all his gums and spices and earths in small boxes—I wonder if anybody at Athens ever made a collection of the coleoptera? Yet in some way they had got the spirit of the earth and sea, the soul of the sun. This never dies; this I wish not to unlearn; this is ever fresh and beautiful as a summer morning :—

Such the golden crocus,
Fair flower of early spring ; the gopher white,

And fragrant thyme, and all the unsown beauty
Which in moist grounds the verdant meadows bear ;
The ox-eye, the sweet-smelling flower of Jove,
The chalca, and the much-sung hyacinth,
And the low-growing violet, to which
Dark Proserpine a darker hue has given.

They come nearest to our own violets and cowslips—the unsown beauty of our meadows—to the hawthorn leaf and the high pinewood. I can forget all else that I have read, but it is difficult to forget these even when I will. I read them in English. I had the usual Latin and Greek instruction, but I read them in English deliberately. For the inflexion of the vowel I care nothing ; I prize the idea. Scholars may regard me with scorn. I reply with equal scorn. I say that a great classic thought is greater to an English mind in English words than in any other form, and therein fits best to this our life and day. I read them in English first, and intend to do so to the end. I do not know what set me on these books, but I began them when about eighteen. The first of all was Diogenes Laertius's ' Lives of the Philosophers.' It was a happy choice ; my good genius, I suppose, for you see I was already fairly well read in modern science, and these old Greek philosophies set me thinking backwards, unwinding and unlearning, and getting at that eidolon which is not to be found in the mechanical heavens of this age. I still read him. I still find new things, quite new, because they are so very, very old, and quite true ; and with his help I seem in a measure to look back upon our thoughts now as if I had projected myself a thousand years forward in space. An imperfect book, say the critics. I do not know about that ; his short paragraphs and chapters in their imperfect state convey more freshness to the mind than the thick, laboured volumes in which modern scholarship professes to describe ancient philosophy. I prefer the imperfect original records. Neither can I read the ponderous volumes of modern history, which are nothing but words. I prefer the incomplete and shattered chronicles themselves, where the swords shine and the armour rings, and all is life though but a broken frieze. Next came Plato (it took me a long time to read Plato, and I have had to unlearn much of him) and Xenophon. Socrates' dialectic method taught me how to write, or rather how to put ideas in sequence. Sophocles, too ; and last, that wonderful encyclopædia of curious things, Athenæus. So that I found, when the idea of the hundred best books came out, that between seventy and eighty of them had been my companions almost from boyhood, those lacking to complete the number being chiefly ecclesiastical or Continental. Indeed, some years before the hundred books were talked of, the idea had occurred to me of making up a catalogue of books that could be bought for ten pounds. In an article in the 'Pall Mall Gazette' on 'The Pigeons at the British Museum' I said, ' It seems as if all the books in the world—really books-—can be bought for 10*l.* Man's whole thought is purchasable at that small price—for the value of a watch, of a good dog.' The idea of making a 10*l.* catalogue was in my mind— I did make a rough pencil one—and I still think that a 10*l.* library is worth the notice of the publishing world. My rough list did not contain a hundred. These old books of nature and nature's mind ought to be chained up, free for every man to read in every parish. These are the only books I do not wish to unlearn, one item only excepted, which I shall not here discuss. It is curious, too, that the Greek philosophers, in the more rigid sense of science, anticipated most of the drift of modern thought. Two chapters in Aristotle might almost be printed without change as summaries of our present natural science. For the facts of nature, of course, neither one hundred books nor a 10*l*. library would be worth mentioning; say five thousand, and having read those, then go to Kew, and spend a year studying the specimens of wood only stored there, such a little slice after all of the whole. You will then believe what I have advanced, that there are no books as yet; they have got to be written; and if we pursue the idea a little further, and consider that these are all about the crude clods of life—for I often feel what a very crude and clumsy clod I am—only of the earth, a minute speck among one hundred millions of stars, how shall we write what is *there*? It is only to be written by the mind or soul, and that is why I strive so much to find what I have called the alchemy of nature. Let us not be too entirely mechanical, Baconian, and experimental only; let us let the soul hope and dream and float on these oceans of accumulated facts, and feel still greater aspiration than it has ever known since first a flint was chipped before the glaciers. Man's mind is the most important fact with which we are yet acquainted. Let us not turn then against it and deny its existence with too many brazen instruments, but remember these are but a means, and that the vast lens of the Californian refractor is but glass—it is the infinite speck upon which the ray of light will fall that is the one great fact of the universe. By the mind, without instruments, the Greeks anticipated almost all our thoughts; by-and-by, having raised ourselves up upon these huge mounds of facts, we shall begin to see still greater things; to do so we must look not at the mound under foot, but at the starry horizon.

THE JULY GRASS.

A JULY fly went sideways over the long grass. His wings made a burr about him like a net, beating so fast they wrapped him round with a cloud. Every now and then, as he flew over the trees of grass, a taller one than common stopped him, and there he clung, and then the eye had time to see the scarlet spots—the loveliest colour—on his wings. The wind swung the burnet and loosened his hold, and away he went again over the grasses, and not one jot did he care if they were *Poa* or *Festuca*, or *Bromus* or *Hordeum*, or any other name. Names were nothing to him ; all he had to do was to whirl his scarlet spots about in the brilliant sun, rest when he liked, and go on again. I wonder whether it is a joy to have bright scarlet spots, and to be clad in the purple and gold of life ; is the colour felt by the creature that wears it ? The rose, restful of a dewy morn before the sunbeams have topped the garden wall, must feel a joy in its own fragrance, and know the exquisite hue of its stained petals. The rose sleeps in its beauty.

The fly whirls his scarlet-spotted wings about and splashes himself with sunlight, like the children on the sands. He thinks not of the grass and sun ; he does not heed them at all—and that is why he is so happy— any more than the barefoot children ask why the sea is there, or why it does not quite dry up when it ebbs. He is unconscious ; he lives without thinking about

living; and if the sunshine were a hundred hours long,
still it would not be long enough.   No, never enough of
sun and sliding shadows that come like a hand over the
table to lovingly reach our shoulder, never enough of the
grass that smells sweet as a flower, not if we could live
years and years equal in number to the tides that have
ebbed and flowed counting backwards four years to every
day and night, backward still till we found out which
came first, the night or the day.   The scarlet-dotted fly
knows nothing of the names of the grasses that grow
here where the sward nears the sea, and thinking of him
I have decided not to wilfully seek to learn any more of
their names either.   My big grass book I have left at
home, and the dust is settling on the gold of the binding.
I have picked a handful this morning of which I know
nothing.   I will sit here on the turf and the scarlet-dotted
flies shall pass over me, as if I too were but a grass.   I
will not think, I will be unconscious, I will live.

Listen ! that was the low sound of a summer wavelet
striking the uncovered rock over there beneath in the
green sea.   All things that are beautiful are found by
chance, like everything that is good.   Here by me is a
praying-rug, just wide enough to kneel on, of the richest
gold inwoven with crimson.   All the Sultans of the East
never had such beauty as that to kneel on.   It is, indeed,
too beautiful to kneel on, for the life in these golden
flowers must not be broken down even for that purpose.
They must not be defaced, not a stem bent ; it is more
reverent not to kneel on them, for this carpet prays itself.
I will sit by it and let it pray for me.   It is so common,
the bird's-foot lotus, it grows everywhere ; yet if I
purposely searched for days I should not have found a
plot like this, so rich, so golden, so glowing with sunshine.   You might pass by it in one stride, yet it is

worthy to be thought of for a week and remembered for
a year. Slender grasses, branched round about with
slenderer boughs, each tipped with pollen and rising in
tiers cone-shaped—too delicate to grow tall—cluster at
the base of the mound. They dare not grow tall or the
wind would snap them. A great grass, stout and thick,
rises three feet by the hedge, with a head another foot
nearly, very green and strong and bold, lifting itself
right up to you; you must say, ' What a fine grass ! '
Grasses whose awns succeed each other alternately ;
grasses whose tops seem flattened ; others drooping over
the shorter blades beneath ; some that you can only find
by parting the heavier growth around them ; hundreds
and hundreds, thousands and thousands. The kingly
poppies on the dry summit of the mound take no heed
of these, the populace, their subjects so numerous they
cannot be numbered. A barren race they are, the proud
poppies, lords of the July field, taking no deep root, but
raising up a brilliant blazon of scarlet heraldry out of
nothing. They are useless, they are bitter, they are
allied to sleep and poison and everlasting night ; yet
they are forgiven because they are not commonplace.
Nothing, no abundance of them, can ever make the
poppies commonplace. There is genius in them, the
genius of colour, and they are saved. Even when they
take the room of the corn we must admire them. The
mighty multitude of nations, the millions and millions
of the grass stretching away in intertangled ranks,
through pasture and mead from shore to shore, have no
kinship with these their lords. The ruler is always a
foreigner. From England to China the native born is
no king ; the poppies are the Normans of the field.
One of these on the mound is very beautiful, a width of
petal, a clear silkiness of colour three shades higher than

the rest—it is almost dark with scarlet. I wish I could do something more than gaze at all this scarlet and gold and crimson and green, something more than see it, not exactly to drink it or inhale it, but in some way to make it part of me that I might live it.

The July grasses must be looked for in corners and out-of-the-way places, and not in the broad acres—the scythe has taken them there. By the wayside on the banks of the lane, near the gateway—look, too, in uninteresting places behind incomplete buildings on the mounds cast up from abandoned foundations where speculation has been and gone. There weeds that would not have found resting-place elsewhere grow unchecked, and uncommon species and unusually large growths appear. Like everything else that is looked for, they are found under unlikely conditions. At the back of ponds, just inside the enclosure of woods, angles of corn-fields, old quarries, that is where to find grasses, or by the sea in the brackish marsh. Some of the finest of them grow by the mere road-side ; you may look for others up the lanes in the deep ruts, look too inside the hollow trees by the stream. In a morning you may easily garner together a great sheaf of this harvest. Cut the larger stems aslant, like the reeds imitated deep in old green glass. You must consider as you gather them the height and slenderness of the stems, the droop and degree of curve, the shape and colour of the panicle, the dusting of the pollen, the motion and sway in the wind. The sheaf you may take home with you, but the wind that was among it stays without.

WINDS OF HEAVEN.

THE window rattled, the gate swung; a leaf rose, and the kitten chased it, 'whoo-oo'—the faintest sound in the keyhole. I looked up, and saw the feathers on a sparrow's breast ruffled for an instant. It was quiet for some time; after a while it came again with heavier purpose. The folded shutters shook; the latch of the kitchen door rattled as if some one were lifting it and dropped it; indefinite noises came from upstairs: there was a hand in the house moving everything. Another pause. The kitten was curled up on the window-ledge outside in the sunshine, just as the sleek cats curled up in the warmth at Thebes of old Egypt five or six thousand years ago; the sparrow was happy at the rose tree; a bee was happy on a broad dandelion disc. 'Soo-hoo!'—a low whistle came through the chink; a handful of rain was flung at the window; a great shadow rushed up the valley and strode the house in an instant as you would get over a stile. I put down my book and buttoned my coat. Soo-hoo! the wind was here and the cloud—soo-hoo! drawing out longer and more plaintive in the thin mouthpiece of the chink. The cloud had no more rain in it, but it shut out the sun; and all that afternoon and all that night the low plaint of the wind continued in sorrowful hopelessness, and little sounds ran about the floors and round the rooms.

Still soo-hoo all the next day and sunlessness, turning the mind, through work and conversation, to pensive notes. At even the edge of the cloud lifted over the forest hill westwards, and a yellow glow, the great beacon fire of the sun, burned out, a conflagration at the verge of the world. In the night, awaking gently as one who is whispered to—listen! Ah! all the orchestra is at work—the keyhole, the chink, and the chimney; whoo-hooing in the keyhole, whistling shrill whew-w-w! in the chink, moaning long and deep in the chimney. Over in the field the row of pines was sighing; the wind lingered and clung to the close foliage, and each needle of the million million leaflets drew its tongue across the organ blast. A countless multitude of sighs made one continued distant undertone to the wild roar of the gable close at hand. Something seemed to be running with innumerable centipede feet over the mouth of the chimney, for the long deep moan, as I listened, resolved itself into a quick succession of touches, just as you might play with your finger-tips, fifty times a second tattooing on the hollow table. In the midst of the clangour the hearing settled down to the sighing of the pines, which drew the mind towards it, and soothed the senses to sleep.

Towards dawn, awake again—another change: the battering-ram at work now against the walls. Swinging back, the solid thickness of the wind came forward—crush! as the iron-shod ram's head hanging from its chains rushed to the tower. Crush! It sucked back again as if there had been a vacuum—a moment's silence, and crush! Blow after blow—the floor heaved; the walls were ready to come together—alternate sucking back and heavy billowy advance. Crush! crush! Blow after blow, heave and batter and hoist, as if it would tear the house up by the roots. Forty miles that battering-ram wind had travelled without so much as a bough to check it till it struck the house on the hill. Thud! thud! as if it were iron and not air. I looked from the window, and the bright morning star was shining—the sky was full of the wind and the star. As light came, the thud, thud sunk away, and nothing remained but the whoo-hoo-hoo of the keyhole and the moan of the chimney. These did not leave us; for four days and nights the whoo-hoo-hoo-whoo never ceased a moment. Whoo-hoo! whoo! and this is the wind on the hill indoors.

Out of doors, sometimes in the morning, deep in the valley, over the tree tops of the forest, there stays a vapour, lit up within by sunlight. A glory hovers over the oaks—a cloud of light hundreds of feet thick, the air made visible by surcharge and heaviness of sunbeams, pressed together till you can see them in themselves and not reflected. The cloud slants down the sloping wood, till in a moment it is gone, and the beams are now focussed in the depth of the narrow valley. The mirror has been tilted, and the glow has shifted; in a moment more it has vanished into space, and the dream has gone from the wood. In the arms of the wind, vast bundles of mist are borne against the hill; they widen and slip, and lengthen, drawing out; the wind works quickly with moist colours ready and a wide brush laying broadly. Colour comes up in the wind; the thin mist disappears, drunk up in the grass and trees, and the air is full of blue behind the vapour. Blue sky at the far horizon— rich deep blue overhead—a dark-brown blue deep yonder in the gorge among the trees. I feel a sense of blue colour as I face the strong breeze; the vibration and blow of its force answer to that hue, the sound of the swinging branches and the rush—rush in the grass is azure in its note; it is wind-blue, not the night-blue, or heaven-blue, a colour of air. To see the colour of the air it needs great space like this—a vastness of concavity and hollow—an equal caldron of valley and plain under, to the dome of the sky over, for no vessel of earth and sky is too large for the air-colour to fill. Thirty, forty, and more miles of eye-sweep, and beyond that the limitless expanse over the sea—the thought of the eye knows no butt, shooting on with stellar penetration into the unknown. In a small space there seems a vacuum, and nothing between you and the hedge opposite, or even across the valley; in a great space the void is filled, and the wind touches the sight like a thing tangible. The air becomes itself a cloud, and is coloured —recognised as a thing suspended; something real exists between you and the horizon. Now full of sun, and now of shade, the air-cloud rests in the expanse.

It is summer, and the wind-birds top the furze; the bright stonechat, velvet-black and red and white, sits on the highest spray of the gorse, as if he were painted there. He is always in the wind on the hill, from the hail of April to August's dry glow. All the mile-long slope of the hill under me is purple-clad with heath down to the tree-filled gorge where the green boughs seem to join the purple. The corn-fields and the pastures of the plain—count them one by one till the hedges and squares close together and cannot be separated. The surface of the earth melts away as if the eyes insensibly shut and grew dreamy in gazing, as the soft clouds melt and lose their outline at the horizon. But dwelling there, the glance slowly finds and fills out something that interposes its existence between us and the further space. Too shadowy for the substance of a cloud, too delicate for outline against the sky, fainter than haze, something of which the eye has consciousness, but cannot put into a word to itself. Something is there. It is the air-cloud adhering like a summer garment to the great downs by the sea. I cannot see the substance of the hills nor their exact curve along the sky; all I can see is the air that has thickened and taken to itself form about them. The atmosphere has collected as the shadow collects in the distant corner of a room—it is the shadow of the summer wind. At times it is so soft, so little more than the air at hand, that I almost fancy I can look through the solid boundary. There is no cloud so faint; the great hills are but a thought at the horizon; I *think* them there rather than see them; if I were not thinking of them, I should scarce know there was even a haze, with so dainty a hand does the atmosphere throw its covering over the massy downs. Riding or passing quickly perhaps you would not observe them; but stay among the heathbells, and the sketch appears in the south. Up from the sea over the corn-fields, through the green boughs of the forest, along the slope, comes a breath of wind, of honey-sweetened air, made more delicate by the fanning of a thousand wings.

The labour of the wind: the cymbals of the aspen clashing, from the lowest to the highest bough, each leaf twirling first forwards and then backwards and swinging to and fro, a double motion. Each lifts a little and falls back like a pendulum, twisting on itself; and as it rises and sinks, strikes its fellow-leaf. Striking the side of the dark pines, the wind changes their colour and turns them paler. The oak leaves slide one over the other, hand above hand, laying shadow upon shadow upon the white road. In the vast net of the wide elm-tops the drifting shadow of the cloud which the wind brings is caught for a moment. Pushing aside the stiff ranks of the wheat with both arms, the air reaches the sun-parched earth. It walks among the mowing-grass like a farmer

feeling the crop with his hand one side, and opening it
with his walking-stick the other. It rolls the wavelets
carelessly as marbles to the shore ; the red cattle redden
the pool and stand in their own colour. The green caterpillar swings as he spins his thread and lengthens his
cable to the tide of air, descending from the tree ; before
he can slip it the whitethroat takes him. With a thrust
the wind hurls the swift fifty miles faster on his way ; it
ruffles back the black velvet of the mole peeping forth
from his burrow. Apple bloom and crab-apple bloom
have been blown long since athwart the furrows over the
orchard wall ; May petals and June roses scattered ;
the pollen and the seeds of the meadow-grasses thrown
on the threshing-floor of earth in basketfuls. Thistle
down and dandelion down, the brown down of the goat's-
beard ; by-and-by the keys of the sycamores twirling
aslant—the wind carries them all on its back, gossamer
web and great heron's vanes—the same weight to the
wind ; the drops of the waterfall blown aside sprinkle the
bright green ferns. The voice of the cuckoo in his season
travels on the zephyr, and the note comes to the most
distant hill, and deep into the deepest wood.

The light and fire of summer are made beautiful by
the air, without whose breath the glorious summer were
all spoiled. Thick are the hawthorn leaves, many deep
on the spray ; and beneath them there is a twisted and
intertangled winding in and out of boughs, such as no
curious ironwork of ancient artist could equal ; through
the leaves and metal-work of boughs the soft west wind
wanders at its ease. Wild wasp and tutored bee sing
sideways on their course as the breeze fills their vanes ;
with broad coloured sails boomed out, the butterfly drifts
alee. Beside a brown coated stone in the shadowed
stream a brown trout watches for the puffs that slay the

May-flies. Their ephemeral wings were made for a more exquisite life ; they endure but one sun ; they bear not the touch of the water ; they die like a dream dropping into the river. To the amethyst in the deep ditch the wind comes ; no petal so hidden under green it cannot find ; to the blue hill-flower up by the sky ; it lifts the guilty head of the passionate poppy that has sinned in the sun for love. Sweet is the rain the wind brings to the wallflower browned in the heat, a-dry on the crumbling stone. Pleasant the sunbeams to the marigold when the wind has carried the rain away and his sun-disc glows on the bank. Acres of perfume come on the wind from the black and white of the bean-field ; the firs fill the air by the copse with perfume. I know nothing to which the wind has not some happy use. Is there a grain of dust so small the wind shall not find it out? Ground in the mill-wheel of the centuries, the iron of the distant mountain floats like gossamer, and is drunk up as dew by leaf and living lung. A thousand miles of cloud go by from morn till night, passing overhead without a sound ; the immense packs, a mile square, succeed to each other, side by side, laid parallel, book-shape, coming up from the horizon and widening as they approach. From morn till night the silent footfalls of the ponderous vapours travel overhead, no sound, no creaking of the wheels and rattling of the chains ; it is calm at the earth, but the wind labours without an effort above, with such ease, with such power. Grey smoke hangs on the hill-side where the couch-heaps are piled, a cumulus of smoke ; the wind comes, and it draws its length along like the genii from the earthen pot ; there leaps up a great red flame shaking its head ; it shines in the bright sunlight ; you can see it across the valley.

A perfect summer day with a strong south wind ; a

cloudless blue sky blown pale, a summer sun blown cool, deep draughts of refreshing air to man and horse, clear definition of red-tile roof and conical oast, perfect colour of soft ash-green trees. In the evening, fourteen black swifts rushing together through the upper atmosphere with shrill cries, sometimes aside and on the tip of one wing, with a whirl descending, a black trail, to the tiled ridge they dwell in. Fine weather after this.

A swooning August day, with a hot east wind, from which there is no escape, which gives no air to the chest —you breathe and are not satisfied with the inspiration ; it does not fill ; there is no life in the killed atmosphere. It is a vacuum of heat, and yet the strong hot wind bends the trees, and the tall firs wrestle with it as they did with Sinis, the Pine-bender, bowed down and rebounding as if they would whirl their cones away like a catapult. Masses of air are moving by, and yet there is none to breathe. No escape in the shadow of hedge or wood, or in the darkened room ; darkness excludes the heat that comes with light, but the heat of the oven-wind cannot be shut out. Some monstrous dragon of the Chinese sky pants his fiery breath upon us, and the brown grass stalks threaten to catch flame in the field. The grain of wheat that was full of juice dries hard in the ears, and water is no more good for thirst. There is not a cloud in the sky ; but at night there is heavy rain, and the flowers are beaten down. There is a thunder-wind that blows at intervals when great clouds are visibly gathering over the hayfield. It is almost a calm ; but from time to time a breath comes, and a low mournful cry sounds in the hollow farmhouse—the windows and doors are open, and the men and women have gone out to make hasty help in the hay ere the storm—a mournful cry in the hollow house, as unhappy a note as if it were soaked February.

In April, six miles away in the valley, a vast cloud came down with swan-shot of hail, black as blackest smoke, overwhelming house and wood, all gone and mixed with the sky ; and behind the mass there followed a white cloud, sunlit, dragging along the ground like a cumulus fallen to the earth. At sunset the sky cleared, and under the glowing rim of the sun a golden wind drove the host of vapour before it, scattering it to the right and left. Large pieces caught and tore themselves in the trees of the forest, and one curved fragment hurled from the ridge fell in the narrow coombe, lit up as it came down with golden sunset rays, standing out bright against the shadowed wood. Down it came slowly as it were with outstretched arms, loth to fall, carrying the coloured light of the sky to the very surface of the earth.

THE COUNTRY SUNDAY.

ROSES bloomed on every bush, and some of the great hawthorns up which the briars had climbed seemed all flowers. The white and pink-white petals of the June roses adhered all over them, almost as if they had been artificially gummed or papered on so as to hide the leaves. Such a profusion of wild-rose bloom is rarely seen. On the Sunday morning, as on a week-day morning, they were entirely unnoticed, and might be said in their turn to take no heed of the sanctified character of the day. With a rush like a sudden thought the white-barred eave-swallows came down the arid road and rose again into the air as easily as a man dives into the water. Dark specks beneath the white summer clouds, the swifts, the black albatross of our skies, moved on their unwearied wings. Like the albatross that floats over the ocean and sleeps on the wing, the swift's scimitar-like pinions are careless of repose. Once now and then they came down to earth, not, as might be supposed, to the mansion or the church tower, but to the low tiled roof of an ancient cottage which they fancied for their home. Kings sometimes affect to mix with their subjects ; these birds that aspire to the extreme height of the air frequently nest in the roof of a despised tenement, inhabited by an old woman who never sees them. The corn was green and tall, the hops looked well, the foxglove was stirring, the delicious atmosphere of summer, sun-laden and scented, filled the deep valleys ; a morning of the richest beauty and deepest repose. All things reposed but man, and man is so busy with his vulgar aims that it quite dawns upon many people as a wonderful surprise how still nature is on a Sunday morning. Nature is absolutely still every day of the week, and proceeds with the most absolute indifference to days and dates.

The sharp metallic clangour of a bell went bang, bang, bang, from one roof ; not far distant a harsher and deeper note—some Tartar-like bell of universal uproar —hammered away. At intervals came the distant chimes of three distinct village churches—ding dong, dong ding, pango, frango, jango—very much jango— bang, clatter, clash—a humming vibration and dreadful stir. The country world was up in arms, I was about to say—I mean in chimney-pot hat and pomade, *en route* to its various creeds, some to one bell, some to another, some to ding dong, and some to dong ding ; but the most of them directed their steps towards a silent chapel. This great building, plain beyond plainness, stood beside a fir copse, from which in the summer morning there floated an exquisite fragrance of pine. If all the angles of the architects could have been put together, nothing could have been designed more utterly opposite to the graceful curve of the fir tree than this red-bricked crass building. Bethel Chapel combined everything that could be imagined contrary to the spirit of nature, which undulates. The largest erection of the kind, it was evidently meant for a large congregation.

Of all the people in this country there are none so devout as the cottagers in the lanes and hamlets. They are as uncompromising as the sectaries who smashed the

images and trampled on the pride of kings in the days
of Charles I. The translation of the Bible cut off
Charles I.'s head by letting loose such a flood of iron-
fisted controversy, and to any one who has read the
pamphlets of those days the resemblance is constantly
suggested. John Bunyan wrote about the Pilgrim. To
this chapel there came every Sunday morning a man
and his wife, ten miles on foot from their cottage home
in a distant village. The hottest summer day or the
coldest winter Sunday made no difference ; they tramped
through dust, and they tramped through slush and mire ;
they were pilgrims every week. A grimly real religion,
as concrete and as much a fact as a stone wall ; a sort of
horse's faith going along the furrow unquestioning. In
their own village there were many chapels, and at least
one church, but these did not suffice. The doctrine at
Bethel was the one saving doctrine, and there they
went. There were dozens who came from lesser distances quite as regularly, the men in their black coats
and high hats, big fellows that did not look ungainly
till they dressed themselves up ; women as red as
turkey-cocks, panting and puffing ; crowds of children
making the road odorous with the smell of pomade ;
the boys with their hair too long behind ; the girls with
vile white stockings, all out of drawing, and without a
touch that could be construed into a national costume
—the cheap shoddy shop in the country lane. All with
an expression of Sunday goodness : 'To-day we are
good, we are going to chapel, and we mean to stay till
the very last word. We have got our wives and families
with us, and woe be to any of them if they dare to look
for a bird's nest ! This is business.' Besides the foot
people there come plenty in traps and pony-carriages,
and some on horseback, for a certain class of farmers

belong to the same persuasion, and there are well-to-do people in the crowd. It is the cast of mind that makes the worshipper, not the worldly position.

It is written, but perhaps it is not true, that in old times—not very old times—the parish clergyman had a legal right, by which every person in the parish was compelled to appear once on a Sunday in the church. Those who did not come were fined a shilling.

Now look at the Shillings this Sunday morning flowing of their own free will along the crooked lanes, and over the stiles, and through the hops, and down the hill to the chapel which can offer no bribe and can impose no fine.

Old women—wonder 'tis how they live on nothing a day—still manage to keep a decent black dress and come to chapel with a penny in their pockets in spite of their age and infirmities. The nearest innkeeper, himself a most godly man, has work enough to do to receive the horses and traps and pony-carriages and stow them away before service begins, when he will stride from the stable to the pew. Then begins the hollow and flute-like modulation of a pitch-pipe within the great building. One of the members of the congregation who is a musician is setting the ears of the people to the tune of the hymn that is about to be given forth. The verse is read, and then rises the full swell of hundreds of voices; and while they sing let us think what a strange thing the old pitch-pipe—no organ, no harmonium—what a strange thing the whole scene is, with its Cromwellian air in the midst of the modern fields.

This is a picture, and not a disputation : as to what they teach or preach inside Bethel, it is nothing to me ; this paper has not the slightest theological bias.

You may tell when the service is nearly over by the

stray boys who steal out and round the walls to throw stones at the sparrows in the roads ; they need a little relaxation ; nature gets even into Bethel. By-and-by out come some bigger lads and tie two long hop-poles together with which to poke down the swallows' nests under the chapel eaves. The Book inside, of which they almost make an idol, seemed to think the life of a sparrow—and possibly of a swallow—was of value ; still it is good fun to see the callow young come down flop on the hard ground.

When the church doors are thrown open by the noiseless vergers, and patchouli and macassar, and the overpowering, rich smell of silks and satins rushes out in a volume of heated air, in a few minutes the whole place is vacant. Bethel is not deserted in this manner. All those who have come from a distance have brought with them their dinner in a black bag or basket, and quietly settle themselves down to take their dinner in the chapel. This practice is not confined to the pilgrims who have walked a long way ; very many of those who live the other side of the village shut up their cottages, bring their provisions, and spend the whole day at their devotions. Now the old woman spends her Sunday penny. At the back of the chapel there is a large room where a person is employed to boil the kettle and supply cups of tea at a halfpenny each. Here the old lady makes herself very comfortable, and waits till service begins again. Halfpenny a cup would not, of course, pay the cost of the materials, but these are found by some earnest member of the body, some farmer or tradesman's wife, who feels it a good deed to solace the weary worshippers. There is something in this primitive hospitality, in this eating their dinners in the temple, and general communion of humanity, which to a philosopher seems very admirable.

It seems better than incense and scarlet robes, unlit candles behind the altar, and vacancy. Not long since a bishop addressed a circular to the clergy of his diocese, lamenting in solemn tones the unhappy position of the labourer in the village churches. The bishop had observed with regret, with very great regret, that the labourer seemed in the background. He sat in the back seats behind the columns, and near the door where he could hardly hear, and where he had none of the comfort of the stove in winter. The bishop feared his position was cold and comfortless, that he did not feel himself to be a member of the Church, that he was outside the pale of its society. He exhorted the country clergy to bring the labourer forward and make him more comfortable, to put him in a better seat among the rest, where he would feel himself to be really one of the congregation.

To those who have sat in country churches this circular read as a piece of most refined sarcasm, so bitter because of its truth. Where had been the clerical eye all these years that Hodge had sat and coughed in the draughts by the door? Was it merely a coincidence that the clerical eye was opened just at the moment when Hodge became a voter?

At Bethel Chapel between the services the cottagers, the farmers, and the tradesmen break their bread together, and converse, and actually seem to recognise one another; they do not turn their backs the instant the organ ceases and return each to his house in proud isolation. There is no dining together, no friendly cup of tea at the parish church. This Bethel is, you see, the church of the poor people, most emphatically *their* church. If the word church means not a building, but a society, then this is the true country church. It is the society of all those who, for want of a better expression, I may term the humble-minded, those who have no aristocratic or exclusive tastes, very simple in their reading and studies even if well-to-do, and simple in their daily habits, rising early and retiring early, and plebeian in their dinner-hour. It is a peculiar cast of mind that I am trying to describe—a natural frame of mind ; these are 'chapel people '—perhaps a phrase will convey the meaning better than explanation. This is *their* church, and whatever the theology may be there is undoubtedly a very strong bond of union among them.

Not only the old women with their Sunday pennies, but great numbers beside, young and old of both sexes, take their cup of tea, for these people take tea with every meal, dinner and supper as well as breakfast and five o'clock, and if they don't feel well they will rise at two in the morning to get a cup of tea. They are as Russian as the Russians in this particular ; they have cheese on the table, too, at every meal. The pastor has, meantime, been entertained with a good dinner at some house adjacent, where he goes every Sunday ; by-and-by the flute begins to tune again, the hymns resound, and the labour of the day is resumed. Somewhere about four o'clock the summer-dusty roads are full again of the returning pilgrims, and the crowd gradually sinks away by footpath and stile. The black albatross is still wheeling in the upper atmosphere, the white-barred swallow rushes along the road and dives upwards, the unwearied roses are still opened to the sun's rays, and calm, indifferent Nature has pursued her quiet course without heed of pitch-pipe or organ, or bell or chalice. Perhaps if you chance to be resting by a gate you may hear one of the cottage women telling her children to let the ants alone and not tease them, for 'thaay be God's

creeturs.' Or possibly the pastor himself may be over-
heard discoursing to a bullet-headed woman, with one
finger on the palm of his other hand, ' That's their serpen-
tine way ; that's their subtlety ; that's their casuistry ;
which arguments you may imagine to refer, as your fancy
pleases, to the village curate, or the tonsured priest of
the monastery over the hill. For the tonsured priest,
and the monastery, and the nunnery, and the mass, and
the Virgin Mary, have grown to be a very great power
indeed in English lanes. Between the Roman missal
and the chapel hymn-book, the country curate with his
good old-fashioned litany is ground very small indeed,
and grows less and less between these millstones till he
approaches the vanishing-point. The Roman has the
broad acres, his patrons have given him the land ; the
chapel has the common people, and the farmers are
banding together not to pay tithes. So that his whole
soul may well go forth in the apostrophe, ' Good Lord,
deliver us ! '

There is no man so feasted as the chapel pastor.
His tall and yet rotund body and his broad red face
might easily be mistaken for the outward man of a sturdy
farmer, and he likes his pipe and glass. He dines every
Sunday, and at least once a week besides, at the house
of one of his stoutest upholders. It is said that at such
a dinner, after a large plateful of black currant pudding,
finding there was still some juice left, he lifted the plate
to his mouth and carefully licked it all round ; the
hostess hastened to offer a spoon, but he declined,
thinking that was much the best way to gather up the
essence of the fruit. So simple were his manners, he
needed no spoon ; and, indeed, if we look back, the
apostles managed without forks, and put their fingers in
the dish. After dinner the cognac bottle is produced,

and the pastor fills his tumbler half full of spirit, and but lightly dashes it with water. It is cognac and not brandy, for your chapel minister thinks it an affront if anything more common than the best French liquor is put before him; he likes it strong, and with it his long clay pipe. Very frequently another minister, sometimes two or three, come in at the same time, and take the same dinner, and afterwards form a genial circle with cognac and tobacco, when the room speedily becomes full of smoke and the bottle of brandy soon disappears. In these family parties there is not the least approach to over-conviviality; it is merely the custom, no one thinks anything of a glass and a pipe; it is perfectly innocent; it is not a local thing, but common and understood. The consumption of brandy and tobacco and the good things of dinner, tea, and supper (for the party generally sit out the three meals), must in a month cost the host a good deal of money, but all things are cheerfully borne for the good of the church. Never were men feasted with such honest good-will as these pastors; and if a budding Paul or Silas happens to come along who has scarce yet passed his ordination, the youthful divine may stay a week if he likes, and lick the platter clean. In fact, so constant is this hospitality, that in certain houses it is impossible to pay a visit at any time of the year without finding one of these young brothers reposing amid the fat of the land, and doubtless indulging in pleasant spiritual communion with the daughters of the mansion. Something in this system of household ministers of religion reminds one of the welcome and reverence said to be extended in the East to the priests, who take up their residence indefinitely, and are treated as visible incarnations of the Deity whose appetites it is meritorious to satisfy. Indeed, these young men, who have perhaps been trained as missionaries, often discourse of Buddha with a very long and unctuous 'Boo.'

The ancient Roman censor who tried by laws and persuasions to induce the inhabitants of Rome to marry, yet could not succeed in inducing them to submit to what they considered a sacrifice for the benefit of the state, would have been delighted with the marrying tendencies of the chapel people. A venerable old gentleman—a great pillar of the body—after the decease of his first wife married her sister, and again, upon her removal, married his cook. Another great prop—elderly indeed, but still upright and iron-grey, a most powerfully made man, who always spoke as if his words were indeed law—rule-of-thumb law—has married three sisters in succession, and has had offspring by all. Their exact degrees of consanguinity I cannot tell you, or whether they call each other brothers and sisters, or cousins. This is certain, however, that whether such marriages be legal or not, they are as such regarded and as such accepted in every sense by the society to which these gentlemen belong. Another gentleman now has his fourth wife, and he, too, is a most strenuous believer, and not his bitterest enemy can rake up the smallest accusation against his character. He, too, is a strong and upright man, fully capable of another wife if time should chance to bring it about. Now, the odd part of it is that, having married four times, and each time in the same village, where all the families are more or less connected, he is more or less related to every single individual in the parish. First, there are his own blood relations and his wives' blood relations, and then there are their relations' relations, and next his sons and daughters have married and introduced a fresh roll, and I really do not think either he or anybody else knows exactly where the list ends.   This is nothing uncommon.   Though clans and tribes no longer settle under their respective chiefs in villages, the families of the same name and blood still present a very close representation of the clan system.   They have all the tribal relationship without any of its feeling.   Instead of forming a strong body and helping each other, these people seemed to detest one another, and to lose no opportunity of snatching some little advantage or telling some scandalous tale.   In fact, this in-and-in breeding seems one of the curses of village life, and a cause of stagnation and narrowness of mind.   This marrying and giving in marriage is not singular to well-to-do leaders of chapel society, but goes on with equal fervour among the lower members.   The cottage girls and cottage boys marry the instant they get a chance, and it is not at all uncommon to find comparatively young labourers who have had two wives.   There is nothing in this to reproach : it is a peculiarity of the cast of mind which I am endeavouring to describe—a cast of mind perhaps not much marked by sentimentality.   Something in this practice reminds one of the Mormons.   Certainly the wives are not taken together, but they are sealed as fast as circumstances permit. Something in it has a Mormonite aspect to an observer, and perhaps the existence of this cast of mind may assist in explaining the inexplicable growth of that strange religion.   Doubtless they would repudiate the suggestion with loud outcries and indignation, for people are always most vigorous in denouncing themselves unconsciously. These numerous wives (who are quite willing), the marrying of sisters, the primitive gatherings at the chapel, so like the religious camps of the Far West, the general relationship, have a distinct flavour of Salt Lake.   Add

to this the immense working power of these pluralist
giants, for you will generally find that the well-to-do cha-
peller with his third wife, or more, is a man who has raised
himself from very much nothing to very much something.   By sheer force of labour and push he has lifted
himself head and shoulders above the village—a career,
too, conspicuous by strict integrity.   Did he live in a
London suburb he would be pointed out to the rising
generation by anxious fathers as the very model for them
to follow.   The village ought to be proud of them, but
the village secretly and aside hates them, being practical
commentaries on the general sloth and stupidity.   This
energy of work, too, is like the saints of Utah, who
have made an oasis and a garden where was a desert.
After labouring from morning till night they like the
sound of a feminine voice and the warmth of a feminine
welcome in the back parlour of rest.

This four times married elder—what work, what a
pyramid of work, his life represents!   The young
labourer left with his mother and brothers and sisters to
keep, learning carpentering, and bettering his wages—
learning mason-work, picking up the way to manage
machinery, inspiring men with confidence, and beginning
to get the leverage of borrowed money, getting a good
name at the bank, managing a little farm, contracting for
building, contracting for hauling—onwards to a larger
farm, larger buildings, big contracts in rising towns,
somehow or other grinding money out of everything by
force of will, bending everything to his purpose by
stubborn sinew, always truthful, straightforward, and
genuine.   Consider what immense labour this represents!
I do not think many such men can be found, rude and
unlettered, yet naturally gentleman-like, to work their
way in the world without the aid of the Lombard Street

financiers; in village life, remember, where all is stagnant and dull—no golden openings such as occur near great towns. On work-days still wearing the same old hat —I wonder what material it was originally?—tough leather probably—its fibres soaked with mortar, its shine replaced by lime, its shape dented by bricks, its rotundity flattened by timber, stuck about with cow's hair—for a milker leans his head against the animal—sodden with rain, and still the same old hat. The same old hat, that Teniers might have introduced, a regular daub of a hat: pity it is that it will never be painted. On Sundays the high silk hat, the glossy black coat of the elder, but there are no gloves to be got on such hands as those; they are too big and too real ever to be got into the artificiality of kid. Everything grew under those hands; if there was a rabbit-hutch in the back yard it became a shed, and a stable sprang up by the shed, and a sawpit out of the stable, and a workshop beyond the sawpit, and cottages to let beyond that; next a market garden and a brick-kiln, and a hop-oast, and a few acres of freehold meadow, and by-and-by some villas; all increasing and multiplying, and leading to enterprises in distant places—such a mighty generation after generation of solid things! A most earnest and conscientious chapel man, welcoming the budding Paul and Silas, steadily feeding the resident apostle, furnishing him with garden produce and a side of bacon when the pig was killed, arranging a vicarage for him at a next-to-nothing rent; lending him horse and trap, providing innumerable bottles of three-star brandy for these men of God, and continual pipes for the prophets; supplying the chapel fund with credit in time of monetary difficulty—the very right arm and defender of the faith.

Let the drama shift a year in one sentence in true

dramatic way, and now imagine the elder and his family proceeding down the road as the Bethel congregation gather. As he approaches they all ostentatiously turn their backs. One or two of the other elders walk inside; being men of some education, they soften down the appearance of their resentment by getting out of the way. Groups of cottage people, on the contrary, rather come nearer the road, and seem to want to make their sentiments coarsely visible. Such is the way with that layer of society; they put everything so very very crudely; they do not understand a gentle intimation, they express their displeasure in the rudest manner, without any consciousness that gruffness and brutality of manner degrades the righteous beneath the level of the wicked who is accused. The women make remarks to each other. Many of them had been visitors at the elder's house, yet now they will not so much as say good morning to his wife and family; their children look over the wall with stolid stare. Farther down the road the elder meets the pastor on his road to chapel. The elder looks the pastor straight in the face; the pastor shuffles his eyes over the hedge; it is difficult to quite forget the good dinners, the bottles, and the pipes. The elder goes on, and he and his family are picked up by a conveyance at the cross-ways and carried to a place of worship in a distant village. This is only a specimen, this is only the Sunday, but the same process goes on all the week. The elder's house, that was once the resort of half the people in the village, is now deserted, no one looks in in passing; the farmers do not stop as they come back from market to tell how much they have lost by their corn, or to lament that So-and-so is going to grub his hops—bad times; the women do not come over of an afternoon with news of births and rumours of marriages. One family, once intimate friends, sent over to say that they liked the elder very much, but they could not call while he was on such terms with their 'dear pastor.' Two or three of the ministers who came by invitation to preach in the chapel, and who had been friendly, did indeed call once, but were speedily given to understand by the leading members of the congregation that dinners and sleeping accommodation had been provided elsewhere, and they must not do so again. The ministers, being entirely in the power of the congregations, had to obey. In short, the elder and his family were excommunicated, spiritually boycotted, interdicted, and cut off from social intercourse; without any of the magical ceremonies of the Vatican, they were as effectually excommunicated as if the whole seventy cardinals and the Pope in person had pronounced the dread sentence. In a great town perhaps such a thing would not be so marked or so much felt; in a little village where everybody knows everybody, where there are no strangers, and where you must perforce come in contact constantly with persons you have known for years, it is a very annoying process indeed. There are no streets of shops to give a choice of butchers and bakers, no competition of tea merchants and cheese-mongers, so that if one man shows a dislike to serving you, you can go on to the next and get better attention. 'Take it or go without it' is village law; no such thing as independence; you must walk or drive into the nearest town, five miles away perhaps, if you wish to avoid a sour face on the other side of the counter. No one will volunteer the smallest service for the excommunicant of the chapel; nothing could more vividly illustrate the command to 'love one another.' No one can imagine the isolation of a house in a country place interdicted like this. If the other inhabitants could find any possible excuse for not doing anything they were asked they would not do it—not for money : they were out of what was wanted, or they had promised it, or they couldn't find it, or they were too busy, and so all through the whole course of daily life.

Now the most remarkable part of this bitter persecution was the fact that the elder had lent money to almost all the principal members of the congregation. The bold speculator had never been appealed to in vain by any one in difficulty.   Some had had a hundred, some fifty, some twenty, some ten—farmers whose corn had been a loss instead of a profit, whose hops had sold for less than the cost of picking them, little tradesmen who had a bill to meet, handicraft men who could not pay the men who worked side by side with them, cottagers who needed an outhouse built, and others who lacked the means to pay for a funeral.   There seemed no one to whom he had not lent money for some purpose, besides the use of his name as security.   Fortune had given to him, and he had given as freely to others, so that it was indeed a bitter trial to the heart :—

> Blow, blow, thou winter wind,
> Thou art not so unkind
>   As man's ingratitude.
> Thy tooth is not so keen,
> Because thou art not seen,
>   Although thy breath be rude.

In his stern pride he did not condescend to put in motion any revenge against these petty poltroons, but went on his way with absolute indifference to all outward seeming.   His family, who were perhaps more nearly touched in the affairs of daily life than he was, consoled themselves with the old country proverb, ' Ah, well, we shall live till we die, if the pigs don't eat us, and then we shall go acorning '—a clear survival of the belief in transmigration, for he who is eaten by a pig becomes a pig, and goeth forth with swine to eat acorns.

There had been some very strong language and straightforward observations at the chapel meetings, the private vestry of the managers ; the elder being one of the founders, and his name on the deed could not be excluded—gall and wormwood—without his signature nothing could be done. Bitterer still, the chapel was heavily in debt to him. Had he chosen, in American phrase, he could have 'shut up the shebang in mighty sudden time.' The elder was tall ; the elder was strong ; the elder was grim ; the elder was a man who could rule hundreds of the roughest labourers ; the elder was a man who would have his say, and said it like throwing down a hod full of bricks. With the irresistible logic of figures and documents he demonstrated the pastor to be a liar, and told him so to his face. With the same engines he proved that two or three of the other managers were hypocrites, and told them so. Neither could pastor nor managers refute it, but stood like sheep. Then he told them what he had done for the chapel and for its minister, and no one could deny him. Indeed, the minister had been heard to weakly confess that the elder had once been a good friend to him. Perhaps his partisans, as is often the case, had taken up the pastor's cause with more violence than he himself desired, and by their vehemence had driven him into a position which he himself would have avoided. Most likely he would have made peace himself ; but the blot on all chapel systems of government is that the minister is but the mouthpiece of his congregation. Having thrown down his load of bricks thump, the elder stalked out with his memoranda and with his cheque-book, leaving them to face the spectre of bank-ruptcy. At least once a week the elder, out of sheer British determination to claim his rights, stepped into the chapel rooms with his private key, just to walk round. They put another lock which his key did not fit, but he heaved the door open with a crowbar, and their case must have been feeble indeed when they could not even bring an action for trespass against him.

The historian knoweth not all things, and how this schism arose is hidden from view. Very likely, indeed, it may have arisen out of the very foundation of the chapel itself, such buildings and land being usually held in some manner by a body of managers or trustees—a sort of committee, in fact—a condition which may easily afford opportunities for endless wrangling. In this particular the Established Church has a great advantage, the land and building being dedicated 'for ever,' so that no dispute is possible. Tales there were of some little feminine disagreement having arisen between the wives of the two men, magnified with the assistance of a variety of tabbies, a sort of thing by no means impossible among two hundred relations. Such affairs often spring from a grain of mustard seed, and by-and-by involve all the fowls of the air that roost in the branches. Idle tales circulated of a discussion among the ministers (visitors) which happened one evening over the pipes and three-star bottles, when the elder, taking down a celebrated volume of sermons, pointed out a passage almost word for word identical with what the pastor had said in his sermon on the previous Sunday—a curious instance of parallel inspiration. Unkind people afterwards spread the gloss that the elder had accused the minister of plagiarism. Mere fiction, no doubt. After a thing has happened people can generally find twenty

causes. The excommunication, however, was real
enough, and ten times more effectual because the sentence was pronounced not by the pastor but by the congregation.

Still nothing disturbed the dignity of the elder. He
worked away as usual, always with tools in his hands.
He would tear away with a plane at a window-frame or
a coffin-lid, and tell the listener his wrongs, and how he
had been scorned and insulted by people whom he had
helped for years, and how they had reversed the teaching of the gospel in their bearing towards him—heavier
blows and longer shavings—as if there were no such
thing as true religion. And, indeed, he would say, in
his business transactions, he had over and over again
found that men who were not 'professors'—*i.e.* who did
not claim to be ' saved '—were more truthful and more
to be depended on in their engagements than those who
constantly talked of righteousness. For all that—with
a tremendous shaving—for all that, the gospel was true.

So he planed and hammered, and got a large contract
on a building estate near a great town, busy as busy
where it was necessary to have a tramway and a locomotive, or ' dirt-engine,' to drag the trucks with the earth
from the excavations. This engine was a source of
never-failing amusement to the steady, quiet farmers
whose domains were being invaded ; very observant
people, but not pushing. One day a part of the engine
was tied up with string ; another day it was blowing off
steam like a volcano, the boiler nearly empty and getting
red-hot, while the men rushed to fetch water with a
couple of buckets ; finally, the funnel rusted off and a
wooden one was put up—a merry joke ! But while
they laughed the contractor pushed ahead in Yankee
style, using any and every expedient, and making

money while they sighed over the slow plough. They must have everything perfect, else they could do nothing ; he could do much with very imperfect materials. He would make a cucumber frame out of a church window, or a church window out of a cucumber frame. One of the residents on the new building estate found his cupboard doors numbered on the panels two, six, eight, in gilt figures inside, and in fact they were made of pew doors which the contractor had got out of some old church he had ransacked and turned topsy-turvy to the order of the vicar. He would have run up a new Salt Lake City cheap, or built a new Rome at five per cent. in a few days.

Meantime, at the little village, various incidents occurred ; the sternly virtuous cottagers, for one thing, had collected from their scattered homes and held a ' Horn Fair.' Some erring barmaid at the inn, accused of too lavish a use of smiles, too much kindness—most likely a jealous tale only—aroused their righteous ire. With shawm and timbrel and ram's-horn trumpet—*i.e.* with cow's horns, poker and tongs, and tea-trays—the indignant and high-toned population collected night after night by the tavern, and made such fearful uproar that the poor girl, really quite innocent, had to leave her situation. Nothing could be more charitable, more truly righteous, after the model of the Man who would not even so much as *say* a harsh word to the woman taken in adultery. One poor man shut up his house and went away with his wife and family, and not being heard of for a little while these backbiters told each other that he had not paid his rent, that his furniture was only on loan, and not a single instalment had been met ; he owed the butcher half a crown, the baker discovered there was one and twopence on his book, the tavern could show a score, everybody knew the wretch was a drunkard and beat his wife, and many knew his wife was no better than she should be.   Nothing was too base to be laid to the charge of the scoundrel who had run away. At the end of a few weeks the wretch and his family returned, looking very healthy and well supplied with money, having been picking in a distant hop-garden. It was common for people to shut their houses and do this at that season of the year, but their blind malice was too eager to remember this. Another person by continually dunning a poor debtor to pay him half a sovereign had driven him to commit suicide ! So ran their bitter tongues. Backbiting is the curse of village life, and seems to keep people by its effects upon the mind far more effectually in the grip of poverty than the lowness of wages. They become so saturated with littleness that they cannot attempt anything, and have no enterprise. To transplant them to the freer atmosphere of a great city, or of the Far West, is the only means of cure. At this particular village they were exceptionally given to backbiting, perhaps because everybody was more than usually related to everybody ; they hated each other and vilified each other with pre-eminent energy. The poorest man, half starving, would hardly do a job for a farmer because—because—because he did not know why, except that nothing was too bad to be said of him ; the poorest washerwoman with hungry children would not go and do a day's work for Mrs. So-and-so, because ' she beant nobody, she beant no better than we ; beant a-going to work for her.' This malice was not directed towards strangers, against whom it is natural to heave half a brick, but against their own old neighbours. They tore each other to pieces, they were perfect cannibals with the tongue, perfect Lestrigonians. They never said 'good morning' to an equal, or lifted their hats to a lady; a jerk of the head, say about half an inch from the perpendicular, was their utmost greeting; their manners were about as pleasant as those of cattle might be could they be dressed like human beings. True, Bethel was of modern date, but they had had resident vicars for centuries; and where had they been, and where was the humanising tendency of much-vaunted Christianity? Could not three centuries soften a little village? I will do something for them if I can, for the credit of the race at large; they shall not be without an excuse if I can help it. Perhaps it was because there were no resident squires, perhaps because a good many of them had little plots of land; still they were Lestrigonians, and no doubt the row between the elder and the pastor was really due to this malice and uncharitableness. How curious it seems to a philosopher that so much religion should be accompanied by such bitter ill-feeling!—true religion, too, for these Lestrigonians were most seriously in earnest in their chapelling. Yet no doubt they fomented the row, for the pastor himself was much too clever a man to proceed to such extremities. By nature he was a fluent speaker, rising to eloquence as eloquence is understood among that kind of audience. He carried them with him, quite swept them away. They came to hear him from miles round about; there were plenty of other chapels, but no one like the man at Bethel. Once they came they always came. Who can name a country clergyman with university training who can do this? The man at Bethel also possessed a natural talent of personally impressing and gaining the good-will of every person with whom he came in contact; it was astonishing with what tenacity people clung to him, so that there must have been something exceptional in his character. His origin was of the humblest; he was drawn from the same class as the apostles, as the great Fisherman, and the great Tentmaker, a man of manual labour lifted entirely by his wit to be a very great power indeed in the community where he was stationed.

Too much credit must not be put upon cottagers' tales: one day they are all so bitter, hanging would not be sufficient, and you would suppose they were going to show a lifelong enmity; in a week or two it is all forgotten, and next month they are taking tea together. Those who know them best say you should never believe anything a cottager tells you. There is sure to be exaggeration, or they tell you half the story, and they catch up the wildest rumour and repeat it as unquestioned truth. No doubt after a while all this sound and fury signifying nothing will blow off, and there will be a reconciliation; the pastor and the elder will be bosom friends, all the congregation will be calling, and eating and drinking; there will be pipes and three-star bottles, and the elect will be made perfect. If the fourth wife disappears in time there will be a fifth, and Christian Mormonism will flourish exceedingly. Very likely the furious fall-out is over before now; there is no stability in this peculiar cast, the chapel mind.

Another curious reflection suggests itself to any one who has seen the fervour of Bethel. Within an easy walk of each other there are eight chapels and three churches and the Salvation Army barracks; a thinly populated country district, too; no squires, the farmers all depressed and ruined, the cottagers howling about starvation wages. One would have thought all of them together could hardly maintain a single spiritual teacher. All this for chapel and church; but no cottage hospital, either for accidents or diseases. If any one fell ill he had to be content with the workhouse doctor; if they required anything else they must go to the clergyman and get a letter of introduction or some kind of certificate for a London hospital, or any infirmary to which he happened to subscribe. The chapellers made no bones about utilising the clergyman in this way; they considered it their right; as he was the parish clergyman, it was his place to supply them with such certificates. There was no provision for the aged labourer or his wife when strength failed—nothing for them but parish relief. There was no library. There was no institute for the teaching of science, or for lectures disseminating the knowledge of the nineteenth century. Every now and then the children died from drinking bad water—ditch water; the women took tea, the men took beer, the children drank water. Good water abounded, but then there was the trouble and expense of digging wells; individuals could not do it, the community did not care. Does it not seem strange? All this fervour and building of temples and rattling of the Salvation Army drum and loud demands for the New Jerusalem, and not a single effort for physical well-being or mental training!

While these pranks are played at Bethel let us glance a moment in another direction down the same green country lane on the same bright summer day. Let it be late in the afternoon of the Sunday, the swifts still wheeling, the roses still blooming, blue-winged jays slipping in and out of the beech trees. These hazel lanes were once the scene of Puritan marchings to and fro, of Fifth Monarchy men who likened the Seven-hilled City to the Beast; furious men with musket and pike, whose horses' hoofs had defaced the mosaic pavements of cathedrals. These hazel lanes, lovely nut-tree boughs,

with 'many an oak that grew thereby,' have been the
scene of historic events down from the days of St. Dun-
stan.   In the quiet of the Sunday afternoon, when the
clashing of the bells was stilled, there walked in the
shade of the oaks a young priest and a lady.   His well-
shaped form seemed the better shown by his flowing
cassock ; his handsome face was refined by its air of
late devotion.   The lady, dressed in the highest style of
aristocratic fashion, that is to say with grace, was evidently a member of good society.   A little picture certainly : only two figures, no pronounced action, no tra-
gedy, yet what a meaning in that cassock !   It spoke of
confession, of ritual, of transubstantiation, of all the great
historic romance of Rome ecclesiastical.   The great
romance of Rome : its holy footsteps of St. Peter, its
aërial dome of Michael Angelo, its Vatican of ancient
manuscripts, of beauteous statue and chariot—the great
romance of Rome, its Borgia, its dungeons and flames of
the Inquisition.   A picture of two figures only, but consider the background.   Consider the thousands of broad
English acres that now support great monasteries and
convents in quiet country places where one could scarce
expect to find a barn.   The buildings are there ; that is
a solid fact, take what view you like of them, or take
none at all.   There are men about country roads with
shaven crown and cassock whose dark Continental faces
have an unmistakable stamp of priesthood ; faces that
might be pictured with those of the monks of old Spain.
Women in long black cloaks, black hoods and white coif,
women with long black rosaries hanging from the girdle,
go to and fro among the wheat and the clover.   One
rubs one's eyes.   Are these the days of Friar Laurence
and Juliet ?   Shall we meet the mitred abbot with his
sumpter mule ?   Shall we meet the mailed knights ?   In

some places whole villages belong to English monks, and there is not a man or woman in them who is not a Catholic ; there are even small country towns which by dint of time, money, and territorial influence have been re-absorbed, and are now as completely Catholic as they were before Henry VIII. In these half-village half-towns you may chance on a busy market day to come across a great building abutting on the street, and may listen to the organ and the chant ; there is incense and gorgeous ceremony, the golden tinkle of the altar-bell. Bow your head, it is the host ; cross yourself, it is the mass. The butcher and the dealer are busy with the sheep, but it is a saint's day. By-and-by no doubt we shall have a village Lourdes at home, and miracles and pilgrimages and offerings and shrines : the village will be right glad to see the pilgrims, if only they come from the West End and have money in the purse. The village would be very glad indeed of a miracle to bring it a shower of gold.

THE COUNTRY SIDE: SUSSEX.

I

ON the wall of an old barn by the great doors there still remains a narrow strip of notice-board, much battered and weather-beaten : 'Beware of steel ——' can be read, the rest has been broken off, but no doubt it was 'traps.' 'Beware of steel traps,' a caution to thieves—a reminiscence of those old days which many of our present writers and leaders of opinion seem to think never existed. When the strong labourer could hardly earn 7s. a week, when in some parishes scarcely half the population got work at all, living, in the most literal sense, on the parish, when bread was dear and the loaf was really life itself, then that stern inscription had meaning enough. The granaries were full, the people half starved. The wheat was threshed by the flail in full view of the wretched, who could gaze through the broad doors at the golden grain ; the sparrows helped themselves, men dare not. At night men tried to steal the corn, and had to be prevented by steel traps, like rats. To-day wheat is so cheap, it scarcely pays to carry it to market. Some farmers have it ground, and sell the flour direct to the consumer ; some have used it for feeding purposes—actually for hogs. The contrast is extraordinary. Better let the hogs eat the corn than

that man should starve. To-day the sparrows are just
as busy as ever of old, chatter, chirp around the old
barn, while the threshing machine hums, and every now
and then lowers its voice in a long-drawn descending
groan of seemingly deep agony. Up it rises again as
the sheaves are cast in—hum, hum, hum ; the note rises
and resounds and fills the yard up to the roof of the
barn and the highest tops of the ricks as a flood fills a
pool, and overflowing, rushes abroad over the fields, past
the red hop-oast, past the copse of yellowing larches,
onwards to the hills. An inarticulate music—a chant
telling of the sunlit hours that have gone and the
shadows that floated under the clouds over the beautiful
wheat. No more shall the tall stems wave in the wind
or listen to the bees seeking the clover-fields. The lark
that sang above the green corn, the partridge that sheltered among the yellow stalks, the list of living things
delighting in it—all have departed. The joyous life of
the wheat is ended—not in vain, for now the grain becomes the life of man, and in that object yet more
glorified. Outwards the chant extending, reaches the
hollows of the valley, rolling over the shortened stubble,
where the plough already begins the first verse of a new
time. A pleasant sound to listen to, the hum of the
threshing, the beating of the engine, the rustle of the
straw, the shuffle shuffle of the machine, the voices of
the men, the occupation and bustle in the autumn afternoon ! I listened to it sitting in the hop-oast, whose
tower, like a castle turret, overlooks and domineers the
yard. In the loft the resounding hum whirled around,
beating and rebounding from the walls, and forcing its
way out again through the narrow window. The edge,
as it were, of a sunbeam lit up the rude chamber crossed
with unhewn beams and roofed above with unconcealed

tiles, whose fastening pegs were visible. A great heap of golden scales lay in one corner, the hops fresh from the drying. Up to his waist in a pocket let through the floor a huge giant of a man trod the hops down in the sack, turning round and round, and now his wide shoulders and now his red cheeks succeeded. The music twirled him about as a leaf by the wind. Without the rich blue autumn sky; within the fragrant odour of hops, the hum of the threshing circling round like the buzz of an immense bee. As the hum of insects high in the atmosphere of midsummer suits and fits to the roses and the full green meads, so the hum of the threshing suits to the yellowing leaf and drowsy air of autumn. The iteration of hum and monotone soothes, and means so much more in its inarticulation than the adjusted chords and tune of written music. Laughing, the children romped round the ricks; they love the threshing and flock to it, they watch the fly-wheel rotating, they look in at the furnace door when the engine-driver stokes his fire, they gaze wonderingly at the gauge, and long to turn the brass taps; then with a shout they rush to chase the unhappy mice dislodged from the corn. The mice hide themselves in the petticoats of the women working at the 'sheening,' and the cottager when she goes home in the evening calls her cat and shakes them out of her skirts. By a blue waggon the farmer stands leaning on his staff. He is an invalid, and his staff, or rather pole, is as tall as himself; he holds it athwart, one end touching the ground beyond his left foot, the other near his right shoulder. His right hand grasps it rather high, and his left down by his hip, so that the pole forms a line across his body. In this way he is steadied and supported and his whole weight relieved, much more so than it would be with an ordinary walking-stick or with one in each hand. When he walks he keeps putting the staff, which he calls a bat, in front, and so poles himself along. There is an invalid boy in the yard, who walks with a similar stick. The farmer is talking with a friend who has looked in from the lane in passing, and carries a two-spean spud, or Canterbury hoe, with points instead of a broad blade. They are saying that it is a 'pretty day,' 'pretty weather' —it is always 'pretty' with them, instead of fine. Pretty weather for the hopping; and so that leads on to climbing up into the loft and handling the golden scales. The man with the hoe dips his brown fist in the heap and gathers up a handful, noting as he does so how the crisp, brittle, leaf-life substance of the hops crackles, and yet does not exactly break in his palm. They must be dry, yet not too dry to go to powder. They cling a little to the fingers, adhering to the skin, sticky. He looks for rust and finds none, and pronounces it a good sample. 'But there beant nothen' now like they old Grapes used to be,' he concludes. The pair have not long gone down the narrow stairs when a waggon stops outside in the lane, and up comes the carter to speak with the 'drier'—the giant trampling round in the pocket—and to see how the hops 'be getting on.' In five minutes another waggoner looks in, then a couple of ploughboys, next a higgler passing by; no one walks or rides or drives past the hop-kiln without calling to see how things are going on. The carters cannot stay long, but the boys linger, eagerly waiting a chance to help the 'drier,' even if only to reach him his handkerchief from the nail. Round and round in the pocket brings out the perspiration, and the dust of the hops gets into the air-passages and thickens on the skin of his face. One of the lads has to push the hops towards him with a

rake. 'Don't you step on 'em too much, that'll break
'em.' On the light breeze that comes now and then a
little chaff floats in at the open window from the threshing. A crooked sort of face appears in the doorway,
the body has halted halfway up—a semi-gipsy face—
and the fellow thrusts a basket before him on the floor.
'Want any herrings?' 'No, thankie—no,' cries the
giant. 'Not to-day, measter; thusty enough without
they.' Herrings are regularly carried round in hop-
time to all the gardens, and there is a great sale for
them among the pickers. By degrees the 'drier'
rises higher in the pocket, coming up, as it were,
through the floor—first his shoulders, then his body, and
now his knees are visible. This is the ancient way of
filling a hop pocket; a machine is used now in large
kilns, but here, where there is only one cone, indicative
of a small garden, the old method is followed.

The steps on which I sit lead up to the door of the
cone. Inside, the green hops lie on the horsehair carpet,
and the fumes of the sulphur burning underneath come
up through them. A vapour hangs about the surface of
the hops; looking upwards, the diminishing cone rises
hollow to the cowl, where a piece of blue sky can be
seen. Round the cone a strip of thin lathing is coiled
on a spiral; could any one stand on these steps and
draw the inside of the cone? Could perspective be so
managed as to give the idea of the diminishing hollow
and spiral? the side opposite would not be so difficult,
but the bit this side, overhead and almost perpendicular,
and so greatly foreshortened, how with that? It would
be necessary to make the spectator of the drawing feel
as if this side of the cone rose up from behind his head;
as if his head were just inside the cone. Would not this
be as curious a bit of study as any that could be found

in the interior of old Continental churches, which people go so many miles to see? Our own land is so full of interest. There are pictures by the oldest Master everywhere in our own country, by the very Master of the masters, by Time, whose crooked signature lies in the corner of the shadowy farmhouse hearth.

Beneath the loft, on the ground-floor, I found the giant's couch. The bed of a cart had been taken off its wheels, forming a very good bedstead, dry and sheltered on three sides. On the fourth the sleeper's feet were towards the charcoal fire. Opening the furnace door, he could sit there and watch the blue and green tongues of sulphur flame curl round about and above the glowing charcoal, the fumes rising to the hops on the horsehair high over. The 'hoppers' in the garden used to bring their kettles and pots to boil, till the practice grew too frequent, and was stopped, because the constant opening of the furnace wasted the heat. The sulphur comes in casks. A sulphur cask sawn down the middle, with a bit left by the head for cover, is often used by the hoppers as a cradle. Another favourite cradle is made from a trug basket, the handle cut off. It is then like half a large eggshell, with cross pieces underneath to prevent it from canting aside. This cradle is set on the bare ground in the garden; when they move one woman takes hold of one end and a second of the other, and thus carry the infant. If you ask them, they will find you a 'hop-dog,' a handsome green caterpillar marked with black velvet stripes and downy bands between. Their labour usually ends early in the afternoon.

The giant at the kiln must watch and bide his time the night through till the hops are ready to be withdrawn from the cone. He is alone. Deep shadows gather round the farmstead and the ricks, and there is not a sound, nothing but the rustle of a leaf falling from the hollow oak by the gateway. But at midnight, just as the drier is drawing the hops, a thunderstorm bursts, and the blue lightning lights up the red cone without, blue as the sulphur flames creeping over the charcoal within. It is lonely work for him in the storm. By day he has many little things to do between the greater labours, to make the pockets (or sacks) by sewing the sackcloth, or to mark the name of the farmer and the date with stencil plates. For sewing up the mouth of the pocket when filled there is a peculiar kind of string used ; you may see it hanging up in any of the country ' stores ;' they are not shops, but stores of miscellaneous articles. He must be careful not to fill his pockets too full of hops, not to tread them too closely, else the sharp folk in the market will suspect that unfair means have been resorted to to increase the weight, and will cut the pocket all to pieces to see if it contains a few bricks. Nor must it be too light ; that will not do.

In this district, far from the great historic hop-fields of Kent, the hops are really grown in gardens, little pieces often not more than half an acre or even less in extent. Capricious as a woman, hops will only flourish here and there ; they have the strongest likes and dis-likes, and experience alone finds out what will suit them. These gardens are always on a slope, if possible in the angle of a field and under shelter of a copse, for the wind is the terror, and a great gale breaks them to pieces ; the bines are bruised, bunches torn off, and poles laid prostrate. The gardens being so small, from five to forty acres in a farm, of course but few pickers are required, and the hop-picking becomes a ' close ' business, entirely confined to home families, to the cottagers working on the farm and their immediate friends. Instead of a scarcity of labour, it is a matter of privilege to get a bin allotted to you. There are no rough folk down from Bermondsey or Mile End way. All staid, stay-at-home, labouring people—no riots ; a little romping no doubt on the sly, else the maids would not enjoy the season so much as they do. But there are none of those wild hordes which collect about the greater fields of Kent. Farmers' wives and daughters and many very respectable girls go out to hopping, not so much for the money as the pleasant out-of-door employment, which has an astonishing effect on the health. Pale cheeks begin to glow again in the hop-fields. Children who have suffered from whooping-cough are often sent out with the hop-pickers ; they play about on the bare ground in the most careless manner, and yet recover. Air and hops are wonderful restoratives. After passing an afternoon with the drier in the kiln, seated close to a great heap of hops and inhaling the odour, I was in a condition of agreeable excitement all the evening. My mind was full of fancy, imagination, flowing with ideas ; a sense of lightness and joyousness lifted me up. I wanted music, and felt full of laughter. Like the half-fabled haschish, the golden bloom of the hops had entered the nervous system ; intoxication without wine, without injurious after-effect, dream intoxication ; they were wine for the nerves. If hops only grew in the Far East we should think wonders of so powerful a plant. At hop-picking a girl can earn about 10s. a week, so that it is not such a highly paid employment as might be supposed from the talk there is about it. The advantages are sideways, so to say ; a whole family can work at the same time, and the sum-total becomes considerable. Hopping happily comes on just after corn harvest, so that the labourers get two harvest-times.

The farmers find it an expensive crop. It costs 50*l.* or 60*l.* to pick a very small garden, and if the Egyptian plague of insects has prevailed the price at market will not repay the expenditure. The people talk much of a possible duty on foreign hops. The hop farmer should have a lady-bird on his seal ring for his sign and token, for the lady-bird is his great friend. Lady-birds (and their larvæ) destroy myriads of the aphides which cause rust, and a flight of lady-birds should be welcomed as much as a flight of locusts is execrated in other countries.

II.

ONE of the hop-picking women told me how she went to church and the parson preached such a curious sermon, all about our 'innerds' (inwards, insides), and how many 'boanes' we had, and by-and-by 'he told us that we were the only beasts who had the use of our hands.' Years since at village schools the girls used to swallow pins; first one would do it, then another, presently half the school were taking pins. Ignorant of physiology! Yet they did not seem to suffer; the pins did not penetrate the pleura or lodge in the processes. Now Anatomy climbs into the pulpit and shakes a bony fist at the congregation. That is the humerus of it, as Corporal Nym might say. At the late election— the cow election —the candidates were Brown, Conservative, and Stiggins, Liberal. The day after the polling a farm labourer was asked how he filled up his voting paper. 'Oh,' said he full of the promised cow, 'I doan't care for that there Brown chap, he bean't no good; zo I jest put a cross agen he, and voted for Stiggins.' The dream of life was accomplished, the labourer had a vote, and—irony—he voted exactly opposite to his intent.

Too-whoo! ooo!—the sound of a horn,—the hunt was up; but this was not the hunting season. Looking out of the kiln door I saw a boy running at full speed down the lane with a small drain-pipe tucked under his arm. He stopped, put the pipe to his mouth, and blew a blast on this 'dread horn,' then jumped through a gap in the hedge and disappeared. They were playing fox and hounds; who but a boy would have thought of using a drain-pipe for a horn? It gave a good note, too. In and about the kiln I learned that if you smash a frog with a stone, no matter how hard you hit him, he cannot die till sunset. You must be careful not to put on any new article of clothing for the first time on a Saturday, or some severe punishment will ensue. One person put on his new boots on a Saturday, and on Monday broke his arm. Some still believe in herbs, and gather wood-betony for herb tea, or eat dandelion leaves between slices of dry toast. There is an old man living in one of the villages who has reached the age of a hundred and sixty years, and still goes hop-picking. Ever so many people had seen him and knew all about him; an undoubted fact, a public fact; but I could not trace him to his lair. His exact whereabouts could not be fixed. I live in hopes of finding him in some obscure 'Hole' yet (many little hamlets are 'Holes,' as Froghole, Foxhole). What an exhibit for London! Did he realise his own value, he would soon come forth. I joke, but the existence of this antique person is firmly believed in. Sparrows are called 'spadgers.' The cat wandering about got caught in the rat-clams—*i.e.* a gin. Another cat was the miller's favourite at the windmill, a well-fed, happy, purring pussy, fond of the floury miller—he as white as snow, she as black as a coal. One day pussy was ingeniously examining the machinery, when the wind suddenly rose, the sails revolved, and she was ground up, fulfilling the ogre's threat—'I'll grind his bones to make my bread.' This was not so sad as the fate of the innkeeper's cow. You have read the 'Arabian Nights'—that book of wisdom, for in truth the stories are no stories; they are the records of ancient experience, the experience of a thousand years, and some of them are as true and as deeply to be pondered on as anything in the holiest books the world reverences. You remember the Three Calenders, each of whom lost an eye—struck out in the most arbitrary and cruel fashion. The innkeeper had a cow, a very pretty, quiet cow, but in time it came about that her left horn, turning inwards, grew in such a manner that it threatened to force the point into her head. To remedy this the top of the horn was sawn off and a brass knob fastened on the tip, as is the custom. The cow passed the summer in the meadows with the rest, till by-and-by it was found that she had gone blind in the left eye. It happened in this way: the rays of the sun heated the brass knob and so destroyed the sight. Unable to call attention to its suffering, the poor creature was compelled to endure, and could not escape. Now the Three Calenders could speak, and had the advantage of human intelligence, and yet each lost an eye, and they were as helpless in the hands of fate as this poor animal.

Down in one of the hamlets there was a forge to which all the workpeople who wanted any tools sharpened carried their instruments, the smith being able to put a better edge on. Other blacksmiths or carpenters, if they required a particularly good edge for some purpose, came to him. This art he had acquired from his grandfather as a sort of heirloom or secret. The grandfather while at work used to trouble and puzzle himself how to get a very sharp edge, and at length one night he dreamed how to do it. From that time he became prosperous. If a celebrated sonata was revealed in a dream, why not the way to sharpen a chisel?

When he was tired the drier said he was 'dreggy.' They were talking of the lambs, and how that dry season they had scarcely any sweetbreads. The sweetbreads were so scanty, the butchers did not even offer them for sale; the lambs had fed on dry food. In seasons when there was plenty of grass and green food they had good large sweetbreads, white as milk. The character of the food does thus under some circumstances really alter the condition of an organ. The sweetbread is the pancreas; now a deficient pancreatic action is supposed to play a great part in consumption and other wasting diseases. Have we here, then, an indication that when the pancreas may be suspected plenty of succulent food and plenty of liquid are nature's remedies? We looked over at the pigs in the sty. They were rooting about in a mess of garbage. 'Oh, what dirty things pigs are!' said a lady. 'Yes, ma'am; they're rightly named,' said he. Some scientific gentleman in the district had a large telescope with which he made frequent observations, and at times would let a labouring man look at the moon. 'Ah,' said our friend, shaking his head in a solemn, impressive way, 'my brother, he see through it; he see great rocks and seas up there. He say he never want to see through it no more. He wish he never looked through him at all.' The poor man was dreadfully frightened at what he had seen in the moon. At first I laughed at the story and the odd idea of a huge, great fellow being alarmed at a glance through a telescope. Since then, however, on reflection, it seems to me perfectly natural. He was illiterate; he had never read of astronomy; to him it was really like a sudden peep into another world, for the instrument was exceptionally powerful, and the view of the sunlight on the peaks and the shadows in the valleys must have been extraordinary to him. There was nothing to laugh at; the incident shows what a great and wonderful thing it is that rocks and mountains should be whirled along over our heads. The idea has become familiarised to us by reading, but the fact is none the less marvellous. This man saw the fact first, before he had the idea, and he had sufficient imagination to realise it. At the village post office they ask for 'Letterhead, please, sir,' instead of a stamp, for it is characteristic of the cottager that whatever words he uses must be different from those employed by other people. Stamp is as familiar to him as to you, yet he prefers to say 'letterhead'—because he does. There are many curious old houses, some of them timbered, still standing in these parts. The immense hearths which were once necessary for burning wood are now occupied with 'duck's-nest' grates, so called from the bars forming a sort of nest. In one of the hamlets the women touched their hats to us.

Not far from the hop-kiln I found a place where charcoal-burning was carried on. The brown charcoal-burner, upright as a bolt, walked slowly round the smouldering heap, and wherever flame seemed inclined to break out cast damp ashes upon the spot. Six or seven water-butts stood in a row for his use. To windward he had built a fence of flakes, or wattles as they are called here, well worked in with brushwood, to break the force of the draught along the hill-side, which would have caused too fierce a fire. At one side stood his hut of poles meeting in a cone, wrapped round with rough canvas. Besides his rake and shovel and a short ladder, he showed me a tool like an immense gridiron, bent half double, and fitted to a handle in the same way as a spade. This was for sifting charcoal when burned, and separating the small from the larger pieces. Every now and then a puff of smoke rose from the heap and drifted along; it has a peculiar odour, a dense, thick smell of smothered wood coal, to me not disagreeable, but to some people so annoying that they have been known to leave their houses and abandon a locality where charcoal-burning was practised. Dim memories of old days come crowding round me, invisible to him, to me visible and alive, of the kings, great hunters, who met with the charcoal-burners in the vast forests or mediæval days, of the noble knights and dames whom the rude charcoal-burners guided to their castles through trackless wastes, and all the romance of old. Scarcely is there a tale of knightly adventure that does not in some way or other mention these men, whose occupation fixed them in the wildernesses which of yore stretched between cultivated places. I looked at the modern charcoal-burner with interest. He was brown, good-looking, upright, and distinctly superior in general style to the common run of working men. He spoke without broad accent and used correct language; he was well educated and up to the age. He knew his own mind, and had an independent expression; a very civil, intel-ligent, and straightforward man. No rude charcoal-burner of old days this. We stood close to the highway road ; a gentleman's house was within stone's throw ; the spot, like the man, was altogether the reverse of what we read in ancient story. Yet such is the force of association that I could not even now divest myself of those dim memories and living dreams of old ; there seemed as it were the clank of armour, a rustle of pennons in the leaves ; it would have been quite natural to hold bow and arrow in the hand. The man was modern, but his office was ancient. The descent was unbroken. The charcoal-burner traced back to the Norman Conquest. That very spot where we stood, now surrounded with meadows and near dwellings, scarcely thirty years since had formed part of one of the largest of the old forests. It was forest land. Woods away on the slope still remained to witness to traditions. As the charcoal-burner worked beside the modern highway, so his trade had come down and was still practised in the midst of modern trades, in these times of sea-coal and steam. He told me that he and his brothers were maintained by charcoal-burning the year through, and, it appeared, in a very comfortable position. They only burned a small quantity here ; they moved about from place to place in the woods, according as the timber was thrown. They often stopped for weeks in the woods, watching the fires all night. A great part of the work was done in the winter, beginning in October—after the hop-picking. Now resting in his lonely hut, now walking round and tending the smoking heap, the charcoal-burner watched out the long winter nights while the stars drifted over the leafless trees, till the grey dawn came with hoar-frost. He liked his office, but owned that the winter nights were very long. Starlight and frost and slow time are the same now as when the red deer and the wild boar dwelt in the forest. Much of the charcoal was prepared for hop-drying, large quantities being used for that purpose. At one time a considerable amount was rebaked for patent fuel, and the last use to which it had been put was in carrying out some process with Australian meat. It was still necessary in several trades. Goldsmiths used charcoal for soldering. They preferred the charcoal made from the thick bark of the butts of birch trees. At the foot or butt of the birch the bark grows very thick, in contrast to the rind higher, which is thinner than on other trees. Lord Sheffield's mansion at Fletching was the last great house he knew that was entirely warmed with charcoal, nothing else being burnt. Charcoal was still used in houses for heating plates. But the principal demand seemed to be for hop-drying purposes—the charcoal burned in the kiln where I had been resting was made on the spot. This heap he was now burning was all of birch poles, and would be four days and four nights completing. On the fourth morning it was drawn, and about seventy sacks were filled, the charcoal being roughly sorted.

The ancient forest land is still wild enough, there is no seeming end to the heath and fern on the ridges or to the woods in the valleys. These moor-like stretches bear a resemblance to parts of Exmoor. The oaks that once reached from here to the sea-shore were burned to smelt the iron in the days when Sussex was the great iron land. For charcoal the vast forests were cut down; it seems strange to think that cannon were once cast— the cannon that won India for us—where now the hops grow and the plough travels slowly, so opposite as they are to the roaring furnace and the ringing hammer. Burned and blasted by the heat, the ground where the furnaces were still retains the marks of the fire. But to-day there is silence; the sunshine lights up the purple heather and the already yellowing fern; the tall and beautiful larches stand graceful in the stillness. Their lines always flow in pleasant curves; they need no wind to bend them into loveliness of form: so quiet and deserted is the place that the wide highway road is green with vegetation, and the impression of our wheels is the only trace upon them. Looking up, the road—up the hill—it appears green almost from side to side. It is well made and firm, and fit for any traffic; but a growth of minute weeds has sprung up, and upon these our wheels leave their marks. Of roads that have become grass-grown in war-desolated countries we have all read, but this is our own unscathed England.

The nature of the ancient forest, its quiet and untrodden silence, adheres to the site. Far down in the valley there is more stirring, and the way is well pulverised. In the hollow there is an open space, backed by the old beech trees of the park, dotted with ashes, and in the midst a farmhouse partly timbered. Here by the road-side they point out to you a low mound, at the very edge of the road, which could easily be passed unnoticed as a mere heap of scrapings overgrown with weeds and thistles. On looking closer it appears more regularly shaped; it is indeed a grave. Of old time an unfortunate woman committed suicide, and according to the barbarous law of those days her body was buried at the cross-roads and a stake driven through it. That was the end so far as the brutal law of the land went. But the road-menders, with better hearts, from that day to this have always kept up the mound. However beautiful the day, however beautiful the beech trees and the ashes that stand apart, there is always a melancholy feeling in passing the place. This thistle-grown mound saddens the whole; it is impossible to forget it; it lies, as it were, under everything, under the beeches, the sunlit sward and fern. The mark of death is there. The dogs and the driven cattle tread the spot; a human being has passed into dust. The circumstance of the mound having been kept up so many years bears curious testimony to the force of tradition. Many writers altogether deny the value of tradition. Dr. Schliemann's spade, however, found Troy. Perhaps tradition is like the fool of the saying, and is sometimes right.

SWALLOW-TIME

THE eave-swallows have come at last with the mid-summer-time, and the hay and white clover and warm winds that breathe hotly, like one that has been running uphill. With the paler hawkweeds, whose edges are so delicately trimmed and cut and balanced, almost as if made by deft human fingers to human design, whose globes of down are like geometrical circles built up of facets, instead of by one revolution of the compasses. With foxglove, and dragon-fly, and yellowing wheat; with green cones of fir, and boom of distant thunder, and all things that say, 'It is summer.' Not many of them even now, sometimes only two in the air together, sometimes three or four, and one day eight, the very greatest number—a mere handful, for these eave-swallows at such times should crowd the sky. The white bars across their backs should be seen gliding beside the dark fir copse a quarter of a mile away. They should be seen everywhere, over the house, and to and fro the eaves, where half last year's nest remains; over the meadows and high up in the blue ether. White breasts should gleam in the azure height, appearing and disappearing as they climb or sink, and wheel and slide through those long boomerang-like flights that suddenly take them a hundred yards aside. They should crowd the sky together with the ruddy-throated chimney-swallows, and the great swifts ; but though it is hay-time and the apples are set, yet eight eave-swallows is the largest number I have counted in one afternoon. They did not come at all in the spring. After the heavy winter cleared away, the delicate willow-wrens soon sang in the tops of the beautiful green larches, the nightingale came, and the cuckoo, the chimney-swallow, the doves softly cooing as the oaks came into leaf, and the black swifts. Up to May 26 there were no eave-swallows at the Sussex hill-side where these notes were taken ; that is more than a month later than the date of their usual arrival, which would be about the middle of April. After this they gradually came back. The chimney-swallows were not so late, but even they are not so numerous as usual. The swifts seem to have come more in their accustomed numbers. Now, the swallows are, of all others, the summer birds. As well suppose the trees without leaves as the summer air without swallows. Ever since of old time the Greeks went round from house to house in spring singing the swallow song, these birds have been looked upon as the friends of man, and almost as the very givers of the sunshine.

> The swallow's come, winging
>   His way to us here ;
> Fair hours is he bringing,
>   And a happy new year !

They had a song for everything, the mill song, the reapers' song, just as in Somerset, the apple country, they still have a cider song, or perhaps, rather, an orchard song. Such rhymes might well be chanted about the hay and the wheat, or at the coming of the green leaf, or the yellowing of the acorns, when the cawing of the rooks is incessant, a kind of autumn festival. It seems so natural that the events of the year should be met with a song. But somehow a very hard and unobservant spirit has got abroad into our rural life, and people do not note things as the old folk did. They do not mark the coming of the swallows, nor any of the dates that make the woodland almanack. It is a pity that there should be such indifference—that the harsh ways of the modern town should press so heavily on the country. This summer, too, there seems a marked absence of bees, butterflies, and other insects in the fields. One bee will come along, calling at every head of white clover. By-and-by you may see one more calling at the heathbells, and nothing else, as in each journey they visit only the flower with which they began. Then there will be quite an interval before a third bee is seen, and a fourth may be found dead perhaps on the path, besides which you may not notice any more. For a whole hour you may not observe a humble-bee, and the wasp-like hover-flies, that are generally past all thought of counting, are scarcely seen. A blue butterfly we found in the dust of the road, without the spirit to fly, and lifted him into a field to let him have a chance of life ; a few tortoiseshells, and so on—even the white butterflies are quite uncommon, the whites that used to drift along like snowflakes. Where are they all ? Did the snow kill them ? Is there any connection between the absence of insects and the absence of swallows ? If so, how did the swallows know beforehand, without coming, that there were no insects for them ? Yet the midsummer hum, the deep humming sound in the atmosphere above, has been loud and persistent over the hayfields, so that there must have been the usual myriads of the insects that cause this sound. While I was thinking in this way a swallow alighted on the turf, picked up a small white moth from among the short grass, and went off with it. In gloomy overcast weather the swallows at the sea-side frequently alight on the pebbles of the beach to pick up the insects which will not rise and fly. Some beaches and sand-banks are much frequented by insects, and black clouds of them sometimes come drifting along, striking the face like small hail.

When swallows fly low, just skimming the ground, it is supposed to be a sign of rain. During the frequent intervals of heavy, overcast weather which have marked this summer, they might have been observed flying low for a week together without a spot of rain falling. Chilly air drives insects downwards, and, indeed, para-lyses a great many of them altogether. It is a fall of temperature, and not wet, that makes the swallows chase their prey low down. Insects are not much afraid of rain if it is warm and soft, so that in the midst of showers, if there is sunshine too, you may see the swallows high in the atmosphere. It is when they fly low, but just missing the grass, that their wonderful powers of flight appear. In the air above there are no obstacles, and if you shoot an arrow it travels to the end of its journey without let or hindrance ; there are no streets there to turn corners, no narrow lanes, no trees or hedges. When the swallow comes down to the earth his path is no longer that of the immortals, his way is as the way of men, constantly obstructed, and made a thousandfold more difficult by the velocity of his passage. Imagine shooting an arrow from the strongest bow in such a manner that it might travel about seven inches above the ground—how far would it go before it would strike a tall buttercup, a wiry bennet, or stick into a slight rise of the turf? You must imagine it given the power to rise over hedges, to make short angles about buildings, slip between the trunks of trees, to avoid moving objects, as men or animals, not to come in contact with other animated arrows, and by some mysterious instinct to know what is or what is not out of sight on the other side of the wall. I was sitting on a log in the narrowest of narrow lanes, a hedge at the back, in front thick fir trees, whose boughs touched the ground, almost within reach, the lane being nothing more than a broader foot-path. It was one of those overcast days when the shelter of the hedge and the furze was pleasant in July. Suddenly a swallow slid by me as it seemed underneath my very hands, so close to the ground that he almost travelled in the rut, the least movement on my part would have stopped him. Almost before I could lift my head he had reached the end of the lane and rose over the gate into the road—not a moments pause before he made that leap over the gate to see if there was a waggon or not in the way; a waggon-load of hay would have blocked the road entirely. How did he know that a man or a horse would not step into his course at the instant he topped the bar?

A swallow never hesitates, never looks before he leaps, threads all day the eyes of needles, and goes on from half-past two in the morning till ten at night, without so much as disturbing a feather. He is the perfection of a machine for falling. His round nest is under the eaves, he throws himself out of window and begins to fall, and keeps on fall, fall, for twenty hours together. His head is bullet-shaped, his neck short, his body all thickened up to the shoulders, tailing out to the merest streak of feather. His form is like a plummet—he is not unlike the heavily weighted minnow used in trolling for pike. Before the bend of the firmly elastic rod, the leaded minnow slides out through the air, running true and sinking without splash into the water. It is proportioned and weighted so that its flight, which is a long fall, may be smooth, and perfectly under control. If wings could be put to the minnow, it would somewhat resemble the swallow. For the swallow is made to fall, and his wings to catch him, and by resisting his descent these outstretched planes lift him again into the sky. He does not fall perpendicularly, the angle of his fall is prolonged and very low, and the swifter he goes the more nearly it approximates to the horizontal. I think he goes swifter when flying just over the ground than when lounging in the easy hammock of the atmosphere. My swallow that came down the lane, in twenty yards opened his wings twenty times and checked his fall, almost grazing the earth, and imperceptibly rose a little, like a flat stone thrown by a boy which suddenly runs up into the air at the end of its flight. He made no blow with his wings; they were simply put out to collect the air in the hollow of their curves, and so prolong his fall. Falling from morn till night, he throws himself on his way, a machine for turning gravity into a motive force. He fits to the circumstances of his flight as water fits to the circumstances of the vessel into which it is poured. No thought, no stop, no rest. If a waggon had been in the way, still he would have got left or right through the very eye of the needle. If a man had been passing, the rush of his wings would not have disturbed the light smoke from his cigar. Farther up the lane there are two gateways opposite without gates. Through these swallows are continually dashing, and I have often felt when coming up the lane as if I must step on them, and half checked myself.

I might as well try to step on lightning. A swallow

came over the sharp ridge of a slate roof and met a slight current of wind which blew against that side of the shed and rose up it. The bird remained there suspended with outstretched wings, resting on the up-current as if the air had been solid, for some moments. He rode there at anchor in the air. So buoyant is the swallow that it is no more to him to fly than it is to the fish to swim ; and, indeed, I think that a trout in a swift mountain stream needs much greater strength to hold himself in the rapid day and night without rest.. The friction of the water is constant against him, and he never folds his fins and sleeps. The more I think the more I am convinced that the buoyancy of the air is very far greater than science admits, and under certain conditions it is superior to water as a supporting medium. Swift and mobile as is the swallow's wing, how much swifter and how much more mobile must be his eye! This rapid and ever-changing course is not followed for pleasure as if it were a mazy dance. The whole time as he floats, and glides, and wheels, his eye is intent on insects so small as to be invisible to us at a very short distance. These he gathers in the air, he sees what we cannot see, his eyes are to our eyes as his wings are to our limbs. If still further we were to consider the flow of the nerve force between the eye, the mind, and the wing, we should be face to face with problems which quite upset the ordinary ideas of matter as a solid thing. How is it that dull matter becomes thus inexpressibly sensitive ? Is not the swallow's eye a miracle ? Then his heart, for he sings as he flies ; he makes love and converses, and all as he rushes along— his hopes, his fears, his little store of knowledge, and his wonderful journey by-and-by to Africa. Remember, he carries his life in his wings as we should say in our hands, for if by chance he should strike a solid object, his great speed renders the collision certain death. It stuns him, and if he recovers from that his beak is usually broken so that he must starve. Happily such accidents are rare. The great rapidity of a bird's heart beating so fast seems to render it peculiarly susceptible to death from shock. Great fright will sometimes kill a bird, as, for instance, when they have wandered inside a room, and been thoughtlessly held in some one's hand. Without visible injury, the heart, after beating excessively violently, almost as rapidly slows, the nictitating membrane is drawn over the eyes, the head falls to one side, and the bird becomes lifeless from nervous exhaustion. The beautiful swallows, be tender to them, for they symbol all that is best in nature and all that is best in our hearts.

BUCKHURST PARK.

AN old beech tree had been broken off about five feet from the ground, and becoming hollow within, was filled with the decay of its own substance. In this wood-sorrel had taken root, and flower and leaf covered the space within, white flower and green leaf flourishing on old age. The wood-sorrel leaf, the triune leaf, is perhaps more lovely even than the flower, like a more delicately shaped clover of a tenderer green, and it lasts far on into the autumn. When the violet leaves are no more looked for, when the cowslips have gone, and the bluebells have left nothing behind them but their nodding seed-cases, still the wood-sorrel leaf stays on the mound, in shape and colour the same, and as pleasantly acid to the taste now under the ripening nuts as in May. At its coming it is folded almost like a green flower; at Midsummer, when you are gathering ferns, you find its trefoil deep under the boughs; it grows, too, in the crevices of the rock over the spring. The whortleberry leaves, that were green as the myrtle when the wood-sorrel was in bloom, have faded somewhat now that their berries are ripening. Another beech has gone over, and lies at full length, a shattered tube, as it were, of timber; for it is so rotten within, and so hollow and bored, it is little else than bark. Others that stand are tubes on end, with rounded knot-holes, loved by the birds, that let air and moisture into the very heart of the wood. They are hardly safe in a strong wind. Others again, very large and much shorter, have sent up four trunks from one root, a little like a banyan, quadruple trees built for centuries, throwing abroad a vast roof of foliage, whose green in the midst of summer is made brown by sacks and sacks of beech nuts. These are the trees to camp by, and that are chosen by painters. The bark of the beech is itself a panel to study, spotted with velvet moss brown-green, made grey with close-grown lichen, stained with its own hues of growth, and toned by time. To these add bright sunlight and leaf shadow, the sudden lowering of tint as a cloud passes, the different aspects of the day and the evening, and the changes of rain and dry weather. You may look at the bark of a beech twenty times and always find it different. After crossing Virgil's Bridge in the deep coombe at the bottom of Marden Hill these great beeches begin, true woodland trees, and somehow more forest-like than the hundreds and hundreds of acres of fir trees that are called forest. There is another spirit among the beech trees; they look like deer and memories of old English life.

The wood cooper follows his trade in a rude shed, splitting poles and making hoops the year through, in warm summer and iron-clad winter. His shed is always pitched at the edge of a great woodland district. Where the road has worn in deeply the roots of the beeches hang over, twisted in and out like a giant matting, a kind of cave under them. Dark yew trees and holly trees stand here and there; a yew is completely barked on one side, stripped clean. If you look close you will see scores in the wood as if made with a great nail.

Those who know Exmoor will recognise these signs in a moment; it is a fraying-post where the stags rubbed the velvet from their horns last summer. There are herds of red deer in the park. At one time there were said to be almost as many as run free and wild over the expanse of Exmoor. They mark the trees very much, especially those with the softer bark. Wire fencing has been put round many of the hollies to protect them. A stag occasionally leaps the boundary and forages among the farmers' corn, or visits a garden, and then the owner can form some idea of what must have been the difficulties of agriculture in mediæval days. Deer more than double the interest of a park. A park without deer is like a wall without pictures. However well proportioned the room, something is lacking if the walls be blank. However noble the oaks and wide the sweep of sward, there is something wanting if antlers do not rise above the fern. The pictures that the deer make are moving and alive; they dissolve and re-form in a distant frame of tree and brake. Lately the herd has been somewhat thinned, having become too numerous. One slope is bare of grass, a patch of yellow sand, which if looked at intently from a distance seems presently to be all alive like mites in cheese, so thick are the rabbits in the warren. Under a little house, as it were, built over a stream is a chalybeate fountain with virtues like those of Tunbridge Wells.

The park is open to visitors—here comes a gay four-in-hand heavily loaded sweeping by on its road to that summer town. There is much ironstone in the soil round about. At the edge of the park stands an old farmhouse of timber and red tile, with red oast-house beside it, built with those gables which our ancestors seemed to think made such excellent rooms within.

Our modern architects try to make their rooms mathe-
matically square, a series of brick boxes, one on the
other like pigeon-holes in a bureau, with flat ceilings
and right angles in the corners, and are said to go
through a profound education before they can produce
these wonderful specimens of art. If our old English
folk could not get an arched roof, then they loved to
have it pointed, with polished timber beams in which
the eye rested as in looking upwards through a tree.
Their rooms they liked of many shapes, and not at right
angles in the corners, nor all on the same dead level of
flooring. You had to go up a step into one, and down
a step into another, and along a winding passage into a
third, so that each part of the house had its individuality.
To these houses life fitted itself and grew to them ; they
were not mere walls, but became part of existence. A
man's house was not only his castle, a man's house was
himself. He could not tear himself away from his
house, it was like tearing up the shrieking mandrake by
the root, almost death itself. Now we walk in and out
of our brick boxes unconcerned whether we live in this
villa or that, here or yonder. Dark beams inlaid in the
walls support the gables ; heavier timber, placed horizontally, forms, as it were, the foundation of the first floor.
This horizontal beam has warped a little in the course
of time, the alternate heat and cold of summers and
winters that make centuries. Up to this beam the
lower wall is built of brick set to the curve of the timber,
from which circumstance it would appear to be a modern
insertion. The beam, we may be sure, was straight
originally, and the bricks have been fitted to the curve
which it subsequently took. Time, no doubt, ate away
the lower work of wood, and necessitated the insertion
of new materials. The slight curve of the great beam

adds, I think, to the interest of the old place, for it is a curve that has grown and was not premeditated ; it has grown like the bough of a tree, not from any set human design. This, too, is the character of the house. It is not large, nor overburdened with gables, not ornamental, nor what is called striking, in any way, but simply an old English house, genuine and true. The warm sunlight falls on the old red tiles, the dark beams look the darker for the glow of light, the shapely cone of the hopoast rises at the end ; there are swallows and flowers, and ricks and horses, and so it is beautiful because it is natural and honest. It is the simplicity that makes it so touching, like the words of an old ballad. Now at Mayfield there is a timber house which is something of a show place, and people go to see it, and which certainly has many more lines in its curves and woodwork, but yet did not appeal to me, because it seemed too purposely ornamental. A house designed to look well, even age has not taken from it its artificiality. Neither is there any cone nor cart-horses about. Why, even a tall chanticleer makes a home look homely. I do like to see a tall proud chanticleer strutting in the yard and barely giving way as I advance, almost ready to do battle with a stranger like a mastiff. So I prefer the simple old home by Buckhurst Park.

The beeches and oaks become fewer as the ground rises, there are wide spaces of bracken and little woods or copses, every one of which is called a ' shaw.' Then come the firs, whose crowded spires, each touching each, succeed for miles, and cover the hill-side with a solid mass of green. They seem so close together, so thickened and matted, impenetrable to footsteps, like a mound of earth rather than woods, a solid block of wood ; but there are ways that wind through and space between the taller trunks when you come near. The odour of firs is variable ; sometimes it fills the air, sometimes it is absent altogether, and doubtless depends upon certain conditions of the atmosphere. A very small pinch of the fresh shoot is pleasant to taste ; these shoots, eaten constantly, were once considered to cure chest disease, and to this day science endeavours by various forms of inhalations from fir products to check that malady. Common rural experience, as with the cow-pox, has often laid the basis of medical treatment. Certain it is that it is extremely pleasant and grateful to breathe the sweet fragrance of the fir deep in the woods, listening to the soft caressing sound of the wind that passes high overhead. The willow-wren sings, but his voice and that of the wind seem to give emphasis to the holy and meditative silence. The mystery of nature and life hover about the columned temple of the forest. The secret is always behind a tree, as of old time it was always behind the pillar of the temple. Still higher, and as the firs cease, and shower and sunshine, wind and dew, can reach the ground unchecked, comes the tufted heath and branched heather of the moorland top. A thousand acres of purple heath sloping southwards to the sun, deep valleys of dark heather ; further slopes beyond of purple, more valleys of heather—the heath shows more in the sunlight, and heather darkens the shadow of the hollows—and so on and on, mile after mile, till the heath-bells seem to end in the sunset. Round and beyond is the immense plain of the air— you feel how limitless the air is at this height, for there is nothing to measure it by. Past the weald lie the South Downs, but they form no boundary, the plain of the air goes over them to the sea and space.

This wild tract of Ashdown Forest bears much

resemblance to Exmoor ; you may walk, or you may ride, for hours and meet no one ; and if black game were to start up it would not surprise you in the least. There seems room enough to chase the red stag from Buckhurst Park with horn and hound till, mayhap, he ended in the sea at Pevensey. Buckhurst Park is the centre of this immense manor. Of old time the deer did run wild, and were hunted till the pale was broken in the great Civil War. The 'Forest' is still in every one's mouth—'on the Forest,' 'by the Forest,' 'in' it, or 'over' it, everything comes from the 'Forest,' even stone to mend the roads, or 'through the Forest,' as up from Brighton. People say this farm used to be forest, or this garden or this house was the first built on the forest. The enclosures are small, and look as if they had been hewn out of wood or stubbed out of heather, and there are numbers of small owners or settlers. Here and there a house stands, as it seems, alone in the world on the Forest ridge, thousands of acres of heather around, the deep weald underneath—as at Duddleswell, a look-out, as it were, over the earth. Forest Row, where they say the courtiers had their booths in ancient hunting days ; Forest Fold, Boar's-head Street, Greenwood Gate—all have a forest sound ; and what prettier name could there be than Sweet-Haws ? Greybirchet Wood, again ; Mossbarn, Highbroom, and so on. Outlying woods in every direction are fragments of the forest, you cannot get away from it ; and look over whatever gate you will, there is always a view. In the vale, if you look over a gate you only see that field and nothing beyond ; the view is bounded by the opposite hedge. Here there is always a deep coombe, or the top of a wood underneath, or a rising slope, or a distant ridge crowned with red-tiled farmstead, red-coned oast-house, and tall spruce firs. Or far away, miles and miles, the fields of the weald pushed close together by distance till in a surface no larger than the floor of a room there are six or seven farms and a village. Clouds drift over; it is a wonderful observatory for cloud studies; they seem so close, the light is so strong, and there is nothing to check the sight as far as its powers will reach. Clouds come up no wider than a pasture-field, but in length stretching out to the very horizon, dividing the blue sky into two halves; but then every day has its different clouds—the fleets of heaven that are always sailing on and know no haven.

HOUSE-MARTINS.

OF five houses, a stable, and chapel wall, much frequented by martins, the aspects were as follows:—House No. 1, nests on the north side, south side, and east, both the south and east very warm; No. 2, on the south and east walls—these walls met in an angle, and as it were enclosed the sunbeams, making it very heated sometimes; No. 3, on the south and west walls, the warmest sides of the building; No. 4, all along under the southern eaves, a very warm wall; No. 5, also under the southern eaves, and not elsewhere. The stable fronted south; there were nests front and back, north and south; the chapel eave that was frequented faced towards the west. In the case of several other houses the nests were on the sunny side; but I am not so well acquainted with the localities. So far as my observation goes, I think the house-martin—with all the swallow tribe—prefers warmth, and, if possible, chooses the sunny side of a building. A consideration, however, that weighs much with this bird is the character of the take-off; he likes a space immediately in front of his nest, free of trees or other obstructions, so that when rushing out from his little doorway he may not strike against anything   For ages it has also been remarked that the house-martin likes the proximity of man, and will build by choice in or over a porch or doorway, whether of house or stable, or over a window—somewhere where man is about. It is curious that in this country, so subject to cold and cold winds, so many houses are built to face north or east, and this fact often compels the house-martin to build that side, the back of a house being frequently obstructed. In the case of house No. 1 there was a clear take-off on the north side, also with the stable. Houses are generally built to face the road, quite irrespective of the aspect, which custom is the origin of many cheerless dwellings. I think that house-martin fledglings and eggs are capable of enduring the utmost heat of our English summer, and the nests found deserted were abandoned for some other reason. More likely that the deficiency of insect food caused by the inclement weather weakened the parent. Sometimes these harmless and useful birds are cruelly shot. I have never seen a nest injured by heats; on the contrary, I should imagine that heat would cause the mortar to cohere more firmly, and that damp would be much more likely to make it unsafe. At house No. 2 the heat in the angle of the two walls was scarcely bearable on a July day If a nest were taken down and put in an oven I should doubt if it would crack. In nature, however, everything depends on locality. The roads in that locality were mended with flint, and the mortar from puddles appeared to make good cement. Possibly in some districts there may be no lime or silicon, and the mortar the birds use may be less adherent. The more one studies nature the more one becomes convinced that it is an error to suppose things proceed by a regular rule always applicable everywhere. All creatures change their habits with circumstances; consequently no observation can be accepted as final.

AMONG THE NUTS.

THE nuts are ripening once more, and it is almost the time to go a-gipsying—the summer passes like the shadow of a cloud which strikes the edge of the yellow wheat and comes over and is gone; it does not give you time to rub out a single ear of corn. Before it is possible to gather the harvest of thought and observation the summer has passed, and we must bind the hastily stitched book with the crimson leaves of autumn. Under these very hazel boughs only yesterday, *i.e.* in May, looking for cuckoo-sorrel, as the wood-sorrel is called, there rolled down a brown last year's nut from among the moss of the bank. In the side of this little brown nut, at its thicker end, a round hole had been made with a sharp tool which had left the marks of its chiselling. Through this hole the kernel had been extracted by the skilful mouse. Two more nuts were found on the same bank, bored by the same carpenter. The holes looked as if he had turned the nut round and round as he gnawed. Unless the nut had shrunk, the hole was not large enough to pull the kernel out all at once; it must have been eaten little by little in many mouthfuls. The same amount of nibbling would have sawn a circle round the nut, and so, dividing the shell in two, would have let the kernel out bodily—a plan more to our fancy; but the mouse is a nibbler, and he preferred to nibble, nibble, nibble. Hard by one afternoon, as the cows were lazily swishing their tails coming home to milking, and the shadow of the thick hedge had already caused the anemones in the grass to close their petals, there was a slight rustling sound. Out into the cool grass by some cowslips there came a small dark head. It was an adder, verily a snake in the grass and flowers. His quick eye—you know the proverb, 'If his ear were as quick as his eye, No man should pass him by'—caught sight of us immediately, and he turned back. The hedge was hollow there, and the mound grown over with close-laid, narrow-leaved ivy. The viper did not sink in these leaves, but slid with a rustling sound fully exposed above them. His grey length and the chain of black diamond spots down his back, his flat head with deadly tooth, did not harmonise as the green snake does with leaf and grass. He was too marked, too prominent—a venomous foreign thing, fit for tropic sands and nothing English or native to our wilds. He seemed like a reptile that had escaped from the glass case of some collection.

The green snake or grass snake, with yellow-marked head, fits in perfectly with the floating herbage of the watery places he frequents. The eye soon grows accustomed to his curves, till he is no more startling than a frog among the water-crowfoot you are about to gather. To the adder the mind never becomes habituated; he ever remains repellent. This adder was close to a house and cowshed, and, indeed, they seem to like to be near cows. Since then a large silvery slowworm was killed just there—a great pity, for they are perfectly harmless. We saw, too, a very large lizard under the heath. Three little effets (efts) ran into one hole on the bank yesterday. Some of the men in spring went off into the woods to 'flawing,' *i.e.* to barking the oak which is thrown in May—the bark is often used now for decoration, like the Spanish cork bark. Some were talking already of the 'grit' work and looking forward to it, that is, to mowing and haymaking, which mean better wages. The farmers were grumbling that their oats were cuckoo oats, not sown till the cuckoo cried, and not likely to come to much. So, indeed, it fell out, for the oats looked very thin and spindly when the nuts turned rosy again. At work hoeing among the 'kelk' or 'kilk,' the bright yellow charlock, the labourers stood up as the cuckoo flew over singing, and blew cuckoo back to him in their hollow fists. This is a trick they have, something like whistling in the fist, and so naturally done as to deceive any one. The children had been round with the May garland, which takes the place of the May-pole, and is carried slung on a stick, and covered with a white cloth, between two little girls. The cloth is to keep the dust and sun from spoiling the flowers—the rich golden kingcups and the pale anemones trained about two hoops, one within the other. They take the cloth off to show you the garland, and surely you must pay them a penny for thought of old England. Yet there are some who would like to spoil this innocent festival. I have heard of some wealthy people living in a village who do their utmost to break up the old custom by giving presents of money to all the poor children who will go to school on that day instead of a-Maying. A very pitiful thing truly! Give them the money, and let them go a-Maying as well. The same bribe they repeat at Christmas to stay the boys from going round mumming. It is in spring that the folk make most use of herbs, such as herb tea of gorse bloom. One cottage wife exclaimed that she had no patience with women so ignorant they did not know how to use herbs, as wood-sage or wood-betony. Most of the gardens have a few plants of the milky-veined holy thistle—good, they say, against inflammations, and in which they have much faith. Soon after the May garlands the meadow orchis comes up, which is called 'dead men's hands,' and after that the 'ram's-horn' orchis, which has a twisted petal ; and in the evening the bat, which they call flittermouse, appears again.

The light is never the same on a landscape many minutes together, as all know who have tried, ever so crudely, to fix the fleeting expression of the earth with pencil. It is ever changing, and in the same way as you walk by the hedges day by day there is always some fresh circumstance of nature, the interest of which in a measure blots out the past. This morning we found a bramble leaf, something about which has for the moment put the record of months aside. This bramble leaf was marked with a grey streak, which coiled and turned and ran along beside the midrib, forming a sort of thoughtless design, a design without an idea. The Greek fret seems to our eyes in its regularity and its repetition to have a human thought in it. The coils and turns upon this leaf, like many other markings of nature, form a design-less design, the idea of which is not traceable back to a mind. They are the work of a leaf-boring larva which has eaten its way between the two skins of the leaf, much like boring a tunnel between the two surfaces of a sheet of paper. If you take a needle you can insert the point in the burrow and pass it along wherever the bore is straight, so that the needle lies between the two sides of the leaf. Off-hand, if any one were asked if it were possible to split a leaf, he would say no. This little creature, however, has worked along inside it, and lived there. The upper surface of the leaf is a darker green, and seems to the touch of firmer texture than the lower; there are no marks on the under surface, which does not seem touched, so that what the creature has really done is to split one surface. He has eaten along underneath it, raising it no doubt a little by the thickness of his body, as if you crept between the carpet and the floor. The softer under surface representing the floor is untouched. The woodbine leaves are often bored like this, and seem to have patterns traced upon them. There is no particle of matter so small but that it seems to have a living thing working at it and resolving it into still more minute atoms; nothing so insignificant but that upon examination it will be found to be of the utmost value to something alive. Upon almost every fir branch near the end there are little fragments like cotton, so thick in places as to quite hang the boughs with threads; these gossamer-like fragments appear to be left by some insect, perhaps an aphis; and it is curious to note how very very busy the little willow-wrens are in the fir boughs. They are constantly at work there; they sing in the firs in the earliest spring, they stay there all the summer, and now that the edge of autumn approaches their tiny beaks are still picking up insects the whole day long. The insects they devour must be as numerous as the fir needles that lie inches thick on the ground in the copse.

Across a broad, dry, sandy path, worn firm, some thousands of ants passing to and fro their nest had left a slight trail. They were hurrying on in full work, when I drew the top of my walking-stick across their road, obliterating about an inch of it. In an instant the work of the nest was stopped, and thousands upon thousands of factory hands were thrown out of employment. The walking-stick had left two little ridges of sand like

minute parallel earthworks drawn across their highway.
Those that came out of the nest on arriving at the little
ridge on their side immediately stopped, worked their
antennæ in astonishment, then went up to the top of it,
and seemed to try to look round.   After a moment they
ran back and touched those that were coming on to
communicate the intelligence.   Every ant that came did
exactly the same thing ; not one of them passed the
little ridge, but all returned.   By-and-by the head of the
column began to spread out and search right and left
for the lost track.   They scouted this way and they
scouted that, they turned and doubled and went through
every possible evolution, hundreds of them, sometimes
a score at once, yet not one of them attempted to go
straight forward, which would have brought them into
their old path.   It was scarcely thrice the length of an
ant's body to where their path began again ; they could
not see or scent, or in any way find out what was so
short a distance in front of them.   The most extraordinary thing was that not one ventured to explore straight
forward ; it was as if their world came to an end at that
little ridge, and they were afraid to step into chaos.
The same actions were going on behind the other ridge
of sand just opposite, an inch away.   There the column
of ants that had been out foraging was met with a like
difficulty, and could not find their way.   There, too, hundreds of ants were exploring right and left in every direction except straight forward, in a perfect buzz of excitement.   Once or twice an ant from either party happened
to mount on the parallel ridges at the same time, and
if they had strained forward and stretched out their
antennæ they could have almost touched each other.
Yet they seemed quite unconscious of each other's presence.   Unless in a well-worn groove a single ant appears

incapable of running in a straight line. At first their motions searching about suggested the action of a pack of hounds making a cast; hounds, however, would have very soon gone forward and so picked up the trail.

If I may make a guess at the cause of this singular confusion, I think I should attribute it to some peculiarity in the brain of the ant, or else to some consideration of which we are ignorant, but which weighs with ants, and not to any absence of the physical senses. Because they do not do as we should do under similar circumstances is no proof that they do not possess the power to hear and see. Experiments, for instance, have been made with bees to find out if they have any sense of hearing, by shouting close to a bee, drawing discordant notes on the violin, striking pieces of metal together, and so on, to all of which the bee remained indifferent. What else could she do? Neither of these sounds hurt if she heard them, nor seemed to threaten danger; they simply conveyed no impression at all to her mind. Observe your favourite pussy curled up in the arm-chair at such time as she knows the dishes have been cleared away, and there is no more chance of wheedling a titbit from you. You may play the piano, or the violin, or knock with a hammer, or shout your loudest, she will take no notice, no more than if she actually had no ears at all. Are you, therefore, to conclude she does not hear you? As well conclude that people do not hear the thunder because they do not shout in answer to it. Such noises simply do not concern her, and she takes no notice. Now, though her eyes be closed, let a strange dog run in, and at the light pad pad of his feet, scarcely audible on the carpet, she is up in a moment, blazing with wrath. That is a sound that interests her. So, too, perhaps, it may be with ants and bees, who may hear and see,

and yet take no apparent notice because the circumstances are not interesting, and the experiment is to
them unintelligible. Fishes in particular have been often,
I think, erroneously judged in this way, and have been
considered deaf, and to have little intelligence, while in
truth the fact is we have not discovered a way of com-
municating with them any more than they have found
a way of talking with us. Fishes, I know, are keener of
sight than I am when they are interested, and I believe
they can hear equally well, and are not by any means
without mind. These ants that acted so foolishly to
appearance may have been influenced by some former
experience of which we know nothing ; there may be
something in the past history of the ant which may lead
them to profoundly suspect interference with their path
as indicative of extreme danger. Once, perhaps, many
ant-generations ago, there was some creature which acted
thus in order to destroy them. This, of course, is merely
an illustration put forward to suggest the idea that there
may be a reason in the brain of the ant of which we
know nothing. I do not know that I myself am any
more rational, for looking back along the path of life
I can see now how I turned and twisted and went to
the right and the left in the most crooked manner, putting
myself to endless trouble, when by taking one single
step straight forward in the right direction, if I had only
known, I might have arrived at once at the goal. Can
any of us look beyond the little ridge of one day and
see what will happen the day after ? Some hours afterwards, towards evening, I found the ants were beginning
to get over their difficulty. On one side an ant would
go forward in a half-circle, on the other another ant
would advance sideways, and meeting together they
would touch their antennæ, and then the first would

travel back with the second, and so the line was re-established. It was very much as if two batsmen at opposite wickets should run forward each halfway, and after shaking hands and conversing, one of them should lead the other safely over.

WALKS IN THE WHEAT-FIELDS.

I.

IF you will look at a grain of wheat you will see that it seems folded up: it has crossed its arms and rolled itself up in a cloak, a fold of which forms a groove, and so gone to sleep. If you look at it some time, as people in the old enchanted days used to look into a mirror, or the magic ink, until they saw living figures therein, you can almost trace a miniature human being in the oval of the grain. It is narrow at the top, where the head would be, and broad across the shoulders, and narrow again down towards the feet; a tiny man or woman has wrapped itself round about with a garment and settled to slumber. Up in the far north, where the dead ice reigns, our arctic explorers used to roll themselves in a sleeping-bag like this, to keep the warmth in their bodies against the chilliness of the night. Down in the south, where the heated sands of Egypt never cool, there in the rock-hewn tombs lie the mummies wrapped and lapped and wound about with a hundred yards of linen, in the hope, it may be, that spices and balm might retain within the sarcophagus some small fragment of human organism through endless ages, till at last the gift of life revisited it. Like a grain of wheat the mummy is folded in its cloth. And I do not know really whether I might not say that these little grains of English corn do not hold within them the actual flesh and blood of man.   Transubstantiation is a fact there.

Sometimes the grains are dry and shrivelled and hard as shot, sometimes they are large and full and have a juiciness about them, sometimes they are a little bit red, others are golden, many white.   The sack stands open in the market—you can thrust your arm in it a foot deep, or take up a handful and let it run back like a liquid stream, or hold it in your palm and balance it, feeling the weight.   They are not very heavy as they lie in the palm, yet these little grains are a ponderous weight that rules man's world.   Wherever they are there is empire.   Could imperial Rome have only grown sufficient wheat in Italy to have fed her legions Cæsar would still be master of three-fourths of the earth.   Rome thought more in her latter days of grapes and oysters and mullets, that change colour as they die, and singing girls and flute-playing, and cynic verse of Horace—anything rather than corn.   Rome is no more, and the lords of the world are they who have mastership of wheat. We have the mastership at this hour by dint of our gold and our hundred-ton guns, but they are telling our farmers to cast aside their corn, and to grow tobacco and fruit and anything else that can be thought of in preference.   The gold is slipping away.   These sacks in the market open to all to thrust their hands in are not sacks of corn but of golden sovereigns, half-sovereigns, new George and the dragon, old George and the dragon, Sydney mint sovereigns, Napoleons, half-Napoleons, Belgian gold, German gold, Italian gold ; gold scraped and scratched and gathered together like old rags from door to door.   Sacks full of gold, verily I may say that all the gold poured out from the Australian fields, every pennyweight of it, hundreds of tons, all shipped over the sea to India, Australia, South Africa, Egypt, and, above all, America, to buy wheat. It was said that Pompey and his sons covered the great earth with their bones, for each one died in a different quarter of the world ; but now he would want two more sons for Australia and America, the two new quarters which are now at work ploughing, sowing, reaping, without a month's intermission, growing corn for us. When you buy a bag of flour at the baker's you pay fivepence over the counter, a very simple transaction. Still you do not expect to get even that little bag of flour for nothing, your fivepence goes over the counter in somebody else's till. Consider now the broad ocean as the counter and yourself to represent thirty-five millions of English people buying sixteen, seventeen, or eighteen million quarters of wheat from the nations opposite, and paying for it shiploads of gold.

So that these sacks of corn in the market are truly filled with gold dust ; and how strange it seems at first that our farmers, who are for ever dabbling with their hands in these golden sands, should be for ever grumbling at their poverty ! 'The nearer the church the farther from God' is an old country proverb ; the nearer to wheat the farther from mammon, I may construct as an addendum. Quite lately a gentleman told me that while he grew wheat on his thousand acres he lost just a pound an acre per annum, *i.e.* a thousand a year out of capital, so that if he had not happily given up this amusement he would now have been in the workhouse munching the putty there supplied for bread.

The rag and bone men go from door to door filling an old bag with scraps of linen, and so innumerable agents of bankers and financiers, vampires that suck gold, are for ever prowling about collecting every golden coin they can scent out and shipping it over sea. And what does not go abroad is in consequence of this great drain sharply locked up in the London safes as reserves against paper, and cannot be utilised in enterprises or manufacture. Therefore trade stands still, and factories are closed, and ship-yards are idle, and beautiful vessels are stored up doing nothing by hundreds in dock ; coal mines left to be filled with water, and furnaces blown out. Therefore there is bitter distress and starvation, and cries for relief works, and one meal a day for Board school children, and the red flag of Socialism is unfurled. All because of these little grains of wheat.

They talked of bringing artillery, with fevered lips, to roar forth shrapnel in Trafalgar Square ; why not Gatling guns ? The artillery did not come for very shame, but the Guards did, and there were regiments of infantry in the rear, with glittering bayonets to prod folk into moving on. All about these little grains of wheat.

These thoughts came into my mind in the winter afternoon at the edge of a level corn-field, with the copper-sheathed spire of the village church on my right, the sun going down on the left. The copper did not gleam, it was dull and brown, no better than discoloured wood, patched with pieces of later date and another shade of dulness. I wish they would glitter, some of these steeples or some of our roofs, and so light up the reddish brown of the elms and the grey lichened oaks. The very rooks are black, and the starlings and the wintry fieldfares and redwings have no colour at a distance. They say the metal roofs and domes gleam in Russia, and even in France, and why not in our rare sunshine ? Once now and then you see a gilded weather-cock shine like a day-star as the sun goes down three miles away, over the dark brown field, where the plough has been going to and fro through the slow hours. I can see the plough and the horses very well at three miles, and know what they are doing.

I wish the trees, the elms, would grow tall enough and thick enough to hide the steeples and towers which stand up so stiff and stark, and bare and cold, some of them blunted and squab, some of them sharp enough to impale, with no more shape than a walking-stick, ferrule upwards—every one of them out of proportion and jarring to the eye. If by good fortune you can find a spot where you cannot see a steeple or a church tower, where you can see only fields and woods, you will find it so much more beautiful, for nature has made it of its kind perfect. The dim sea is always so beautiful a view because it is not disfigured by these buildings. In the ships men live; in the houses among the trees they live; these steeples and towers are empty, and no spirit can dwell in that which is out of proportion. Scarcely any one can paint a picture of the country without sticking in one of these repellent structures. The oast-houses, whose red cones are so plentiful in Kent and Sussex, have quite a different effect; they have some colour, and by a curious felicity the builders have hit upon a good proportion, so that the shape is pleasant; these, too, have some use in the world.

Westward the sun was going down over the sea, and a wild west wind, which the glow of the sun as it touched the waves seemed to heat into fury, brought up the distant sound of the billows from the beach. A line of dark Spanish oaks from which the sharp pointed acorns were dropping, darkest green oaks, shut out the shore. A thousand starlings were flung up into the air out of these oaks, as if an impatient hand had cast them into the sky ; then down they fell again, with a ceaseless whistling and clucking ; up they went and down they came, lost in the deep green foliage as if they had dropped in the sea. The long level of the wheat-field plain stretched out from my feet towards the far-away Downs, so level that the first hedge shut off the fields beyond ; and every now and then over these hedges there rose up the white forms of sea-gulls drifting to and fro among the elms. White sea-gulls—birds of divination, you might say—a good symbol of the times, for now we plough the ocean. The barren sea ! In the Greek poets you may find constant reference to it as that which could not be reaped or sowed. Ulysses, to betoken his madness, took his plough down to the shore and drew furrows in the sand—the sea that even Demeter, great goddess, could not sow nor bring to any fruition. Yet now the ocean is our wheat-field and ships are our barns. The sea-gull should be painted on the village tavern sign instead of the golden wheatsheaf.

There could be no more flat and uninteresting surface than this field, a damp wet brown, water slowly draining out of the furrows, not a bird that I can see. No hare certainly, or partridge, or even a rabbit—nothing to sit or crouch—on that cold surface, tame and level as the brown cover of a book. They like something more human and comfortable ; just as we creep into nooks and corners of rooms and into cosy arm-chairs, so they like tufts or some growth of shelter, or mounds that are dry, between hedges where there is a bite for them. I can trace nothing on this surface, so heavily washed by late rain. Let now the harriers come, and instantly the hounds' second sense of smell picks up the invisible sign of the hare that has crossed it in the night or early dawn, and runs it as swiftly as if he were lifting a clue of thread. The dull surface is all written over with hieroglyphics to the hound, he can read and translate to us in joyous tongue. Or the foxhounds carry a bee-line straight from hedge to hedge, and after them come the hoofs, prospecting deeply into the earth, dashing down fibre and blade, crunching up the tender wheat and battering it to pieces. It will rise again all the fresher and stronger, for there is something human in wheat, and the more it is trampled on the better it grows. Despots grind half the human race, and despots stronger than man—plague, pestilence, and famine—grind the whole; and yet the world increases, and the green wheat of the human heart is not to be trampled out.

The starlings grew busier and busier in the dark green Spanish oaks, thrown up as if a shell had burst among them ; suddenly their clucking and whistling ceased, the speeches of contention were over, a vote of confidence had been passed in their Government, and the House was silent. The pheasants in the park shook their wings and crowed ' kuck, kuck—kow,' and went to roost ; the water in the furrows ceased to reflect ; the dark earth grew darker and damper ; the elms lost their reddish brown ; the sky became leaden behind the ridge of the Downs, and the shadow of night fell over the field.

Twenty-five years ago I went into a camera obscura, where you see miniature men and women, coloured photographs alive and moving, trees waving, now and then dogs crossing the bright sun picture. I was only there a few moments, and I have never been in one since, and yet so inexplicable a thing is memory, the picture stands before me now clear as if it were painted and tangible. So many millions of pictures have come and gone upon the retina, and yet I can single out this one in an instant, and take it down as you would a book from a shelf. The millions of coloured etchings that have fixed themselves there in the course of those years are all in due order in the portfolio of the mind, and yet they cannot occupy the space of a pin's point. They have neither length, breadth, nor thickness, none of the qualifications of mathematical substance, and yet they must in some way be a species of matter. The fact indicates the possibility of still more subtle existences. Now I wish I could put before you a coloured, living, moving picture, like that of the camera obscura, of some other wheat-fields at a sunnier time. They were painted on the surface of a plain, set round about with a margin of green downs. They were large enough to have the charm of vague, indefinite extension, and yet all could be distinctly seen. Large squares of green corn that was absorbing its yellow from the sunlight , chess squares, irregularly placed, of brown furrows ; others of rich blood-red trifolium ; others of scarlet sainfoin and blue lucerne, gardens of scarlet poppies here and there. Not all of these, of course, at once, but they followed so quickly in the summer days that they seemed to be one and the same pictures, and had you painted them altogether on the same canvas, together with ripe wheat, they would not have seemed out of place. Never was such brilliant colour ; it was chalk there, and on chalk the colours are always clearer, the poppies deeper, the yellow mustard and charlock a keener yellow ; the air, too, is pellucid. Waggons going along the tracks ; men and women hoeing ; ricks of last year still among clumps of trees, where the chimneys and gables of farm-houses are partly visible ; red-tiled barns away yonder ; a shepherd moving his hurdles ; away again the black funnel of an idle engine, and the fly-wheel above hawthorn bushes—all so distinct and close under that you might almost fear to breathe for fear of dimming the mirror. The few white clouds sailing over seemed to belong to the fields on which their shadows were now foreshortened, now lengthened, as if they were really part of the fields, like the crops, and the azure sky so low down as to be the roof of the house and not at all a separate thing. And the sun a lamp that you might almost have pushed along his course faster with your hand ; a loving and interesting sun that wanted the wheat to ripen, and stayed there in the slow-drawn arc of the summer day to lend a hand. Sun and sky and clouds close here and not across any planetary space, but working with us in the same field, shoulder to shoulder, with man. Then you might see the white doves yonder flutter up suddenly out of the trees by the farm, little flecks of white clouds themselves, and everywhere all throughout the plain an exquisite silence, a delicious repose, not one clang or harshness of sound to shatter the beauty of it. There you might stand on the high down among the thyme and watch it, hour after hour, and still no interruption ; nothing to break it up. It was something like the broad folio of an ancient illuminated manuscript, in gold, gules, blue, green ; with foliated scrolls and human figures, somewhat clumsy and thick, but quaintly drawn, and bold in their intense realism.

There was another wheat-field by the side of which I used to walk sometimes in the evenings, as the grains in the ears began to grow firm. The path ran for a mile beside it—a mile of wheat in one piece—all those million million stalks the same height, all with about the same number of grains in each ear, all ripening together. The hue of the surface travelled along as you approached ; the tint of yellow shifted farther like the reflection of sunlight on water, but the surface was really much the same colour everywhere. It seemed a triumph of culture over such a space, such regularity, such perfection of myriads of plants springing in their true lines at the same time, each particular ear perfect, and a mile of it. Perfect work with the plough, the drill, the harrow in every detail, and yet such breadth. Let your hand touch the ears lightly as you walk—drawn through them as if over the side of a boat in water—feeling the golden heads. The sparrows fly out every now and then ahead; some of the birds like their corn as it hardens, and some while it is soft and full of milky sap. There are hares within, and many a brood of partridge chicks that cannot yet use their wings. Thick as the seed itself the feathered creatures have been among the wheat since it was sown. Finches more numerous than the berries on the hedges; sparrows like the finches multiplied by finches, linnets, rooks, like leaves on the trees, wood-pigeons whose crops are like bushel baskets for capacity; and now as it ripens the multitude will be multiplied by legions, and as it comes to the harvest there is a fresh crop of sparrows from the nests in the barns, you may see a brown cloud of them a hundred yards long. Besides which there were the rabbits that ate the young green blades, and the mice that will be busy in the sheaves, and the insects from spring-time to granary, a nameless host uncounted. A whole world, as it were, let loose upon the wheat, to eat, consume, and wither it, and yet it conquers the whole world. The great field you see was filled with gold corn four feet deep as a pitcher is filled with water to the brim. Of yore the rich man is said, in the Roman classic, to have measured his money, so here you might have measured it by the rood. The sunbeams sank deeper and deeper into the wheatears, layer upon layer of light, and the colour deepened by these daily strokes. There was no bulletin to tell the folk of its progress, no Nileometer to mark the rising flood of the wheat to its hour of overflow. Yet there went through the village a sense of expectation, and men said to each other, 'We shall be there soon.' No one knew. the day—the last day of doom of the golden race; every one knew it was nigh. One evening there was a small square piece cut at one side, a little notch, and two shocks stood there in the twilight. Next day the village sent forth its army with their crooked weapons to cut and slay. It used to be an era, let me tell you, when a great farmer gave the signal to his reapers; not a man, woman, or child that did not talk of that. Well-to-do people stopped their vehicles and walked out into the new stubble. Ladies came, farmers, men of low degree, everybody—all to exchange a word or two with the workers. These were so terribly in earnest at the start they could scarcely acknowledge the presence even of the squire. They felt themselves so important, and were so full, and so intense and one-minded in their labour, that the great of the earth might come and go as sparrows for aught they cared. More men and more men were put on day by day, and women to bind the sheaves, till the vast field held the village, yet they seemed but a handful buried in the tunnels of the golden mine: they were lost in it like the hares, for as the wheat fell, the shocks rose behind them, low tents of corn. Your skin or mine could not have stood the scratching of the straw, which is stiff and sharp, and the burning of the sun, which blisters like red-hot iron. No one could stand the harvest-field as a reaper except he had been born and cradled in a cottage, and passed his childhood bareheaded in July heats and January snows.

I was always fond of being out of doors, yet I used to wonder how these men and women could stand it, for the summer day is long, and they were there hours before I was up. The edge of the reap-hook had to be driven by force through the stout stalks like a sword, blow after blow, minute after minute, hour after hour ; the back stooping, and the broad sun throwing his fiery rays from a full disc on the head and neck. I think some of them used to put handkerchiefs doubled up in their hats as pads, as in the East they wind the long roll of the turban about the head, and perhaps they would have done better if they had adopted the custom of the South and wound a long scarf about the middle of the body, for they were very liable to be struck down with such internal complaints as come from great heat. Their necks grew black, much like black oak in old houses. Their open chests were always bare, and flat, and stark, and never rising with rounded bust-like muscle as the Greek statues of athletes.

The breast-bone was burned black, and their arms, tough as ash, seemed cased in leather. They grew visibly thinner in the harvest-field, and shrunk together —all flesh disappearing, and nothing but sinew and muscle remaining. Never was such work. The wages were low in those days, and it is not long ago, either—I mean the all-year-round wages ; the reaping was piece-work at so much per acre—like solid gold to men and women who had lived on dry bones, as it were, through the winter. So they worked and slaved, and tore at the wheat as if they were seized with a frenzy ; the heat, the aches, the illness, the sunstroke, always impending in the air—the stomach hungry again before the meal was over, it was nothing. No song, no laugh, no stay— on from morn till night, possessed with a maddened desire to labour, for the more they could cut the larger the sum they would receive ; and what is man's heart and brain to money ? So hard, you see, is the pressure of human life that these miserables would have prayed on their knees for permission to tear their arms from the socket, and to scorch and shrivel themselves to charred human brands in the furnace of the sun.

Does it not seem bitter that it should be so ? Here was the wheat, the beauty of which I strive in vain to tell you, in the midst of the flowery summer, scourging them with the knot of necessity ; that which should give life pulling the life out of them, rendering their exist-ence below that of the cattle, so far as the pleasure of living goes. Without doubt many a low mound in the churchyard—once visible, now level—was the sooner raised over the nameless dead because of that terrible strain in the few weeks of the gold fever. This is human life, real human life—no rest, no calm enjoyment of the scene, no generous gift of food and wine lavishly offered by the gods—the hard fist of necessity for ever battering man to a shapeless and hopeless fall.

The whole village lived in the field ; a corn-land village is always the most populous, and every rood of land thereabouts, in a sense, maintains its man. The reaping, and the binding up and stacking of the sheaves, and the carting and building of the ricks, and the glean-ing, there was something to do for every one, from the ' olde, olde, very olde man,' the Thomas Parr of the hamlet, down to the very youngest child whose little eye could see, and whose little hand could hold a stalk of wheat. The gleaners had a way of binding up the collected wheatstalks together so that a very large quantity was held tightly in a very small compass. The gleaner's sheaf looked like the knot of a girl's hair woven in and bound. It was a tradition of the wheat field handed down from generation to generation, a thing you could not possibly do unless you had been shown the secret—like the knots the sailors tie, a kind of hand art. The wheatstalk being thick at one end makes the sheaf heavier and more solid there, and so in any manner of fastening it or stacking it, it takes a rounded shape like a nine-pin ; the round ricks are built thick in the middle and lessen gradually toward the top and toward the ground. The warm yellow of the straw is very pleasant to look at on a winter's day under a grey sky ; so, too, the straw looks nice and warm and comfortable, thrown down thickly in the yards for the roan cattle.

After the village has gone back to its home still the work of the wheat is not over ; there is the thatching with straw of last year, which is bleached and contrasts with the yellow of the fresh-gathered crop. Next the threshing ; and meantime the ploughs are at work, and very soon there is talk of seed-time.

I used to look with wonder when I was a boy at the endless length of wall and the enormous roof of a great tithe barn. The walls of Spanish convents, with little or no window to break the vast monotony, somewhat resemble it : the convent is a building, but does not look like a home ; it is too big, too general. So this barn, with its few windows, seemed too immense to belong to any one man. The tithe barn has so completely dropped out of modern life that it may be well to briefly mention that its use was to hold the tenth sheaf from every wheat-field in the parish. The parson's tithe was the real actual tenth sheaf bodily taken from every field of corn in the district. A visible tenth, you see ; a very solid thing. Imagine the vast heap they

would have made, imagine the hundreds and hundreds
of sacks of wheat they filled when they were threshed.
I have often thought that it would perhaps be a good
thing if this contribution of the real tenth could be
brought back again for another purpose.   If such a barn
could be filled now, and its produce applied to the help
of the poor and aged and injured of the village, we
might get rid of that blot on our civilisation—the workhouse.   Mr. Besant, in his late capital story, ' The Children of Gibeon,' most truly pointed out that it was custom
which rendered all men indifferent to the sufferings of
their fellow-creatures.   In the old Roman days men
were crucified so often that it ceased even to be a show ;
the soldiers played at dice under the miserable wretches ;
the peasant women stepping by jested and laughed and
sang.   Almost in our own time dry skeletons creaked
on gibbets at every cross-road :—

> When for thirty shillings men were hung,
>   And the thirst for blood grew stronger,
> Men's lives were valued then at a sheep's—
>   Thank God that lasts no longer.

So strong is custom and tradition, and the habit of
thought it weaves about us, that I have heard ancient
and grave farmers, when the fact was mentioned with
horror, hum, and ah ! and handle their beards, and mutter
that ' they didn't know as 'twas altogether such a bad
thing as they was hung for sheep-stealing.'   There were
parsons then, as now, in every rural parish preaching and
teaching something they called the Gospel.   Why did
they not rise as one man and denounce this ghastly ini-
quity, and demand its abolition ?   They did nothing of
the sort ; they enjoyed their pipes and grog very comfortably.

The gallows at the cross-roads is gone, but the work-house stands, and custom, cruel custom, that tyrant of the mind, has inured us (to use an old word) to its existence in our midst. Apart from any physical suffering, let us only consider the slow agony of the poor old reaper when he feels his lusty arm wither, and of the grey bowed wife as they feel themselves drifting like a ship ashore to that stony waiting-room. For it is a waiting-room till the grave receives them. Economically, too, the workhouse is a heavy loss and drag.

Could we, then, see the tithe barn filled again with golden wheat for this purpose of help to humanity, it might be a great and wonderful good. With this tenth to feed the starving and clothe the naked ; with the tenth to give the little children a midday meal at the school— that would be natural and true. In the course of time, as the land laws lessen their grip, and the people take possession of the earth on which they stand, it is more than probable that something of this kind will really come about. It would be only simple justice after so many centuries—it takes so many hundreds of years to get even that.

'Workhouse, indeed!' I have heard the same ancient well-to-do greybeards ejaculate, 'workhouse! they ought to be very thankful they have got such a place to go to!'

All the village has been to the wheat-field with reaping-hooks, and waggons and horses, the whole strength of man has been employed upon it; little brown hands and large brown hands, blue eyes and dark eyes have been there searching about; all the intelligence of human beings has been brought to bear, and yet the stubble is not empty. Down there come again the ever-increasing clouds of sparrows ; as a cloud rises here

another cloud descends beyond it, a very mist and
vapour as it were of wings. It makes one wonder to
think where all the nests could have been ; there could
hardly have been enough eaves and barns for all these
to have been bred in. Every one of the multitude has
a keen pair of eyes and a hungry beak, and every single
individual finds something to eat in the stubble. Something that was not provided for them, crumbs that have
escaped from this broad table, and there they are every
day for weeks together, still finding food. If you will
consider the incredible number of little mouths, and the
busy rate at which they ply them hour by hour, you
may imagine what an immense number of grains of
wheat must have escaped man's hand, for you must
remember that every time they peck they take a whole
grain. Down, too, come the grey-blue wood-pigeons and
the wild turtle-doves. The singing linnets come in
parties, the happy greenfinches, the streaked yellowhammers, as if any one had delicately painted them in
separate streaks, and not with a wash of colour, the
brown buntings, chaffinches—out they come from the
hazel copses, where the nuts are dropping, and the hedge
berries turning red, and every one finds something to his
liking. There are the seeds of the charlock and the
thistle, and a hundred other little seeds, insects, and
minute atom-like foods it needs a bird's eye to know.
They are never still, they sweep up into the hedges and
line the boughs, calling and talking, and away again to
another rood of stubble without any order or plan of
search, just sowing themselves about like wind-blown
seeds. Up and down the day through with a zest never
failing. It is beautiful to listen to them and watch them,
if any one will stay under an oak by the nut-tree
boughs, where the dragon-flies shoot to and fro in the

shade as if the direct rays of the sun would burn their delicate wings; they hunt chiefly in the shade. The linnets will suddenly sweep up into the boughs and converse sweetly over your head. The sunshine lingers and grows sweeter as the autumn gives tokens of its coming in the buff bryony leaf, and the acorn filling its cup. They are so happy, the birds, yet there are few to listen to them. I have often looked round and wondered that no one else was about hearkening to them. Altogether, perhaps, they lead safer lives in England than anywhere else. We do not shoot them; the fowlers do mischief, still they make but little impression; there are few birds of prey, and there is not that fearful bloodthirstiness that makes a tropical forest so terrible in fact, under its outward show of glowing colour. There, with cruel hawks and owls, and serpents, and beasts of prey, a bird's life is one long terror. They are ever on the watch here, but they are not so fearfully harassed, and are not certain as it were beforehand to be torn to pieces. The land is well cultivated, and the more the culture the more the food for them. Frost and snow are their greatest enemies, but even these do not often last a great while. It is a land of woods, and above all of hedges, which are much more favourable to birds than forests, so that they are better off in England than in other countries. From the sowing to the reaping, the wheat-field gives a constant dole like the monasteries of old, only here it is no crust, but a free and bountiful largess. Then the stubble must be broken up by the plough, and again there is a fresh helping for them. Brown partridge, and black rook, and yellowhammer, all hues and degrees, come to the wheat-field.

II.

EVERY day something new is introduced into farming, and yet the old things are not driven out. Every one knows that steam is now used on the farm for ploughing and threshing and working machinery at the farmstead, and one would have thought that by this time it would have superseded all other motive powers. Yet this very day I counted twenty great cart-horses at work in one ploughed field. They were all in pairs, harnessed to harrows, rollers, and ploughs, and out of the twenty, nineteen were dark-coloured. Huge great horses, broad of limb, standing high up above the level surface of the open field, great towers of strength, almost prehistoric in their massiveness. Enough of them to drag a great cannon up into a battery on the heights. The day before, passing the same farm—it was Sunday—a great bay cart-horse mare standing contentedly in a corner of the yard looked round to see who it was going by, and the sun shone on the glossy hair, smooth as if it had been brushed, the long black mane hung over the arching neck, the large dark eyes looked at us so quietly—a real English picture. The black funnel of the steam-engine has not driven the beautiful cart-horses out of the fields. They have been there for centuries, and there they stay ; the notched, broad wheel of the steam-plough has but just begun to leave its trail on the earth. New things come, but the old do not go away. One life is but a summer's day compared with the long cycle of years of agriculture, and yet it seems that a whole storm, as it were, of innovations has burst upon the fields ever since I can recollect, and, as years go, I am still in the green leaf. The labouring men used to tell me how they went reaping, for although you may see what is called reaping still going on at harvest-time, it is not reaping. True reaping is done with a hook alone and the hand; all the present reaping is 'vagging,' with a hook in one hand and a bent stick in the other, and instead of drawing the hook towards him and cutting it, the reaper chops at the straw as he might at an enemy. Then came the reaping machines, that simply cut the wheat, and left it lying flat on the ground, which were constantly altered and improved. Now there are the wire and string binders, that not only cut the corn, but gather it together and bind it in sheaves—a vast saving in labour. Still the reaping-hook endures and is used on all small farms, and to some extent on large ones, to round off the work of the machine; the new things come, but the old still remains. In itself the reaping-hook is an enlarged sickle, and the sickle was in use in Roman times, and no man knows how long before that. With it the reaper cut off the ears of the wheat only, leaving the tall straw standing, much as if it had been a pruning-knife. It is the oldest of old implements— very likely it was made of a chip of flint at first, and then of bronze, and then of steel, and now at Sheffield or Birmingham in its enlarged form of the 'vagging' hook. In the hand of Ceres it was the very symbol of agriculture, and that was a goodly time ago. At this hour they say the sickle is still used in several parts of England where the object is more to get the straw than the ear.

On the broad page of some ancient illuminated manuscript, centuries old, you may see the churl, or farmer's man, knocking away with his flail at the grain on the threshing-floor. The knock knocking of the

flail went on through the reigns of how many kings and
queens I do not know, they are all forgotten, God wot,
down to the edge of our own times.   The good old days
when there was snow at Christmas, and fairs were held
and pamphlets printed on the frozen Thames, when
comets were understood as fate, and when the corn laws
starved half England—those were the times of the flail.
Every barn—and there were then barns on every farm,
think of the number—had its threshing-floor opposite the
great open doors, and all the dread winter through the
flail resounded.   Men looked upon it as their most
cherished privilege to get that employment in the bitter
dark hours of the hungry months.   It was life itself to
them : to stand there swinging that heavy bit of wood
all day meant meat and drink, or rather cheese and drink,
for themselves and families.   It was a post as valued as
a civil list pension nowadays, for you see there were
crowds of men in these corn villages, but only a few
of them could get barns to snop away in.

The flail is made of two stout staves of wood jointed
with leather.   They had flails of harder make than that,
harder than the iron flails used in the wars of old times,
i.e. Hunger, Necessity, Fate, to beat them on the back,
and thresh them on the floor of the earth.   The corn
laws are gone, half the barns are gone, our granaries
now are afloat, steam threshes our ricks—in a few days
doing what used to take months, and you would think
that this simple implement would have disappeared for
ever.   Instead of which flails are still in use on small
farms—which it is now the cry to multiply—for knocking
out little quantities of grain for feeding purposes.   The
gleaners used to use them to thresh out their collections.
There would be no difficulty in getting a flail if anybody
had a mind to make a museum of such things ; and if

the force of modern ideas should succeed in dividing the land among small occupiers, the flail will become as common as ever.

There was an old waggon shown at the Royal Agricultural Show in London said to be two hundred years old ; probably it had had so many new wheels, and shafts, and sides, as to have physiologically changed its constitution—still there were waggons in those days, and there are waggons now.   Express trains go by in a great hurry—the slow waggons gather up the warm hay and the yellow wheat, just as they did hundreds of years since.   The broad-browed oxen guided by the ancient goad draw the old wooden plough over the slopes of the Downs, though the telegraph wires are in sight.   You may see men sowing broadcast just as they did a thousand years ago on the broad English acres.   Yet the light iron plough, and the heavy drill with its four horses, the steam-plough, winnowing machines, root-pulpers, are manufactured and cast out into the fields, and machinery, machinery, machinery, still increases.

If I were a painter I should like to paint all this ; I should like to paint a great steam-ploughing engine and its vast wheels, with its sweep of smoke, sometimes drifting low over the fallow, sometimes rising into the air in regular shape, like the pine tree of Pliny over Pompeii's volcano.   A wonderful effect it has in the still air ; sweet white violets in a corner by the hedge still there in all their beauty.   For I think that the immense realism of the iron wheels makes the violet yet more lovely ; the more they try to drive out Nature with a fork the more she returns, and the soul clings the stronger to the wild flowers.   I should like to paint the lessening square of the wheat-field, the reaping machine continually cutting the square smaller, as if it traversed the Greek fret. People of the easel would not find it easy to depict the half-green, half-made hay floating in the air behind a haymaking machine. Sunlight falls on the modern implements just the same as on the old wooden plough and the oxen. To be true, pictures of our fields should have them both, instead of which all the present things are usually omitted, and we are presented with landscapes that might date from the first George. Turner painted the railway train and made it at once ideal, poetical, and classical. His 'Rain, Steam, and Speed,' which displays a modern subject, is a most wonderful picture. If a man chose his hour rightly, the steam-plough under certain atmospheric conditions would give him as good a subject as a Great Western train. He who has got the sense of beauty in his eye can find it in things as they really are, and needs no stagey time of artificial pastorals to furnish him with a sham nature. Idealise to the full, but idealise the real, else the picture is a sham.

All the old things remain on the farm, but the village is driven out—the village that used to come as one man to the reaping. Machinery has not altered the earth, but it has altered the conditions of men's lives, and as work decreases, so men decrease. Some go the cities, some emigrate ; the young men drift away, and there is none of that home life that there used to be. They are going to try to re-settle our land by altering the laws. Most certainly the laws ought to be altered, and must be altered, still it is evident to any one of dispassionate thought, while such immense quantities of gold are sent away from us, profit cannot be made in farming either small or great. The crop is the same in either case, and if there is no sale for the produce, it matters very little whether you farm four acres or four hundred.

New hats and jackets, but the same old faces. A stout old farmer sat at the side of his barn door on the hatch leaning against the post. His body was as rotund as a full sack of wheat, his great chin and his great cheeks were full; a man very solidly set as it were, and he eyed me, a stranger, as I passed down the lane, with mistrust and suspicion in every line of his face. Out of the hunting season a stranger might perhaps have been seen there once in six months, and this was that once. The British bull-dog growled in his countenance—very likely pleasantness itself to those he knew, grimness itself to others. The sunlight fell full into the barn, the great doors wide open; there were sacks on the other side of the door piled up inside, a heap of grain, and two men turning the winches of a winnowing machine. New hats, but old faces. Could his great-great-grandfather have been dug up and set in that barn door, he would have looked just the same, so would the sacks, and the wheat, and the sunshine. At the market town, where the auctioneer's hammer goes tap tap over bullocks and sheep, crowds of men gather together, —farmers, and bailiffs, and shepherds, drovers and labourers—and their clothes are different, but there are the same old weather-beaten faces. Faces that you may see in the ancient illuminated manuscripts, in the realistic wood engravings of early printed books, in the etchings of last century, the same lines and expression. The earth has marked them all. In a modern country sketch or picture you would *not* find them, they would be smoothed away—drawing-room faces, made transparent, in attitudes like easy-limbed girls delicately proportioned These are not country people. Country people are the same now in appearance as when the old artists honestly drew them; sturdy and square, bulky and slow, no attitudes, no drawing-room grace, no Christmas card glossiness ; somewhat stiff of limb, with a distinct flavour of hay and straw about them, and no enamel. In the villages cottagers have no ideas of tastefully disposing their mantles about their shoulders, or of dressing for the occasion. I do not know how to describe the form of a middle-aged cottage woman on a stormy day with a large, greenish umbrella, a round bonnet, huge and enclosing all the head, back, and sides, like the vast helm of the knights, a sort of circular cloak, stout ankles well visible, and sometimes pattens ; the wearer inside all this decidedly bulky, and the whole apparatus coming along through mud and rain with great deliberation. Inside the round bonnet a ruddy, apple-cheeked face, just such a one as used to go to mass in Sir John the priest's time, before the images were knocked out of the rood-loft at the church there. The boys and girls play in the ditches till they go to school, and they play in the hedges and ditches every hour they can get out of school, and the moment their time is up they go to work among the hedges and ditches, and though they may have had to read standard authors at school, no sooner do they get among the furrows than they talk hedge and ditch language. They do not talk Pope, or Milton, or Addison ; they 'knaaws,' 'they be a-gwoin thur,' it's a 'geat,' and a 'vield,' and a 'vurrow.' These are the old faces you see, the same old powers are at work to fashion them. Heavy, blind blows of the Wind, the Rain, Frost, and Heat, have beaten up their faces in rude *repoussé* work. They have nails in their boots, but new hats on their heads ; he who paints them aright should paint the old nailed boots, but also the new hats and the Waltham watches. Why do they not read ? All have been taught, and curious as the inconsistency may seem, they all value the privilege

of being *able* to read and write, and yet they do not
exercise it, except in a casual, random way.   I for one,
when the public schools began all through the rural districts, thought that at last the printing-press was going to
reach the country people.   In a measure it has done so,
but in a flickering, uncertain manner ; they read odd
bits which come drifting to their homes in irregular ways,
just as people on the coast light their fires with fragments
of wreck, chance-thrown by the stormy spring-tides on
the beach. So the fire of the mind in country places is fed
with chips and splinters, and shapeless pieces that do not
fit together, and no one sits down to read.   I think I see
two reasons why country people do not read, the first of
which, thanks be to Allah, will endure for ever ; the
second may perhaps disappear in time, when those who
make books come to see what is wanted.

First, nature has given them so much to read out of
doors, such a vast and ever-changing picture-book, that
white paper stained with black type indoors seems dry
and without meaning.   A barnyard chanticleer and his
family afford more matter than the best book ever
written.   His coral red comb, his silvery scaled legs, his
reddened feathers, and his fiery attitudes, his jolly crow,
and all his ways—there's an illustrated pamphlet, there's
a picture-block book for you in one creature only !
Reckon his family, the tender little chicks, the enamelled
eggs, the feeding every day, the roosting, the ever-present
terror of the red wood-dog (as the gipsies call the fox)—
here's a Chronicon Nurembergense with a thousand wood-
cuts ; a whole history.   This seems a very simple matter,
and yet it is true that people become intensely absorbed
in watching and living with such things.   Add to these
the veined elms, whose innumerable branches divide like
the veins or the nerves of a physiological diagram, or like

sprays of delicate seaweed slow turning from their winter outline to the soft green shading of summer ; add to these the upspringing of the wheat and its slow coming to that maturity of gold which marks the fulness of the year ; consider, then, the incomparable beauty of the mowing grass. Now remember that they live among these things, and by daily iteration the dullest mind becomes wrapped up in and welded to them. Black type on white paper is but a flat surface after these. Secondly, the books and papers themselves, made and printed in such enormous quantities, do not touch a country mind. They have such a cityfied air. Very correct, very scientific, and extremely well edited, but thin in the matter. Something so stagey —you may see it, for instance, in the books for children introducing fairies, which fairies have short skirts, and caper about exactly like a pantomime among stage frogs and stage mushrooms, and it is quite clear that the artist who drew them, and the author who wrote of them, actually drew their inspiration from the boards of a theatre. They have never dreamed among the cowslips of the real fields, they have never watched the ways of the birds from under an oak. Children instinctively see that these toy-books are not natural, and do not care for them ; they may be illustrated in gold and colours, sumptuously got up, and yet they are failures. Children do not take these to bed with them. I have seen this myself ; I bought so many books to please children, but could never do it till by chance some one sent a little American toy-book, 'The History of the Owl and his Little One, and the Manœuvres of the Fox.' This had a little of the spirit of the woods in it, and was read and re-read for a year. Only the other day a lady was telling me much the same thing, how she had bought book after book but could never hit on anything to please her little boy, till at last she found an American publication, roughly illustrated, which he always had by him.   It is very strange that the art of the old-fashioned book for children has gone over to New York, which seems to us the land of newness.

For grown-up people the modern books which are sent out in such numbers, often very cheap, have likewise an artificial cityfied air so obviously got up and theatrical, such a mark of machinery on them, all stamped and chucked out by the thousand, that they have no attraction for a people who live with nature, and even in old age retain a certain childlike faith in honesty and genuine work.   The reprints of good old authors, too, which may be had for a few pennies now, are so edited away that all the golden ring of the metal is clipped out of them.   Overlaid with notes, and analyses, and critical exegesis, the original throb of the author's heart has disappeared from these polished bones.   Just to suggest the book that would please the country reader, look for a moment at those works which came into existence at the very first dawn of printing— those volumes with strongly drawn and Dürer-like illustrations, very rough, and without perspective, but whose meaning is at once understood, and which somehow convey what I may call a genuine impression.   Any countryman would tell you at once that the illustrations of half the books of the present day are mere vamped-up shallowness, drawn from a city man's mind in a city room by gaslight.   You must consider that the countryman who lives out of doors, and always with nature, is, as regards his reading, very much in the same mental position as the people who lived four hundred years ago—in the days when costly and rare manuscripts, few and far between, chained to the desk, were just being superseded by printed books at a fifth the price, which could be actually bought and carried home. Till quite lately so few books have circulated in country places that they may be said to have been like these old manuscripts. The early printed books were simply the manuscripts printed, and that is why they remain to this day the finest specimens of typography, quite incomparable and not to be approached by present-day printers. The art of the scribe, elaborated through centuries, had reached a marvellous perfection ; the first printer copied them—the magic Fust actually sold his first books as manuscripts. Since printers have only copied printers, books have steadily declined in excellence. I have been obliged to use the outside to suggest the inside—country readers want that which is genuine, honest, and, in a word, really good ; you cannot please them with vamped-up book-making. Two books occur to me at this moment which would be greatly appreciated in every country home, from that of the peasant who has just begun to read to the houses of well-educated and well-to-do people, if they only knew of their existence and their contents—of course provided they were cheap enough, for country people have to be careful of their money nowadays. I allude to Darwin's 'Climbing Plants' and to his 'Earthworms ; ' these are astonishing works of singular patience and careful observation. The first gives most fascinating facts about such a common plant, for example, as the hedge bryony and the circular motion of its tendrils. Any farmer, for instance, will tell you that the hop-bine will insist upon going round the pole in one direction, and you cannot persuade it to go the other. These circular movements seem almost to resemble those of the planets about their centre, all things down to the ether seem to have a rotatory motion ; and some foreign plants which he grew send their far-extended tendrils round and round with so patent a movement that you can see it hour by hour like the hand of a clock. Perhaps the little book on earthworms is a yet more wonderful achievement of this great genius, who had not only untiring patience to observe and verify, but also possessed imagination, and could thereby see the motive idea at work behind the facts. At first it has a repellent sound, but we quickly learn how clumsy and prejudiced have been our views of the despised worm thrown up by every ploughshare.

I have spoken of the veined elms and their thousand thousand branches that divide like the nerves ; from each of these nerves of living wood there has fallen its breathing lungs of leaf. Where are these million leaves? By night the worm has drawn them into his gallery beneath the surface, and they have formed his food to again become the richest guano, to help the succulent growth of green grass and corn. Merely for profit alone, the profit of this digested food for plants, the agriculturist should preserve some trees that their leaves may thus be applied. The despised worm, the lowly worm, is actually so exquisitely organised that the whole of its body is sensitive to light, and is as conscious of the ray as the pupil of your own eye. Here is great and good work like that of those classics, the manuscripts of which were the first to be copied by the early printers, and books like this would be well thumbed of the country reader.

In a degree the interior of the country bears a certain resemblance to the state of Spain. Of that sunny land, travellers tell us the strangest inconsistencies of the people and natural products. It is an arid land, without verdure, nothing but prickly aloes and scattered orange groves, mere dots in a sunburnt expanse. Silver and gold abound, and every other metal, yet none of the mines pay except the quicksilver. A rich soil is uncultivated, and every natural advantage thrown away. There are railways, and engines, and telegraphs, and books, but the populace are still Spaniards, conservative in traditions, and wedded to old customs; often nominally Republican, but in fact of the ancient creeds and ways. Like this in lesser degree, everything among our green leaves and golden wheat is in a confused mixture, at once backwards and forwards, progressive and retrograde Here is some of the best soil in the world, numerous natural advantages, close proximity to immense markets, such as London. There seem mines of gold and silver in every acre, yet there is a crushing poverty among the farmers, and exacting poverty among their dependants the labourers. Every farm may be said to be within reach of railway communication, yet the producers know nothing of their customers. The country wishes new land laws to abolish the last vestiges of feudalism, and is beginning to unite against tithes, and in the same breath votes Conservative and places a Conservative Government in office. It would break down the monopoly of the railways, and at the same time would like a monopoly of protection for itself. It has learned to read and does not buy books. Science has been shouted over the length and breadth of the land, and chemistry, and I know not what, called to the assistance of the farmer, and every day we are drifting more and more backwards into the rule-of-thumb methods of our forefathers. No anarchy, happily— omitting that there is a strong resemblance to Spain. For an instance, in the daily papers it has become as common as possible to see an advertisement of farm-house apartments to let. Numbers of farm people look forward to their letting season in the same way as at the sea-side and in London. This is an immense breach in the ancient isolated manners of country life. The old farmers, and only a very little time ago, would as soon have thought of flying as of opening their doors to strangers, and indeed their rooms were scarcely furnished in a way to receive them. On the other hand, many farmhouses are empty altogether, and the land is un-tilled, because it cannot be let at any price, and lapsing backwards into barbarism. Everything used to be so fixed : there was a sort of caste of farmers. A man born in a farmhouse never thought of anything else but farming, and waited and waited, perhaps till he was grey, to get a farm ; now there are few who have such fixed ideas, they are ready to take a chance at home or abroad. Yet it is the same old country, and with the new ways and science, and learning, and civilisation, it is as with the machinery, they are all sunk and lost in the firm old lines. It is all changed and just the same. What a clamour there used to be about the damage done by the hares and rabbits to the crops ! By-and-by Parliament said, 'Shoot the hares and rabbits.' To work they went and demolished them, and now, lo! there is a feeling getting about that we don't want to be rid of all the hares and rabbits. Hares are almost formed on purpose to be good sport, and make a jolly good dish, a pleasant addition to the ceaseless round of mutton and beef to which the dead level of civilisation reduces us. Coursing is capital, the harriers first-rate. Now every man who walks about the fields is more or less at heart a sportsman, and the farmer having got the right of the gun he is not unlikely to become to some extent a game preserver. When they could not get it they wanted to destroy it, now they have got it

they want to keep it. The old feeling coming up again
—the land reasserting itself, Spain you see—down with
feudalism, but let us have the game. Look down the
long list of hounds kept in England, not one of which
could get a run were it not for the good-will of the
farmers, and indeed of the labourers. Hunting is a
mimicry of the mediæval chase, and this is the nineteenth century of the socialist, yet every man of the
fields loves to hear the horn and the burst of the hounds.
Never was shooting, for instance, carried to such perfection, perfect guns made with scientific accuracy, plans
of campaign among the pheasants set out with diagrams
as if there was going to be a battle of Blenheim in the
woods. To be a successful sportsman nowadays you
must be a well-drilled veteran, never losing presence of
mind, keeping your nerve under fire—flashes to the left
of you, reports to the right of you, shot whistling from
the second line—a hero amid the ceaseless rattle of
musketry and the 'dun hot breath of war.' Of old time
the knight had to go through a long course of instruc-
tions. He had to acquire the *manège* of his steed, the
use of the lance and sword, how to command a troop,
and how to besiege a castle. Till perfect in the arts of
war and complete in the minutiæ of falconry and all the
terms of the chase, he could not take his place in the
ranks of men. The English country gentleman who
now holds something the same position socially as the
knight, is not a sportsman till he can use the breechloader with terrible effect at the pheasant-shoot, till he
can wield the salmon-rod, or ride better than any
Persian. Never were people—people in the widest
sense—fonder of horses and dogs, and every kind of
animal, than at the present day. The town has gone out
into the country, but the country has also penetrated

the mind of the town. No sooner has a man made a little money in the city, than away he rushes to the fields and rivers, and nothing would so deeply hurt the pride of the *nouveaux riches* as to insinuate that he was not quite fully imbued with the spirit and the knowledge of the country. If you told him he was ignorant of books he might take that as a compliment; if you suggested in a sidelong way that he did not understand horses he would never more be friends with you again.

Nothing has died out, but everything has grown stronger that appertains to the land. Heraldry, for instance, and genealogy, county history—people don't want to be sheriffs now, but they would very much like to be able to say one of their ancestors was sheriff so many centuries ago. The old crests, the old coats of arms, are more thought of than ever; every fragment of antiquity valued. Almost everything old is of the country, either of the mansion or of the cottage; old silver plate, and old china, and works of the old masters in the one, old books, old furniture, old clocks in the other.

The sweet violets bloom afresh every spring on the mounds, the cowslips come, and the happy note of the cuckoo, the wild rose of midsummer, and the golden wheat of August. It is the same beautiful old country always new. Neither the iron engine nor the wooden plough alter it one iota, and the love of it rises as constantly in our hearts as the coming of the leaves. The wheat as it is moved from field to field, like a quarto folded four times, gives us in the mere rotation of crops a fresh garden every year. You have scented the bean-field and seen the slender heads of barley droop. The useful products of the field are themselves beautiful; the sainfoin, the blue lucerne, the blood-red trifolium, the clear yellow of the mustard, give more definite colours, and all these are the merely useful, and, in that sense, the plainest of growths. There are, then, the poppies, whose wild brilliance in July days is not surpassed by any hue of Spain. Wild charlock—a clear yellow—pink pimpernels, pink-streaked convolvulus, great white convolvulus, double-yellow toadflax, blue borage, broad rays of blue chicory, tall corn-cockles, azure corn-flowers, the great mallow, almost a bush, purple knapweed—I will make no further catalogue, but there are pages more of flowers, great and small, that grow at the edge of the plough, from the coltsfoot that starts out of the clumsy clod in spring to the white clematis. Of the broad surface of the golden wheat and its glory I have already spoken, yet these flower-encircled acres, these beautiful fields of peaceful wheat, are the battle-fields of life. For these fertile acres the Romans built their cities and those villas whose mosaics and hypocausts are exposed by the plough, and formed straight roads like the radii of a wheel or the threads of a geometrical spider's web. Thus like the spider the legions from their centre marched direct and quickly conquered. Next the Saxons, next the monk-slaying Danes, next the Normans in chain-mail—one, two, three heavy blows—came to grasp these golden acres. Dearly the Normans loved them; they gripped them firmly and registered them in 'Domesday Book.' They let not a hide escape them; they gripped also the mills that ground the corn. Do you think such blood would have been shed for barren wastes? No, it was to possess these harvest-laden fields. The wheat-fields are the battle-fields of the world. If not so openly invaded as of old time, the struggle between nations is still one for the ownership or for the control of corn. When Italy became a vineyard and could no more feed the armies, slowly power slipped away and the great empire of Rome split into many pieces. It has long been foreseen that if ever England is occupied with a great war the question of our corn supply, so largely derived from abroad, will become a weighty matter. Happy for us that we have wheat-growing colonies! As persons, each of us, in our voluntary or involuntary struggle for money, is really striving for those little grains of wheat that lie so lightly in the palm of the hand. Corn is coin and coin is corn, and whether it be a labourer in the field, who no sooner receives his weekly wage than he exchanges it for bread, or whether it be the financier in Lombard Street who loans millions, the object is really the same—wheat. All ends in the same: iron mines, coal mines, factories, furnaces, the counter, the desk—no one can live on iron, or coal, or cotton—the object is really sacks of wheat. Therefore to the eye of the mind they are not sacks of wheat, but filled to the brim, like those in the magic caves of the 'Arabian Nights,' with gold.

JUST BEFORE WINTER.

A RICH tint of russet deepened on the forest top, and
seemed to sink day by day deeper into the foliage like
a stain; riper and riper it grew, as an apple colours.
Broad acres these of the last crop, the crop of leaves; a
thousand thousand quarters, the broad earth will be
their barn. A warm red lies on the hill-side above the
woods, as if the red dawn stayed there through the day;
it is the heath and heather seeds; and higher still, a
pale yellow fills the larches. The whole of the great hill
glows with colour under the short hours of the October
sun; and overhead, where the pine-cones hang, the sky
is of the deepest azure. The conflagration of the woods
burning luminously crowds into those short hours a
brilliance the slow summer does not know.

The frosts and mists and battering rains that follow
in quick succession after the equinox, the chill winds
that creep about the fields, have ceased a little while,
and there is a pleasant sound in the fir trees. Everything is not gone yet. In the lanes that lead down to
the 'shaws' in the dells, the 'gills,' as these wooded
depths are called, buckler ferns, green, fresh, and elegantly
fashioned, remain under the shelter of the hazel-lined
banks. From the tops of the ash wands, where the
linnets so lately sang, coming up from the stubble, the

darkened leaves have been blown, and their much-divided branches stand bare like outstretched fingers. Black-spotted sycamore leaves are down, but the moss grows thick and deeply green ; and the trumpets of the lichen seem to be larger, now they are moist, than when they were dry under the summer heat. Here is herb Robert in flower—its leaves are scarlet ; a leaf of St. John's-wort, too, has become scarlet ; the bramble leaves are many shades of crimson ; one plant of tormentil has turned yellow. Furze bushes, grown taller since the spring, bear a second bloom, but not perhaps so golden as the first. It is the true furze, and not the lesser gorse ; it is covered with half-opened buds ; and it is clear, if the short hours of sun would but lengthen, the whole gorse hedge would become aglow again. Our trees, too, that roll up their buds so tightly, like a dragoon's cloak, would open them again at Christmas ; and the sticky horse-chestnut would send forth its long ears of leaves for New Year's Day. They would all come out in leaf again if we had but a little more sun ; *they* are quite ready for a second summer.

Brown lie the acorns, yellow where they were fixed in their cups ; two of these cups seem almost as large as the great acorns from abroad. A red dead-nettle, a mauve thistle, white and pink bramble flowers, a white strawberry, a little yellow tormentil, a broad yellow dandelion, narrow hawkweeds, and blue scabious, are all in flower in the lane. Others are scattered on the mounds and in the meads adjoining, where may be collected some heath still in bloom, prunella, hypericum, white yarrow, some heads of red clover, some beautiful buttercups, three bits of blue veronica, wild chamomile, tall yellowweed, pink centaury, succory, dock cress, daisies, fleabane, knapweed, and delicate blue harebells.

Two York roses flower on the hedge : altogether, twenty-six flowers, a large bouquet for October 19, gathered, too, in a hilly country.

Besides these, note the broad hedge-parsley leaves, tunnelled by leaf-miners ; bright masses of haws gleaming in the sun ; scarlet hips ; great brown cones fallen from the spruce firs ; black heart-shaped bindweed leaves here, and buff bryony leaves yonder ; green and scarlet berries of white bryony hanging thickly on bines from which the leaves have withered ; and bunches of grass, half yellow and half green, along the mound. Now that the leaves have been brushed from the beech saplings you may see how the leading stem rises in a curious wavy line ; some of the leaves lie at the foot, washed in white dew, that stays in the shade all day ; the wetness of the dew makes the brownish red of the leaf show clear and bright. One leaf falls in the stillness of the air slowly, as if let down by a cord of gossamer gently, and not as a stone falls—fate delayed to the last. A moth adheres to a bough, his wings half open, like a short brown cloak flung over his shoulders. Pointed leaves, some drooping, some horizontal, some fluttering slightly, still stay on the tall willow wands, like bannerets on the knights' lances, much torn in the late battle of the winds. There is a shower from a clear sky under the trees in the forest ; brown acorns rattling as they fall, and rich coloured Spanish chestnuts thumping the sward, and sometimes striking you as you pass under ; they lie on the ground in pocketfuls. Specks of brilliant scarlet dot the grass like some bright berries blown from the bushes ; but on stooping to pick them, they are found to be the heads of a fungus. Near by lies a black magpie's feather, spotted with round dots of white.

At the edge of the trees stands an old timbered farmstead, whose gables and dark lines of wood have not been painted in the memory of man, dull and weather-beaten, but very homely ; and by it rises the delicate cone of a new oast-house, the tiles on which are of the brightest red. Lines of bluish smoke ascend from among the bracken of the wild open ground, where a tribe of gipsies have pitched their camp. Three of the vans are time-stained and travel-worn, with dull red roofs ; the fourth is brightly picked out with fresh yellow paint, and stands a marked object at the side. Orange-red beeches rise beyond them on the slope ; two hoop-tents, or kibitkas, just large enough to creep into, are near the fires, where the women are cooking the gipsy's *bouillon*, that savoury stew of all things good : vegetables, meat, and scraps, and savouries, collected as it were in the stock-pot from twenty miles round. Hodge, the stay-at-home, sturdy carter, eats bread and cheese and poor bacon sometimes ; he looks with true British scorn on all scraps and soups, and stock-pots and *bouillons*—not for him, not he ; he would rather munch dry bread and cheese for every meal all the year round, though he could get bits as easy as the other and without begging. The gipsy is a cook. The man with a gold ring in his ear ; the woman with a silver ring on her finger, coarse black snaky hair like a horse's mane ; the boy with naked olive feet ; dark eyes all of them, and an Oriental, sidelong look, and a strange inflection of tone that turns our common English words into a foreign language—there they camp in the fern, in the sun, their Eastern donkeys of Syria scattered round them, their children rolling about like foals in the grass, a bit out of the distant Orient under our Western oaks.

It is the nature of the oak to be still, it is the nature

of the hawk to roam with the wind. The Anglo-Saxon labourer remains in his cottage generation after generation, ploughing the same fields; the express train may rush by, but he feels no wish to rush with it; he scarcely turns to look at it; all the note he takes is that it marks the time to 'knock off' and ride the horses home. And if hard want at last forces him away, and he emigrates, he would as soon jog to the port in a waggon, a week on the road, as go by steam; as soon voyage in a sailing ship as by the swift Cunarder. The swart gipsy, like the hawk, for ever travels on, but, like the hawk, that seems to have no road, and yet returns to the same trees, so he, winding in circles of which we civilised people do not understand the map, comes, in his own times and seasons, home to the same waste spot, and cooks his savoury *bouillon* by the same beech. They have camped here for so many years that it is impossible to trace when they did not; it is wild still, like themselves. Nor has their nature changed any more than the nature of the trees.

The gipsy loves the crescent moon, the evening star, the clatter of the fern-owl, the beetle's hum. He was born on the earth in the tent, and he has lived like a species of human wild animal ever since. Of his own free will he will have nothing to do with rites or litanies: he may perhaps be married in a place of worship—to make it legal, that is all. At the end, were it not for the law, he would for choice be buried beneath the 'fireplace' of their children's children. He will not dance to the pipe ecclesiastic, sound it who may—Churchman, Dissenter, priest, or laic. Like the trees, he is simply indifferent. All the great wave of teaching and text and tracts and missions and the produce of the printing-press has made no impression upon his race any more than upon the red deer that roam in the forest behind his camp. The negroes have their fetich, every nation its idols ; the gipsy alone has none—not even a superstitious observance ; they have no idolatry of the Past, neither have they the exalted thought of the Present. It is very strange that it should be so at this the height of our civilisation, and you might go many thousand miles and search from Africa to Australia before you would find another people without a Deity. That can only be seen under an English sky, under English oaks and beeches.

Are they the oldest race on earth? and have they worn out all the gods? Have they worn out all the hopes and fears of the human heart in tens of thousands of years, and do they merely live, acquiescent to fate? For some have thought to trace in the older races an apathy as with the Chinese, a religion of moral maxims and some few joss-house superstitions, which they themselves full well know to be nought, worshipping their ancestors, but with no vital living force, like that which drove Mohammed's bands to zealous fury, like that which sent our own Puritans over the sea in the *Mayflower.* No living faith. So old, so very, very old, older than the Chinese, older than the Copts of Egypt, older than the Aztecs ; back to those dim Sanskrit times that seem like the clouds on the far horizon of human experience, where space and chaos begin to take shape, though but of vapour. So old, they went through civilisation ten thousand years since ; they have worn it all out, even hope in the future ; they merely live acquiescent to fate, like the red deer. The crescent moon, the evening star, the clatter of the fern-owl, the red embers of the wood fire, the pungent smoke blown round about by the occasional puffs of wind, the shadowy trees, the sound of the horses cropping the grass, the night that steals on till the stubbles alone are light among the fields—the gipsy sleeps in his tent on mother earth ; it is, you see, primeval man with primeval nature. One thing he gains at least—an iron health, an untiring foot, women whose haunches bear any burden, children whose naked feet are not afraid of the dew.

By sharp contrast, the Anglo-Saxon labourer who lives in the cottage close by and works at the old timbered farmstead is profoundly religious.

The gipsies return from their rambling soon after the end of hop-picking, and hold a kind of informal fair on the village green with cockshies, swings, and all the clumsy games that extract money from clumsy hands. It is almost the only time of the year when the labouring people have any cash ; their weekly wages are mortgaged beforehand ; the hop-picking money comes in a lump, and they have something to spend. Hundreds of pounds are paid to meet the tally or account kept by the pickers, the old word tally still surviving, and this has to be charmed out of their pockets. Besides the gipsies' fair, the little shopkeepers in the villages send out circulars to the most outlying cottage announcing the annual sale at an immense sacrifice ; anything to get the hop-pickers' cash ; and the packmen come round, too, with jewelry and lace and finery. The village by the forest has been haunted by the gipsies for a century ; its population in the last thirty years has much increased, and it is very curious to observe how the gipsy element has impregnated the place. Not only are the names gipsy, the faces are gipsy ; the black coarse hair, high cheek-bones, and peculiar forehead linger ; even many of the shopkeepers have a distinct trace, and others that do not show it so much are known to be nevertheless related.

Until land became so valuable—it is now again

declining—these forest grounds of heath and bracken were free to all comers, and great numbers of squatters built huts and inclosed pieces of land. They cleared away the gorse and heath and grubbed the fir-tree stumps, and found, after a while, that the apparently barren sand could grow a good sward. No one would think anything could flourish on such an arid sand, exposed at a great height on the open hill to the cutting winds. Contrary, however, to appearances, fair crops, and sometimes two crops of hay are yielded, and there is always a good bite for cattle. These squatters consequently came to keep cows, sometimes one and sometimes two—anticipating the three acres and a cow; and it is very odd to hear the women at the hop-picking telling each other they are going to churn to-night. They have, in fact, little dairies. Such are the better class of squatters. But others there are who have shown no industry, half-gipsies, who do anything but work—tramp, beg, or poach; sturdy fellows, stalking round with toy-brooms for sale, with all the blackguardism of both races. They keep just within the law; they do not steal or commit burglary; but decency, order, and society they set utterly at defiance. For instance, a gentleman pleased with the splendid view built a large mansion in one spot, never noticing that the entrance was opposite a row of cottages, or rather thinking no evil of it. The result was that neither his wife nor visitors could go in or out without being grossly insulted, without rhyme or reason, merely for the sake of blackguardism. Now, the pure gipsy in his tent or the Anglo-Saxon labourer would not do this; it was the half-breed. The original owner was driven from his premises; and they are said to have changed hands several times since from the same cause. All over the parish this half-breed element shows its presence by the extraordinary and unusual coarseness of manner. The true English rustic is always civil, however rough, and will not offend you with anything unspeakable, so that at first it is quite bewildering to meet with such behaviour in the midst of green lanes. This is the explanation—the gipsy taint. Instead of the growing population obliterating the gipsy, the gipsy has saturated the English folk.

When people saw the red man driven from the prairies and backwoods of America, and whole states as large as Germany without a single Indian left, much was written on the extermination of the aborigines by the stronger Saxon. As the generations lengthen, the facts appear to wear another aspect. From the intermarriage of the lower orders with the Indian squaws the Indian blood has got into the Saxon veins, and now the cry is that the red man is exterminating the Saxon, so greatly has he leavened the population. The typical Yankee face, as drawn in *Punch*, is indeed the red Indian profile with a white skin and a chimney-pot hat. Upon a small scale the same thing has happened in this village by the forest; the gipsy half-breed has stained the native blood. Perhaps races like the Jew and gipsy, so often quoted as instances of the permanency of type, really owe that apparent fixity to their power of mingling with other nations. They are kept alive as races by mixing; otherwise one of two things would happen—the Jew and the gipsy must have died out, or else have supplanted all the races of the globe. Had the Jews been so fixed a type, by this time their offspring would have been more numerous than the Chinese. The reverse, however, is the case; and therefore we may suppose they must have become extinct, had it not been for fresh supplies of Saxon, Teuton,

Spanish, and Italian blood. It is, in fact, the inter-marriages that have kept the falsely so-called pure races of these human parasites alive. The mixing is continually going on. The gipsies who still stay in their tents, however, look askance upon those who desert them for the roof. Two gipsy women, thorough-bred, came into a village shop and bought a variety of groceries, ending with a pound of biscuits and a Guy Fawkes mask for a boy. They were clad in dirty jackets and hats, draggle-tails, unkempt and unwashed, with orange and red kerchiefs round their necks (the gipsy colours). Happening to look out of window, they saw a young servant girl with a perambulator on the opposite side of the 'street;' she was tidy and decently dressed, looking after her mistress's children in civilised fashion; but they recognised her as a deserter from the tribe, and blazed with contempt. ' Don't *she* look a figure !' exclaimed these dirty creatures.

The short hours shorten, and the leaf-crop is gathered to the great barn of the earth ; the oaks alone, more tenacious, retain their leaves, that have now become a colour like new leather. It is too brown for buff—it is more like fresh harness. The berries are red on the holly bushes and holly trees that grow, whole copses of them, on the forest slopes—'the Great Rough ;' the half-wild sheep have polished the stems of these holly trees till they shine, by rubbing their fleeces against them. The farmers have been drying their damp wheat in the oast-houses over charcoal fires, and wages are lowered, and men discharged. Vast loads of brambles and thorns, dead firs, useless hop-poles and hop-bines, and gorse are drawn together for the great bonfire on the green. The 5th of November bonfires are still vital institutions, and from the top of the hill you may see them burning in all directions, as if an enemy had set fire to the hamlets.

LOCALITY AND NATURE.

By the side of the rivers of Exmoor there grows a great leaf, so large it almost calls to mind those tropical leaves of which umbrellas and even tents are made. This is of a rounder shape than those of the palm, it is an elephant's ear among the foliage. The sweet river slips on with a murmuring song, for these are the rivers of the poets, and talk in verse for ever. Purple-tinted stones are strewn about the shallows flat like tiles, and out among the grass and the white orchis of the meadow. The floods carried them there and left them dry in the sun. Among these grows a thick bunch of mimulus or monkey-plant, well known in gardens, here flourishing alone beside the stream. These two plants greatly interested me : the last because it had long been a favourite in an old garden and I had not before seen it growing wild ; the other because though I knew its large leaf by repute, this was the first time I had come upon it. Now that little spot in the bend of the river by means of these two plants is firmly impressed in my memory, and is a joy to me whenever I think of it. The sunshine, the song of the water, the pleasant green grass, the white orchis, and the purplish stones were thereby rendered permanent to me. Such is the wonderful power of plants. To any one who takes a delight in wild flowers some spot or other of the earth is always becoming consecrated.

There is, however, something curious about this butterbur. It is related to the coltsfoot of the arable fields, and the coltsfoot sends up a stalk without a leaf, and flowers before any green appears. So, too, the butterbur of the river flowers before its great leaf comes. Nothing is really common either, for everything is so local that you may spend years, and in fact a lifetime, in a district and never see a flower plentiful enough in another. Just where I am staying now the pennywort grows on every wall attached to the mortar between the cobbles. In some places you may search the roads in vain for this little plant, which has this merit, that its rounded leaf presents a fresh green in February. It does not die away, it appears as green as spring, and pieces of the wall are ornamented with it as thickly as the iron-headed nails in old doors. One plant grows out of the hard stem of a hawthorn tree, as if it were a parasite like the mistletoe ; probably there is some crack which the plant itself has hidden. If every plant and every flower were found in all places the charm of locality would not exist. Everything varies, and that gives the interest. These purplish stones, where they lie in the water, seem to have a kind of growth upon them—small knobs on the surface. On examination each small roughness or knob will be found composed of a number of very minute fragments of stone. It is a sort of cell, probably built by a species of caddis. There was hardly a stone in the rivers that was not dotted with these little habitations, so that it seemed difficult to overlook them ; but upon showing one to a mighty hunter to know the local name, he declared he had never noticed it before, and added that he did not care for such little things. It is of such little things that great nature is made.

On the highest part of the Forest Ridge in Sussex, where the soil is sandy and covered with heath, fern, and fir trees, there never seemed to be any rooks. These birds, so very characteristic of the country, appeared to be almost absent over several miles. They went by sometimes, sailing down into the vale, but never stopped on the hill, not even to walk the furrows behind the plough. This would seem to indicate a remarkable absence of the food they like, for it is very rare indeed for a piece of ground to be fresh ploughed without rooks coming to it. There were rookeries beneath in the plains where the elms and beeches grew tall, but the birds never came up to forage. Crows could be found, and stopped on the hill all the year. Wood-pigeons, like the rooks, went over, but did not stay. Starlings were not at all plentiful; blackbirds and thrushes were there, but not nearly so numerous as is usually the case; fieldfares and redwings drifted by in the winter, but never stopped. Slow-worms lived in the sand under the heath, and lizards, but no snakes and only a few adders. Inquiring of an old man if there were many snakes about, he said no; the soil was too poor for them; but in some places down in the vale he had dug up a gallon of snakes' eggs in the 'maxen.' The word was noticeable as a survival of the old English 'mixen' for manure heap. Swallows, martins, and swifts abounded; and as for insects, they were countless—honey-bees, wild bees, humble-bees, varieties of wasps, butterflies—an endless list. So common a plant as the arum did not seem to exist; on the other hand, ferns literally made up the hedges, growing in such quantities as to take the place of the grasses There was, too, a great variety of moss and fungi. The soil looked black and fertile, and new-comers thought they were going to have good crops, but when these failed they found, upon examining the earth, that it was little more than black sand, and the particles of silica glittered if a handful were held in the sun. Such a sand would give the impression of dryness, instead of which it was extremely damp—damp all the year round.

For contrast, a place on the coast just opposite, as it were, and almost within view, at the same time of year seemed to have no bees. A great field of clover in flower was silent; there was no hum, nor glistening of wings. Butterflies rarely came along. Swallows were not common. In the rich loam it was curious to note mussel-shells, quite recent, in good preservation, and a geologist might wonder at the layers of them in such an earth; the farmer would smile, and say the mussels were carted there for manure. Another place, again, in the same county is full of rooks, and the arum is green on the banks. These items in a small area show how different places are, and if you move from locality to locality everything you have read about is by degrees seen in reality. In an old book, the History of North-ampton, which I chanced to look at, among other curiosities, the author a hundred years ago mentioned a substance called star shot, which appeared in the meadows overnight, and seemed to have dropped from the sky. This I had not then seen, but many years afterwards came suddenly, by a copse, on a quantity of jelly-like substance with a most unpleasant aspect, but which did not in any other way offend the senses. It had shot up in the night, and was gone next day. It is a fungus unnoticed till it suddenly swells; I suppose this was the old chronicler's star shot. Nor do I think it too small a thing that the common snail makes a straight track over everything ; if he comes to the wall of a house he goes straight up without the smallest hesitation, and explores a good height before he comes down again ; if he finds a loaf of bread in the cellar he never thinks of going round it, but travels in a Roman road up and over. So do the armies of ants in warmer climates, and this proceeding in an invariable line irrespective of obstacles seems to be peculiar to many creatures, and is the reason why such ' plagues ' were and are so dreaded. Nothing could divert the straight march of the locusts ; nothing could divert the course of the millions of butterflies that sometimes cross the Channel and arrive here from the Continent.

The tenacity of insects in anything they have once begun is shown in many ways ; you cannot drive away a fly or a gnat, and if a colony of ants take up their home in the garden they will hardly move till all are destroyed. Aristotle mentions the diseases of swine, so it will not be amiss to record that in the country swine are supposed to suffer from water-brash, and to relieve themselves by eating dry earth, for which purpose those that run loose are continually tearing up the ground. Human beings so affected show a similar tendency for dry food, as oatmeal. Sometimes the liver of calves and bullocks is small and dry, of very little use for food ; this is found to be due to the neglect of providing them with dry standing-ground when fattening. To ensure their fattening properly they should stand on dry and high ground, and they should be plentifully supplied with dry litter. This fact may be of value to some suffering person ; it points to the necessity of dry warm feet, dry subsoil, and drainage if the liver is to be in good order. Popular suspicion, if not science, attaches many other diseases besides those that actually consume that organ to the abnormal action of the liver, possibly lung disease. Such trifling circumstances are not so trifling as they appear. A case came under my notice quite recently when a person had been helpless from paralysis for several years. Chance compelled removal to another house, and very soon the paralysis began to disappear. The first house may have been damp, or there may have been some minute conditions besides. It certainly is a marked fact that in the country, at all events, one house is noted for its healthiness and another close by for its unhealthiness, and the cause is not traceable to the usual and obvious reason of drainage or water. Any one who has noticed the remarkable influence of locality in the more evident vegetation—such, for instance, as lichens—will be able to suppose the possibility of minute organisms—microbe, bacteria, whatever you like to call them—being more persistent in one spot than in another. I have often thought of the half-magical art of the Chinese, Feng-shui, by which they discover if a place be fortunate and fit for a house. It seems to suggest something of this kind, and I think there is a great deal yet to be discovered by the diligent observation of localities. The experience of the rudest country rustic is not to be despised ; an observation is an observation, whoever makes it ; there has been an air of too much science in the affected derision of our forefathers' wisdom

COUNTRY PLACES.

I.

HIGH up and facing every one who enters a village there still remains an old notice-board with the following inscription :—'All persons found wandering abroad, lying, lodging, or being in any barn, outhouse, or in the open air, and not giving a good account of themselves, will be apprehended as rogues and vagabonds, and be either publicly whipt or sent to the house of correction, and afterwards disposed of according to law, by order of the magistrates. Any person who shall apprehend any rogue or vagabond will be entitled to a reward of ten shillings.' It very often happens that we cannot see the times in which we actually live. A thing must be gone by before you can see it, just as it must be printed before it is read. This little bit of weather-stained board may serve, perhaps, to throw up the present into a picture so that it may be visible. For this inhuman law still holds good, and is not obsolete or a mere relic of barbarism. The whipping, indeed, is abrogated for very shame's sake ; so is the reward to the informer ; but the magistrate and the imprisonment and the offence remain. You must not sleep in the open, either in a barn or a cart-house or in a shed, in the country, or on a door-step in a town, or in a boat on the beach ; and if you have no coin in your pocket you are still more diabolically wicked—you are a vagrom man, and the cold cell is your proper place. This is the Jubilee year, too, of the mildest and best reign of the Christian era. Something in this weather-beaten board to be very proud of, is it not? Something human and comforting and assuring to the mind that we have made so much progress. The pagan Roman Empire reached from the wall of Severus in the north of England to Athens of the philosophers; it included our islands, France, Germany, Spain, Italy, Austria, Greece, Turkey in Europe and Asia, Egypt— the whole world of those days. No one could escape from it, because it enclosed all; you could not take refuge in Spain on account of the absence of an extradition treaty; no forger, no thief, no political offender could get out of it. A crushing power this, quite unknown in our modern world, with all our engines, steamers, and telegraphs. A man may hide himself somewhere now, but from the power of old Rome there was no running away. And all this, too, was under the thumb of one irresponsible will, in an age when human life was of no value, and there was no State institution preaching gentleness in every village. Yet even then there was no such law as this, and in this respect we are more brutal than was the case nineteen centuries ago. This weather-beaten board may also serve to remind us that in this Jubilee year the hateful workhouse still endures; that people are imprisoned for debt under the mockery of contempt of court; that a man's household goods, down to the bed on which he sleeps, and the tools warm from his hand, may be sold. In the West End of London a poor woman, an ironer, being in debt, her six children's clothes were seized. What a triumph for the Jubilee year! Instead of building a

Church House to add another thousand tons to the enormous weight of ecclesiastical bricks and mortar that cumbers the land, would it not be more human to signalise the time by the abolition of these cruel laws, and by the introduction of some system to gradually emancipate the poor from the workhouse, which is now their master?

In the gathering dusk of the afternoon I saw a mouse rush to a wall—a thick stone wall,—run up it a few inches, and disappear in a chink under some grey lichen. The poor little biter, as the gipsies call the mouse, had a stronghold wherein to shelter himself, and close by there was a corn-rick from which he drew free supplies of food. A few minutes afterwards I was interested in the movements of a pair of wrens that were playing round the great trunk of an elm, flying from one to another of the little twigs standing out from the rough bark. First one said something in wren language, and then the other answered; they were husband and wife, and after a long consultation they flew to the corn-rick and crept into a warm hole under the thatch. So both these, the least of animals and the least of birds, have a resource, and man is the only creature that punishes his fellow for daring to lie down and sleep.

Up in the plain there were some mounds, or *tumuli*, about which nothing seemed to be known, though they had evidently been cut into and explored. At last, however, a farmer—Mr. Nestor Hay, who knew everything—told me something about them. He cut them open. He had an old county history and several other volumes which had somehow accumulated in the Manor-house Farm, and, like many country people, he was extremely fond of studying the past. He fancied there might have been a battle in that locality, and hence

these mounds, but could find no reference to them anywhere, so he dug through one or two of them himself,
without success ; the soil did not seem to have ever been
disturbed, consequently they might have been natural.
'Perhaps I should have found out something though,'
he said, with a smile, 'if it had not been for that there
old dog as we used to keep in the tub at the back of the
house. Such a lot of folk used to come to our back
door all day long after victuals, some out of the village,
and some from the next parish, and some as went round
regular, and gipsy chaps, and chaps as pretended to
come from London—you never saw such a crowd,—just
because the old man and the missus was rather good to
'em. So there they was a-clacking at that door all day
long. But this 'ere dog in the tub used to sarve 'em out
sometimes if they didn't mind. (Chuckle.) She never
barked, or nothing of that sort, never let 'em know as
there was a dog there at all ; there she'd lie as quiet till
they was just gone by a little—then out she'd slip without a word behind them, and snip 'em by the leg. Lord,
how they did jump and holler ! (Chuckle.) See, they
had the pinch afore they knowed as she was there.
Lord, what a lot she did bite to be sure ! (thoughtfully) ;
I can't tell 'e how many, her did it so neat. That kept
folk away a little, else I suppose we shouldn't have had
anything to eat ourselves. None of 'em never went
wrong, you know, never went mad or anything of that
sort—never had to send nobody to Paris in them days
to be dog-vaccinated. Curious, wasn't it? Must have
been something different about folk then. However,
this here dog was desperate clever at it. As I was
telling you, I dug through them mounds ; couldn't find
no coins or anything ; so I heard of a big archæologist
chap that was writing a new book about the antiquities

of the country, and I wrote to him about it, and he said he would come and see them. The day he come was rather roughish and cold : he seemed sort of bad when he come into the house, and had to have some brandy. By-and-by he got better, and out we started ; but just as we was going through the yard this old dog nips him by the hand—took him right through his hand—made him look main straight. However, washed his hand and bound it up, and started out again. (Chuckle.) Hadn't gone very far, and was getting through a hedge, and dalled if he didn't fall into the pond, flop ! (Chuckle.) I suppose he didn't like it, for he never said nothing about the mounds in his book when it come out—left 'em out altogether.'

This pond still exists, and Mr. Nestor Hay had noted a curious thing about it. Across the middle of the pond a tree had fallen ; it was just on a level with the surface of the water. A pair of water-rats always ate their food on this tree. They would go out into the grass of the meadow, bite off the vegetation that suited their taste, and carry it back in their mouths to the tree, and there eat it in safety, with water, as it were, all round them like a moat. This they did a hundred times—in fact, every day. 'But,' said Mr. Hay, 'you can't watch nothing now a minute without some great lout coming along with a stale baccy pipe in his mouth, making the air stink ; they spoils everything, these here half-towny fellows ; everybody got a neasty stale pipe in their mouths, and they gets over the hedges anywhere, and disturbs everything.' It is common on the banks of a stream or a pond to see half a dozen of these little beaver-like water-voles out feeding in the grass, and they eat it where they find it. At this particular pond the two rats diverged from the custom of their race, and always took their food to a place of safety first. If he is alarmed the water-rat instantly dives, and his idea of security is a spot where he can drop like a stone under the surface without a moment's reflection. Mr. Hay could not understand why the water-rats were so timid at this pond till he recollected that the preceding summer two schoolboys used to get up in an oak that overhung the water, each with a catapult, and, firing bullets from these india-rubber weapons on the water-rats underneath, slew nearly every one of them. The few left had evidently learnt extreme caution from the misfortune of their friends, and no longer trusted themselves away from the water, into which they could slip at the movement of a shadow.

Mr. Hay disliked to see the slouching fellows making tracks across his fields, every one of which he looked on with as much jealousy as if it had been a garden—a wild garden they were too, strewn sometimes with the white cotton of the plane tree, hung about with roses and sweet with mowing grass. Those who love fields and every briar in the hedge dislike to see them entered irreverently. I have just the same feeling myself even of fields and woods in which I have no personal interest ; it jars upon me to see nature profaned. These fellows were a ' Black George ' lot, in hamlet language. Nestor Hay knew everybody in the village round about, their fathers and grandfathers, their politics and religious opinions, and whether they were new folk or ancient inhabitants—an encyclopædic knowledge not written, an Homeric memory. For I imagine in ancient days when books were scarce that was how men handed down the history of the chiefs of Troy. An Homeric memory for everything—superstitions, traditions, anecdotes ; the only difficulty was that you could not command it. You could not turn to letter A or B and demand information direct about this or that; you must wait till it came up incidentally in conversation. In one of the villages there was a young men's club, and, among other advantages, when they were married they could have a cradle for nothing. A cottager had a child troubled with a slight infirmity; the doctor ordered the mother to prepare a stew of mice and give him the gravy. There happened to be some threshing going on, and one of the men caught her nine mice, which she skinned and cooked. She did not much like the task, but she did it, and the child never knew but that it was beef gravy. It cured him completely. This is the second time I have come across this curious use of mice. I had heard of it as a traditional resource among the country people, but in this case it seemed to have been ordered by a medical practitioner. Perhaps, after all, there may be something in the strange remedies and strange mixtures of remedies so often described in old books, and what we now deride may not have been without its value. If an empirical remedy will cure you, it is of more use than a scientific composition which ought to cure you but does not. How much depends on custom! The woman felt a repugnance to skinning the mice, yet they are the cleanest creatures, living on grain; she would have skinned a hare or rabbit without hesitation, and have cooked and eaten bacon, though the pig is not a cleanly feeder. It is a country remark that the pig's foot—often seen on the table—has as many bones as there are letters of the alphabet. The grapnel kept at every village draw-well is called the grabhook; the plant called honesty (because both sides of the flower are alike) is old woman's penny. If you lived in the country you might be alarmed late in the evening by hearing the tramp of feet round your house. But it is not burglars; it is young fellows with a large net and a lantern after the sparrows in the ivy. They have a prescriptive right to enter every garden in the village. They cry 'sparrow catchers' at the gate, and people sit still, knowing it is all right. In the jealous suburb of a city the dwellers in the villas would shrink from this winter custom, the constable would soon have orders to stop it; in the country people are not so rigidly exclusive. Now it is curious that the sparrows and blackbirds, yellowhammers and greenfinches, that roost in the bushes, fly into the net and are easily captured, but the starlings—thanks to their different ways in daylight—always fly out at the top of the bush, and so escape.

II.

A BLACK cannon ball lies in a garden, an ornament like a shell or a fossil, among blue lobelia and green ferns. It is about as big as a cricket ball—a mere trifle to look at. What a contrast with the immense projectiles thrown by modern guns! Yet it is very heavy—quite out of proportion to its size. Imagine iron cricket balls bounding along the grass and glancing at unexpected angles, smashing human beings instead of wickets. This cannon ball is not a memorial of the Civil War. It was shot at a carter with his waggon. Our grandfathers had no idea of taking care of other people's lives. Every man had to look out for himself; if you got in the way, that was your fault. A battery was practising, and they did not trouble themselves about the highway road which skirted the range; and as the carter was coming home with his waggon one of the balls ricocheted and rolled along in front of

his horses.   He picked it up and brought it home, and
there it has lain many a long year, a silent witness, like
the bricks Jack Cade put in the chimney, to the extraordinary change of ideas which has taken place.   We
are all expected nowadays to think not only of ourselves
but of others, and if a man fires a gun without due pre-
cautions, and injures or even might have injured another,
he is liable.   All our legislation and all the drift of public
opinion goes in this direction.   Men were the same then
as now ; the change in this respect shows the immense
value of ideas.   They were then quite strangers to the
very idea of taking any thought for those who might
chance to be in the way.   That has been inculcated of
recent years.   Those were the days when there was an
irresponsible tyrant in every village, who could not
indeed hang men at his castle gate by feudal right of
gallows, but who could as effectually silence them by
setting in motion laws made by the rich for the rich.   It
is on record how a poor carrier, whose only fortune was
a decrepit horse, dared presumptuously, against the will
of the lord of the manor, to water his horse at a roadside
pond.   For this offence he was taken before the justices
and fined, his goods seized,—

> And the knackers had his silly old horse,
> And so John Harris was bowled out !

Then there was a still more terrible offence—a hungry
man picked up a rabbit.   ' How dared John Bartlett for
to venture for to go for to grab it ? '   But they put him
in gaol and cured him of ' that there villanous habit,'
which rhymes, and the tale thereof may be found by the
student of old times in the 'Punch' of the day—a good true
honest manly Punch, who brought his staff down heavily
on the head of abuses and injustice.   We do things every

day in the present age equally unjust and cruel, only we cannot see them ; as some one observed, one cannot see the eye because it is so close to the sight. In the almost sacred name of education tyrannies are being enacted surpassing anything recorded in the most outlying village in the most outlying time. One constantly sees cases of poor people sent to prison because they happen to have children. No other reason can be detected.

Our great-grandfathers' doctors never used to trouble themselves to write prescriptions for their poorer patients ; they used to keep two or three mixtures always made up ready in great jars, and ladle them out. There was the bread and cheese mixture, very often called for, as the ailments of the labourers are commonly traceable to a heavy diet of cheese. As an old doctor used to say when he was called to a cottage, ' Hum ; s'pose you've been eating too much fat bacon and cabbage ! ' Another was the club mixture, called for about May, when the village clubs are held and extra beer disturbs the economy. In factory towns, where the mechanics have dispensaries and employ doctors, something of the same sort of story has got about at the present day. The women are constantly coming for physic, and the 'assistants are stated to gravely measure a little peppermint and colour it pink or yellow, which does as well. Great invalids with long pockets, who have paid their scores of guineas and gone the round of fashionable physicians, do not seem to have received much more benefit than if they had themselves chosen the yellow or pink hue of their tinted water. It is wonderful what value the country poor set on a bottle of physic ; they are twice as grateful for it as for a good dinner. Some of the doctors of old are said to have had an eye for an old book, or an old clock, or an old bit of furniture or china in the cottage, and when the patient was recovering they would take a fancy to it and buy it at their own valuation, for of course the humble labourer was obliged to regard such a wish as a command. The workhouse system puts the labourer completely under the thumb of the clergyman and the doctor. It was in this way that many good old pieces of work gradually found their destination in great London collections. Once now and then, however, the eager collector would come across some one independent, and meet with a sharp refusal to part with the old china bowl. The wife of a small farmer naïvely remarked about the tithes, ' You know it is such a lot to pay, and we never go there to church ; you know it is too far to walk.' It was not the doctrine to which she objected—it was the paying for nothing ; paying and never having anything. The farmers, staunch upholders of Church and State, are always grumbling because the clergy are constantly begging. One man took a deep oath that if the clergyman ever came to his house without asking for money he would cut a deep notch with his knife in the oaken doorpost. Ten years went by, still more years, and still no notch was cut. Odd things happen in odd places. There is a story of an old mansion where a powerful modern stove was put in an ancient hearth under a mantelpiece supported by carved oak figures of knights. The unwonted heat roasted the toes of these martyrs till their feet fell off. Another story relates how in our grandfathers' days a great man invited his friends to dinner, promising them a new dish that had never before been set upon the table. The fillet came in on the shoulders of several men, and when the cover was removed, lo an actress in a state of nature ! One farmer lent his friend his dogcart. Time went on, and the dog-cart was not returned ; a year went by, still no cart.

Country people are very peculiar in this respect, and do not like to remind their friends of obligations. Two years went by, and still no return, though the parties were in constant intercourse. I have known people borrow a hundred pounds in the country, and debtor and creditor meet several times a week for years, and nothing said about it on either side. No strained relations were caused—it seemed quite forgotten till executors came. Three years went by, still no dogcart, though it was seen daily on the roads in use. I was driving with a man once when we met a woman walking, and as we passed she put up her umbrella so as not to be able to see us. 'That's So-and-so,' said he; 'they borrowed some money from me a long time ago; they have never said anything about it. Whenever she meets me she always puts up her umbrella so as not to see me.' Four years went by, and still no dogcart. By this time it was looking shabby and getting shaken by rough usage; perhaps they did not like to return it in such a condition. Five years went by, and after that they seem to have lost all count of the dogcart, which faded away like a phantom. One farmer had been telling another something which his companion seemed to consider doubtful, and disputed; however, he finished up by saying, 'That's no lie, I can assure you.' 'Well, no; but I should certainly have taken it as such.' One fellow happening by chance in the hunting-field to come across the Prince of Wales, took off his hat with *both* hands to express his deep humility. Here is a cottage nursery rhyme, genuinely silly :—

> Right round my garden
> There I found a farden,
> Gave it to my mother
> To buy a little brother,

Brother was so cross
Sat him on a horse,
Horse was so randy
Gave him some brandy,
Brandy was so strong
Put him in the pond,
Pond was so deep
Put him in the cradle and
    rocked him off to sleep.

It is curious that there seems to be a distinct race of flat heads among the cottagers; the children look as if the front part of the head had been sat upon and compressed. Straw hats, the common sort, seem to be made to fit these shallow crowns. In some parts they cook dates; others cook oranges, making them into dumplings and also stewing them. These are favourite sweets. To go out singing from door to door at Christmas is called wassailing—a relic of the ancient time when wassail was a common word. When I was a boy, among other out-of-the-way pursuits, I took an interest in astrology. The principal work on astrology, from which all the others have been more or less derived, is Ptolemy's 'Tetrabiblos,' and there, pointing out the mysterious influence of one thing upon another, it mentions that the virtues of the magnet may be destroyed by rubbing it with garlic. This curious statement has been thrown against Ptolemy and held to invalidate his theories, because upon experiment garlic is not found to affect the magnet. Possibly, however, the plant Ptolemy meant may not have been the plant we now call garlic, for there is nothing so uncertain as the names of plants. There is a great confusion, and it is difficult to identify with certainty apparently well-known herbs with those used by the ancients. Possibly, too, the experiment was performed in a different manner. It happened one day, many years after reading this, I chanced to be talking to a village clock-maker about watches. We were discussing what a difficulty it was sometimes to get a watch to go right. I said I had heard that watches sometimes got magnetised, and went on in the most erratic manner until the magnetism was counteracted. Ah yes, he said, he recollected a case in the shop where he learnt his trade ; they had a watch brought to them which had got magnetised, and he believed the influence was at last removed by the use of onions. Instantly memory ran back to Ptolemy's garlic ; perhaps after all there was something in his statement ; at all events, it is very curious that the subject should come up again in this unexpected way, in the darkness, as it were, of a village where the very name of the great mathematician was unknown. The clockmaker fumbled with an anecdote, and tried to tell me of another sort of magnetism which had got into a watch. The watch would not keep time, nothing would make it ; till by-and-by it occurred to him to suggest to the owner to wind it up at breakfast-time instead of at night. For he fancied the owner became a little magnetised himself at night over the genial bowl, and so was irregular in winding his watch.

THE robin, 'jolly Robin!' is an unlucky bird in some places. When the horse-chestnut leaves turn scarlet the redbreast sings in a peculiarly plaintive way, as if in tone with the dropping leaves and the chill air that follows the early morning frost. You may tell how much moisture there is in the air in a given place by the colours of the autumn leaves ; the horse-chestnut, scarlet near a stream, is merely yellowish in drier soils. Cock robin sings the louder for the silence of other birds, and if he comes to the farmstead and pipes away day by day on a bare cherry tree or any bough that is near the door, after his custom, the farmer thinks it an evil omen. For a robin to sing persistently near the house winter or summer is a sign that something is about to go wrong. Yet the farmer will not shoot him. The roughest poaching fellows who would torture a dog will not kill a robin ; it is bad luck to have anything to do with it. Most people like to see fir boughs and holly brought into the house to brighten the dark days with their green, but the cottage children tell you that they must not bring a green fir branch indoors, because as it withers their parents will be taken ill and fade away. Indeed the labouring people seem in all their ways and speech to be different, survivals perhaps of a time when their words and superstitions were the ways of a ruder England. The lanes and the gateways in the fields, as they say, are 'slubby' enough in November, and those who try to go through get 'slubbed' up to their knees. This expresses a soft, plastic, and adhesive condition of the mud which comes on after it has been 'raining hop-poles' for a week. The labourer has little else to do but to chop up disused hop-poles into long fagots with a hand-bill—in other counties a bill-hook. All his class bitterly resent the lowering of wages which takes place in winter; it is a shame, they say, and they evidently think that the farmers ought to be forced to pay them more—they are starvation wages. On the other hand, the farmer, racked in every direction, and unable to sell his produce, finds the labour bill the most difficult to meet, because it comes with unfailing regularity every Saturday. A middle-aged couple of cottagers left their home, and the wife told us how they had walked and walked day after day, but the farmers said they were too poor to give them a job. So at last the man, as they went grumbling on the highway, lost his temper, and hit her a 'clod' in the head, 'and I never spoke to him for an *hour* afterwards; no, that I didn't; not for an hour.' A clod is a heavy, lumping blow. Their home was 'broad' of Hurst—that is, in the Hurst district, but at some little distance.

'There a' sets' is a constant expression for there it lies. A dish on the table, a cat on the hearth, a plough in the field, 'there a' sets,' there it is. 'No bounds' is another. It may rain all day long, 'there's no bounds;' that is, no knowing. 'I may go to fair, no bounds,' it is uncertain, I have not made up my mind. A folk so vague in their ideas are very fond of this 'no bounds;' it is like the 'Quien sabe?' of the Mexicans, who knows? and accompanies every remark. An avaricious person is very 'having;' wants to have everything. What are usually called dog-irons on the hearth are called brand-irons, having to support the brand or burning log. Where every one keeps fowls the servant girls are commonly asked if they can cram a chicken, if they understand how to fatten it by filling its crop artificially. 'Sure,' pronounced with great emphasis on the 'su,' like the 'shure' of the Irish, comes out at every sentence. 'I shan't do it all, sure;' and if any one is giving a narration, the polite listener has to throw in a deep 'sure' of assent at every pause. 'Cluttered up' means in a litter, surrounded with too many things to do at once. Of a little girl they said she was pretty, but she had 'bolted' eyes; a portrait was a good one, but 'his eyes bolt so,' meaning thereby full, staring eyes, that seem to start out of the head. A drunken man, says the poor wife, is not worth a hatful of crab apples. The boys go hoop-driving, never bowling. If in any difficulty they say, 'I hope to match it out to the end of the week,' to make the provisions last, or fit the work in. Most difficult of all to express is the way they say yes and no. It is neither yes nor no, nor yea nor nay, but a cross between it somehow. To say yes they shut their lips and then open them as if gasping for breath and emit a sort of 'yath' without the 'th,' more like 'yeah,' and better still if to get the closing of the lips you say 'em' first—'em-yeah.' The no is 'nah' with a sort of jerk on the h; 'na-h.' This yeah and nah is most irritating to fresh ears; you do not seem to know if your servant has taken any notice of what you said, or is making a mouth at you in derision.

The farmers are always complaining that the men crawl through their work and put no energy into anything, just as if they were afraid to use their hands. More particularly, if there is any little extra thing to be done, they could not possibly do it. A wheat rick was threshed one day, and when it was finished in the afternoon there were the sacks in a great heap about twenty or thirty yards from the barn. So soon as the rick was finished, the men asked for their money as usual, when the farmer said he wanted them to carry the sacks into the barn before they left. Oh no, they couldn't do that. 'Well, then,' said he, 'I can't pay you till you have done it.' No, they couldn't do it, couldn't be expected to carry sacks of wheat across the rickyard and into the barn like that, it was too much for any man to do; why couldn't he send for the cart? The farmer replied that the cart was two miles away, engaged in other labour; the night was coming on, and if it rained in the night the wheat would be damaged. No, they couldn't do it. The farmer would not pay them, and so the dispute continued for a long time. At length the farmer said, 'Well, if you won't do it, perhaps you will at least help me as far as this : will you lift up a sack and place it on another high enough for me to get it on my back, and I will myself carry them to the barn?' So small a favour they could not refuse, and having raised up a sack for him in this manner, he took it on his back and made off with it to the barn. He was anything but a strong man—far less able to carry a sack of wheat than the labourers—but determined not to be beaten. He carried one sack, then another and another, till he had got eight safely housed, when on coming back for the ninth he met a labourer with a sack on his back, shamed into giving assistance. After him a second man took a sack, and one by one they all followed, till in about half an hour all the wheat was in the barn. This is the spirit in which they work if the least little difficulty occurs, or they are asked to do anything that varies from what they did yesterday or the day before, they cannot possibly accomplish it.

Since, however, the farmers have been unable to sell their produce and winter wages have gone down, and work is scarce, the position of the labourer is a very dull one, and it is feared the present winter will be a hard time for many homes. Numbers talk of emigrating, and some have taken the first step, and will sell their furniture and leave a land where neither farmer nor labourer has any hope. One middle-aged cottage woman, married, kept harping upon the holiday they should have during the voyage to America. That seemed to her the great beauty of emigration, the great temptation. For ten days, while the voyage lasted, she would have nothing to do, but could rest! She had never had such a holiday in all her life. How hard must be the life which makes such a trifling circumstance as a week's rest appear so heavenly!

COTTAGE IDEAS.

PASSING by the kitchen door, I heard Louisa, the maid, chanting to a child on her knee:

> Feyther stole th' Paason's sheep;
> A merry Christmas we shall keep;
> We shall have both mutton and beef—
> *But we won't say nothing about it.*

To rightly understand this rhyme you must sing it with long-drawn emphasis on each word, lengthening it into at least two syllables; the first a sort of hexameter, the second a pentameter of sound:

> Fey-ther sto-ole th' Paa-son's sheep.

The last line is to come off more trippingly, like an 'aside.' This old sing-song had doubtless been handed down from the times when the labourers really did steal sheep, a crime happily extinct with cheap bread. Louisa was one of the rare old sort—hard-working, and always ready; never complaining, but satisfied with any food there chanced to be; sensible and sturdy; a woman who could be thoroughly depended on. Her boxes were full of good dresses, of a solid, unassuming kind, such as would wear well—a perfect wardrobe. Her purse was always well supplied with money; she had money saved up, and she sent money to her parents: yet her wages, until late years, had been small. In doing her duty to others she did good to herself. A duchess would have been glad to have her in her household. She had been in farmhouse service from girlhood, and had doubtless learned much from good housewives ; farmers' wives are the best of all teachers : and the girls, for their own sakes, had much better be under them than wasting so much time learning useless knowledge at compulsory schools.

> Freckles said, when he came in,
> He never would enter a tawny skin,

was another of her rhymes. Freckles come in with summer, but never appear on a dark skin, so that the freckled should rejoice in these signs of fairness.

> Your father, the elderberry,
> Was not such a gooseberry
> As to send in his bilberry
> Before it was dewberry.

Some children are liable to an unpleasant complaint at night ; for this there is a certain remedy. A mouse is baked in the oven to a 'scrump,' then pounded to powder, and this powder administered. Many ladies still have faith in this curious medicine ; it reminds one of the powdered mummy, once the great cure of human ills. Country places have not always got romantic names—Wapse's Farm, for instance, and Hog's Pudding Farm. Wapse is the provincial for wasp.

Country girls are not all so shrewd as Louisa : we heard of two—this was some time since—who, being in service in London, paid ten shillings each to Madame Rachel for a bath to be made beautiful for ever. Half a sovereign out of their few coins ! On the other hand, town servants are well dressed and have plenty of finery, but seldom have any reserve of good clothing, such as Louisa possessed. All who know the country regret the change that has been gradually coming over the

servants and the class from which they are supplied.
' Gawd help the pore missis as gets hold of *you* !' exclaimed a cottage woman to her daughter, whose goings
on had not been as they should be: ' God help the poor
mistress who has to put up with you !'   A remark that
would be most emphatically echoed by many a farmer's
wife and country resident.   ' Doan't you stop if her hol-
lers at 'ee,' said another cottage mother to her girl, just
departing for service—that is, don't stop if you don't like
it ; don't stop if your mistress finds the least fault. ' Come
along home if you don't like it.' Home to what ? In this
instance it was a most wretched hovel, literally built in
a ditch ; no convenience, no sanitation ; and the father a
drunkard, who scarcely brought enough money indoors
to supply bread.

You would imagine that a mother in such a position
would impress upon her children the necessity of endeavouring to do something.   For the sake of that spirit of
independence in which they seem to take so much pride,
one would suppose they would desire to see their children able to support themselves.   But it is just the
reverse ; the poorer folk are, the less they seem to care
to try to do something. ' You come home if you don't
like it ;' and stay about the hovel in slatternly idleness, tails bedraggled and torn, thin boots out at the toes
and down at the heels, half starved on potatoes and weak
tea—stay till you fall into disgrace, and lose the only
thing you possess in the world—your birthright, your
character.   Strange advice it was for a mother to give.

Nor is the feeling confined to the slatternly section,
but often exhibited by very respectable cottagers indeed.

' My mother never would go out to service—she
wouldn't go,' said a servant to her mistress, one day talking confidentially.

'Then what did she do?' asked the mistress, knowing they were very poor people.

'Oh, she stopped at home.'

'But how did she live?'

'Oh, her father had to keep her. If she wouldn't go out, of course he had to somehow.'

This mother would not let her daughter go to one place because there was a draw-well on the premises; and her father objected to her going to another because the way to the house lay down a long and lonely lane. The girl herself, however, had sense enough to keep in a situation; but it was distinctly against the feeling at her home; yet they were almost the poorest family in the place. They were very respectable, and thought well of in every way, belonging to the best class of cottagers.

Unprofitable sentiments! injurious sentiments— self-destroying; but I always maintain that sentiment is stronger than fact, and even than self-interest. I see clearly how foolish these feelings are, and how they operate to the disadvantage of those whom they influence. Yet I confess that were I in the same position I should be just as foolish. If I lived in a cottage of three rooms, and earned my bread by dint of arm and hand under the sun of summer and the frost of winter; if I lived on hard fare, and, most powerful of all, if I had no hope for the future, no improvement to look forward to, I should feel just the same. I would rather my children shared my crust than fed on roast beef in a stranger's hall. Perhaps the sentiment in my case might have a different origin, but in effect it would be similar. I should prefer to see my family about me— the one only pleasure I should have—the poorer and the more unhappy, the less I should care to part with them. This may be foolish, but I expect it is human nature.

English folk don't 'cotton' to their poverty at all; they don't eat humble-pie with a relish; they resent being poor and despised. Foreign folk seem to take to it quite naturally; an Englishman, somehow or other, always feels that he is wronged. He is injured; he has not got his rights. To me it seems the most curious thing possible that well-to-do people should expect the poor to be delighted with their condition. I hope they never will be; an evil day that—if it ever came—for the Anglo-Saxon race.

One girl prided herself very much upon belonging to a sort of club or insurance—if she died, her mother would receive ten pounds. Ten pounds, ten golden sovereigns was to her such a magnificent sum, that she really appeared to wish herself dead, in order that it might be received. She harped and talked and brooded on it constantly. If she caught cold it didn't matter, she would say, her mother would have ten pounds. It seemed a curious reversal of ideas, but it is a fact that poor folk in course of time come to think less of death than money. Another girl was describing to her mistress how she met the carter's ghost in the rickyard; the waggon-wheel went over him; but he continued to haunt the old scene, and they met him as commonly as the sparrows.

'Did you ever speak to him?'

'Oh no. You mustn't speak to them; if you speak to them they'll fly at you.'

In winter the men were allowed to grub up the roots of timber that had been thrown, and take the wood home for their own use; this kept them in fuel the winter through without buying any. 'But they don't get *paid*

for that work.' She considered it quite a hardship that
they were not paid for taking a present. Cottage people
do look at things in such a curious crooked light! A
mother grumbled because the vicar had not been to see
her child, who was ill. Now, she was not a church-goer,
and cared nothing for the Church or its doctrines—that
was not it ; she grumbled so terribly because 'it was his
place to come.'

A lady went to live in a village for health's sake,
and having heard so much of the poverty of the farmer's
man, and how badly his family were off, thought that she
should find plenty who would be glad to pick up extra
shillings by doing little things for her. First she wanted
a stout boy to help to draw her Bath chair, while the
footman pushed behind, it being a hilly country. Instead
of having to choose between half a dozen applicants, as
she expected, the difficulty was to discover anybody
who would even take such a job into consideration.
The lads did not care about it ; their fathers did not care
about it ; and their mothers did not want them to do it.
At one cottage there were three lads at home doing
nothing ; but the mother thought they were too delicate
for such work. In the end a boy was found, but not
for some time. Nobody was eager for any extra shilling
to be earned in that way. The next thing was somebody to fetch a yoke or two of spring water daily. This
man did not care for it, and the other did not care for
it ; and even one who had a small piece of ground, and
kept a donkey and water-butt on wheels for the very
purpose, shook his head. He always fetched water for
folk in the summer when it was dry, never fetched none
at that time of year—he could not do it. After a time
a small shopkeeper managed the yoke of water from the
spring for her—*his* boy could carry it ; the labourer's

could not. He was comparatively well-to-do, yet he was not above an extra shilling.

This is one of the most curious traits in the character of cottage folk—they do not care for small sums ; they do not care to pick up sixpences. They seem to be *afraid of obliging people*—as if to do so, even to their own advantage, would be against their personal honour and dignity. In London the least trifle is snapped up immediately, and there is a great crush and press for permission to earn a penny, and that not in very dignified ways. In the country it is quite different. Large fortunes have been made out of matches ; now your true country cottager would despise such a miserable fraction of a penny as is represented by a match. I heard a little girl singing—

Little drops of water, little grains of sand.

It is these that make oceans and mountains ; it is pennies that make millionaires. But this the countryman cannot see. Not him alone either ; the dislike to little profits is a national characteristic, well marked in the farmer, and indeed in all classes. I, too, must be humble, and acknowledge that I have frequently detected the same folly in myself, so let it not be supposed for an instant that I set up as a censor ; I do but delineate. Work for the cottager must be work to please him ; and to please him it must be the regular sort to which he is accustomed, which he did beside his father as a boy, which *his* father did, and *his* father before him ; the same old plough or grub-axe, the same milking, the same identical mowing, if possible in the same field. He does not care for any new-fangled jobs : he does not recognise them, they have no *locus standi*—they are not established. Yet he is most anxious for work, and works well, and is indeed the best labourer in the world. But it is the national character. To understand a nation you must go to the cottager.

The well-to-do are educated, they have travelled, if not in their ideas, they are more or less cosmopolitan. In the cottager the character stands out in the coarsest relief ; in the cottager you get to 'bed-rock,' as the Americans say ; there's the foundation. Character runs upwards, not downwards. It is not the nature of the aristocrat that permeates the cottager, but the nature of the cottager that permeates the aristocrat. The best of us are polished cottagers. Scratch deep enough, and you come to that ; so that to know a people, go to the cottage, and not to the mansion. The labouring man cannot quickly alter his ways. Can the manufacturer? All alike try to go in the same old groove, till disaster visits their persistence It is English human nature.

APRIL GOSSIP.

THE old woman tried to let the cuckoo out of the basket at Heathfield fair as usual on the 14th; but there seems to have been a hitch with the lid, for he was not heard immediately about the country. Just before that two little boys were getting over a gate from a hop-garden, with handfuls of Lent lilies—a beautiful colour under the dark sky. They grow wild round the margin of the hop-garden, showing against the bare dark loam; gloomy cloud over and gloomy earth under. 'Sell me a bunch?' 'No, no, can't do that; we wants these yer for granmer.' 'Well, get me a bunch presently, and I will give you twopence for it.' 'I dunno. We sends the bunches we finds up to Aunt Polly in Lunnon, and they sends us back sixpence for every bunch.' So the wild flowers go to Lunnon from all parts of the country, bushels and bushels of them. Nearly two hundred miles away in Somerset a friend writes that he has been obliged to put up notice-boards to stay the people from tearing up his violets and primroses, not only gathering them but making the flowery banks waste; and notice-boards have proved no safeguard. The worst is that the roots are taken, so that years will be required to repair the loss. Birds are uncertain husbandmen, and sow seeds as fancy leads their wings. Do the violets get sown by ants? Sir John Lubbock says they carry violet seeds into their nests.

The lads, who still pelt the frogs in the ponds, just as they always did, in spite of so much schooling, call them chollies. Pheasants are often called peacocks. Bush-harrows, which are at work in the meadows at this time of year, are drudges or dredges. One sunny morning I noticed the broken handle of a jug on the bank of the road by the garden. What interested me was the fine shining glaze of this common piece of red earthenware. And how had the potter made that peculiar marking under the surface of the glaze? I touched it with my stick, when the pot-handle drew itself out of loop shape and slowly disappeared under some dead furze, showing the blunt tail of a blindworm. I have heard people say that the red ones are venomous, but the grey harmless. The red are spiteful, and if you see them in the road you should always kill them. It is curious that in places where blindworms are often seen their innocuous nature should not be generally known. They are even called adders sometimes. At the farm below, the rooks have been down and destroyed the tender chickens not long hatched; they do not eat the whole of the chicken, but disembowel it for food. Rooks are very wide feeders, especially at nesting-time. They are suspected of being partial to the young of partridge and pheasant, as well as to the eggs.

Looking down upon the tree-tops of the forest from a height, there seemed to come from day to day a hoariness in the boughs, a greyish hue, distinct from the blackness of winter. This thickened till the eye could not see into the wood; until then the trunks had been visible, but they were now shut out. The buds were coming; and presently the surface of the tree-tops took a dark reddish-brown tint. The larches lifted their branches, which had drooped, curving upwards as a man raises his arms above his shoulders, and the slender boughs became set with green buds. At a distance the corn is easily distinguished from the meadows beside it by the different shade of green ; grass is a deep green, corn appears paler and yet brighter—perhaps the long winter has given it the least touch of yellow. Daisies are up at last—very late indeed. Big humble-bees, grey striped, enter the garden and drone round the banks, searching everywhere for a fit hole in which to begin the nest. It is pleasant to hear them ; after the dreary silence the old familiar burr-rr is very welcome. Spotted orchis leaves are up, and the palm-willow bears its yellow pollen. Happily, the wild anemones will not bear the journey to London, they wither too soon ; else they would probably be torn up like the violets. Neither is there any demand for the white barren strawberry blossom, or the purplish ground-ivy among the finely marked fern moss.

The rain falls ; and in the copses of the valley, deep and moist, where grey lichen droops from the boughs, the thrushes sing all day—so delighted are they to have the earth soft again, and so busy with the nesting. At four o'clock in the morning the larks begin to sing : they will be half an hour earlier next month, adjusting their time nicely by the rising of the sun. They sing on till after the lamps are lit in the evening. Far back in the snow-time a pair of wagtails used to come several times a day close to the windows, their black markings showing up singularly well against the snow on the ground. They seemed to have just arrived. But now the weather is open and food plentiful they have left us. The wagtails appear to be the first of the migrant birds to return, long before the hail of April rattles against the windows and leaps up in the short grass. Out in the hop-gardens the poles are placed ready for setting, in conical heaps

—at a distance resembling the tents of an army. Never were the labouring men so glad to see the spring, for never have so many of them been out of work or for longer periods. Yet, curiously enough, even if out of work and suffering, every sort of job will not suit them. One applicant for work was offered hop-pole shaving at 3s. a hundred—said to be a fair price; but the work did not please him, and he would not do it. On the other hand, a girl sent out 'to service' turned her back on domestic duties, ran away from her mistress, and joined her father and brother in the woods where they were shaving hop-poles. There she worked with them all the winter—the roughest of rough winters—preferring the wild freedom of the snow-clad woods, with hard food, to the indoor employment. No mistress there in the snow: one woman does not like another over her. A man stood idling at the cross-roads in the village for weeks, hands in pockets, waiting for work. Some one took pity on him, and said he could come and dig up an acre of grass-land to make a market garden; 15s. a week was the offer, with spade found, and not long hours. 'Thank you, sir; I'll go and look at it,' said the labourer. He went; and presently returned to say that he did not care about it. In some way or other it did not fall in with his notions of what work for him ought to be. I do not believe he was a bad sort of fellow at all; but still there it is. No one can explain these things. A distinct line, as it were, separates the cottager, his ways and thoughts, from others. In a cottage with which I am acquainted an infant recently died. The body was kept in the parents' bedroom close to their bed, day and night, until burial. This is the custom. The cottage wife thinks that not to have the body of her child by her bed would be most unfeeling—most cruel to lay it by itself in a cold room away from her.

A BLACK humble-bee came to the white hyacinths in the garden on the sunny April morning when the yellow tulip opened, and as she alighted on the flower there hovered a few inches in the rear an eager attendant, not quite so large, more grey, and hovering with the shrillest vibration close at hand. The black bee went round the other side of a bunch of hyacinths, and was hidden in the bell of a purple one. At thus temporarily losing sight of her, the follower, one might say, flew into a state of extreme excitement, and spun round and round in the air till he caught sight of her again and resumed his steady hovering. Then she went to the next bunch of hyacinths ; he followed her, when, with a furious, shrill cry of swiftly beating wings, a second lover darted down, and then the two followed the lady in black velvet—buzz, buzz, buzz, pointing like hounds stationary in the air—buzz, buzz—while she without a moment's thought of them worked at the honey. By-and-by one rushed at her—a too eager caress, for she lost her balance and fell out of the flower on to the ground. Up she got and pursued him for a few angry circles, and then settled to work again. Presently the rivals darted at each other and whirled about, and in the midst of the battle off went the lady in velvet to another part of the garden, and the combatants immediately rushed after her. Every morning that the tulip opened its great yellow bell, these black humble-bees came, almost always followed by one lover, sometimes, as on the first occasion, by two. A bright row of polyanthus and oxlips seemed to be the haunt of the male bees. There they waited, some on the leaves and some on the dry clods heated by the sun, in ambush till a dark lady should come. The yellow tulip was a perfect weather-meter ; if there was the least bit of harshness in the air, the least relic of the east wind, it remained folded. Sunshine alone was not sufficient to tempt it, but the instant there was any softness in the atmosphere open came the bell, and as if by a magic key all the bees and humble-bees of the place were unlocked, and forth they came with joyous note—not to visit the tulip, which is said to be a fatal cup of poison to them.

Any one delicate would do well to have a few such flowers in spring under observation, and to go out of doors or stop in according to their indications. I think there were four species of wild bee at these early flowers, including the great bombus and the small prosopis with orange-yellow head. It is difficult to scientifically identify small insects hastily flitting without capturing them, which I object to doing, for I dislike to interfere with their harmless liberty. They have all been named and classified, and I consider it a great cruelty to destroy them again without special purpose. The pleasure is to see them alive and busy with their works, and not to keep them in a cabinet. These wild bees, particularly the smaller ones, greatly resented my watching them, just the same as birds do. If I walked by they took no heed ; if I stopped or stooped to get a better view they were off instantly. Without doubt they see you, and have some idea of the meaning of your various motions. The wild bees are a constant source of interest, much

more so than the hive bee, which is so extremely regular
in its ways. With an explosion almost like a little
bomb shot out of a flower; with an immense hum,
almost startling, boom! the great bombus hurls himself
up in the air from under foot; well named—boom—
bombus. Is it correct or is it only a generalisation, that
insects like ants and hive bees, who live in great and
well-organised societies, are more free from the attacks
of parasites than the comparatively solitary wild bees?
Ants are, indeed, troubled with some parasites, but these
do not seem to multiply very greatly, and do not
seriously injure the populousness of the nest. They
have enemies which seize them, but an enemy is not a
parasite. On the other hand, too, they have mastered a
variety of insects, and use them for their delectation and
profit. Hive bees are likewise fairly free from parasites,
unless, indeed, their so-called dysentery is caused by
some minute microbe. These epidemics, however, are
rare. Take it altogether, the hive bee appears comparatively free of parasites. Enemies they have, but that is
another matter.

Have these highly civilised insects arrived in some
manner at a solution of the parasite problem? Have
they begun where human civilisation may be said to
have ended, with a diligent study of parasitic life? All
our scientific men are now earnestly engaged in the
study of bacteria, microbes, mycelium, and yeast, infini-
tesimally minute fungi of every description, while meantime the bacillus is eating away the lives of a heavy
percentage of our population. Ants live in communities
which might be likened to a hundred Londons dotted
about England, so are their nests in a meadow, or, still
more striking, on a heath. Their immense crowds, the
population of China to an acre, do not breed disease.

Every ant out of that enormous multitude may calculate on a certain average duration of life, setting aside risks from battle, birds, and such enemies. Microbes are unlikely to destroy her. Now this is a very extraordinary circumstance. In some manner the ants have found out a way of accommodating themselves to the facts of their existence ; they have fitted themselves in with nature and reached a species of millennium. Are they then more intelligent than man ? We have certainly not succeeded in doing this yet ; they are very far ahead of us. Are their eyes, divided into a thousand facets, a thousand times more powerful than our most powerful microscopes, and can they see spores, germs, microbes, or bacilli where our strongest lenses find nothing ? I have some doubts as to whether ants are really shut out of many flowers by hairs pointing downwards in a fringe and similar contrivances. The ant has a singularly powerful pair of mandibles : put one between your shirt and skin and try ; the nip you will get will astonish you. With these they can shear off the legs or even the head of another ant in battle. I cannot see, therefore, why, if they wished, they could not nip off this fringe of hairs, or even sever the stem of the plant. Evidently they do not wish, and possibly they have reasons for avoiding some plants and flowers, which besides honey may contain spores—just as they certainly contain certain larvæ, which attach themselves to the bodies of bees.

Possibly we may yet use the ants or some other clever insects to find out the origin of the fatal parasite which devours the consumptive. Some reason exists for imagining that this parasite has something to do with the flora, for phthisis ceases at a certain altitude, and it is very well known that the floras have a marked line of demarcation. Up to a certain height certain flowers

will grow, but not beyond, just as if you had run a separating ditch round the mountain.   With the flora the insects cease ; whether the germ comes from the vegetation or from the insect that frequents the vegetation
does not seem known.   Still it would be worth while to
make a careful examination of the plant and insect life
just at the verge of the line of division.   The bacillus
may spring from a spore starting from a plant or starting from an insect.   Most of England had an Alpine
climate probably once, and some Alpine plants and
animals have been stranded on the tops of our highest
hills and remain there to this day.   In those icy times
English lungs were probably free of disease.   Has formic
acid ever been used for experiments on bacilli ?   It is
the ant acid ; they are full of it, and it is extracted and
used for some purposes abroad.   Perhaps its strong
odour is repellent to parasites.   To return : while the
honey-bees live in comparative safety, the more or less
solitary wild bees have a great struggle to repel various
creatures that would eat them or their young, and, be as
watchful as they may, all their efforts at nest-building
are often rendered nugatory by the success of a parasite.
So it is not worth while to catch them just for the purpose of identification, for they have enough enemies in
the field without man and his heartless cabinets.   The
collector is the most terrible parasite of all.   Let them
go on with a happy hum, while the tulip opens in the
sunshine.

THE TIME OF YEAR.

THE Emperor moth came out on the 2nd of April, and suddenly filled the cardboard box like the noonday phantom in the sunshine, so unexpected and wonderful. His wings, which as he rests are spread open, stretched from one side of the box to the other, hovering over his old home, a beautiful grey tipped with pink, and peacock-eyed, ring within ring   He clung to the piece of heather upon which the caterpillar was found seven months before, and which he had fixed in the threads of his cocoon. The immense dark green caterpillar banded with black and spotted with gold was found on the 29th of August among the heather on the hill-side ; the sun burning, the air all alight with the fire of the beams, a day of flame —as if the keen tips of the pine needles would take fire in the glow.   The caterpillar in its colour and size seemed almost tropical ; those who have not seen it would scarcely believe that a caterpillar could be so magnificent ; but indoors in the cardboard box he lost his sun-burnished colour and half his glory.   Immediately afterwards he spun his cocoon, and there he stayed for seven long months, so that the moth thus suddenly appearing, without any cracking or opening of the cocoon, appeared to be created on the spot.   At first, indeed, some thought it was a moth that had entered by the window, there being no rent or place of exit from the perfect case.   Within, however, was the broken and blackened skin of the caterpillar and the detached thorax : the cocoon is like the baskets for taking fish at weirs, only the willows merely touch at the tip, and through these he had crept out, and they closed behind him.

The pale purple heather bloom still lies in the bottom of the box.   Never again shall I see a day of such glory of light, of air burning with light ; the very ferns in the shade were bright with the glow, despite their soft green. A sad hour it was to me, yet I could see all its beauty ; sad, too, to think it will never return.   So the Emperor moth came out on the 2nd of April, and the same day there was a yellow and a white butterfly in the garden. There had come a gleam of sunshine after two months of bitter north wind, and the insects took life immediately.   Early in the morning the greenfinches were screaming at each other in the elm—they were in such a hurry to get out their song, they screamed ; the chaffinches were challenging, and the starlings fluttering their wings at the high window, and all this excitement at one gleam of sun.   A friend asked me what bird it was that always finished up its song with a loud call for 'ginger-beer'—whatever he sang he always said 'ginger-beer' at the end of it ; it is the chaffinch, and a very good rendering of the notes.   'Quawk ! Quoak !' the rooks as they went by were so contented enjoying the sunshine, they took out the harsh 'c' or 'k' and substituted the softer 'q '—' quawk ! quowk !'   Another perched on a tree made a short speech, perhaps he thought it was a song.   Sea-gulls have curiously rook-like habits in some respects, following the plough like them, and in spring wheeling for hours round and round in the sky as the rooks do.

The blackbirds and thrushes that had been singing

freely previously suddenly ceased singing about December 15, and remained silent for a month, and as suddenly began singing again about January 15. Where they all came from I cannot think, there seemed such an increase in their numbers ; one wet morning in a small meadow there were forty-five feeding in sight that could be easily counted. They say the thrushes dig up and eat the roots of the arum, yet they are not root-eaters. Possibly it may have a medicinal effect ; the whole plant has very strong properties, and is still much gathered, I suppose for the herbalists. The root is set rather deep, quite a dig with a pocket knife sometimes ; one would fancy it was only those which had become accidentally exposed that are eaten by the thrushes. I have never seen them do it, and some further testimony would be acceptable. The old naturalists said the bear on awakening from its winter sleep dug up and ate the roots of the arum in order to open the tube of the intestine which had flattened together during hibernation. The blackbirds are the thrushes' masters, and drive them from any morsel they fancy. There is very little humanity among them : one poor thrush had lost the joint of its leg, and in order to pick up anything had to support itself with one wing like a crutch. This bird was hunted from every spot he chose to alight on ; no sooner did he enter the garden than one of the stronger birds flew at him—'so misery is trodden on by many.' There was a drone-fly on a sunny wall on January 20, the commonest of flies in summer, quite a wonder then ; the same day a house-sparrow was trying to sing, for they have a song as well as a chirp ; on January 22 a tit was sharpening his saw and the gnats were jumping up and down in crowds—this up-and-down motion seems peculiar to them and may-flies. Then the snowdrops flowered and a hive-bee came to them ; next the yellow crocus ; bees came to these, too, and so eager were they that one bee would visit the same flower five or six times before finally going away. Bees are very eager for water in the early year ; you may see them in crowds on the wet mud in ditches ; there was a wild bee drowning in a basin of water the other day till I took him out.

Before the end of January the woodbine leaf was out, always the first to come, and never learning that it is too soon ; whether the woodbine came over with 'Richard Conqueror' or the Romans, it still imagines itself ten degrees further south, so that some time seems necessary to teach a plant the alphabet. Immediately afterwards down came a north wind and put nature under its thumb for two months ; the drone-fly hid himself, the bees went home, everything became shrivelled, dry, inhuman. The local direction of the wind might vary, but it was still the same polar draught, the blood-sucker ; for, like a vampire, it sucks the very blood and moisture out of delicate human life, just as it dries up the sap in the branch. While this lasted there were no notes to make, the changes were slower than the hour hand of a clock ; still it was interesting to see the tree-climber come every morning at eleven o'clock to the cobble-stone wall and ascend it exactly as he ascends trees, peering into chinks among the moss and the pennywort. He seemed almost as fond of these walls as of his tree trunks. He came regularly at eleven and again at three in the afternoon, and a barn owl went by with a screech every evening a little after eight. The starlings told the time of the year as accurately as the best chronometer at Whitehall. When I saw the last chimney swallow, November 30, they went by to their sleeping-trees about three o'clock in the afternoon

—a long night, a short day for them. So they continued till in January the day had grown thirty minutes longer, when they went to roost so much the later; in February, four o'clock; in March, by degrees their time for passing by the window *en route* drew on to five o'clock. Let the cold be never so great or the sky so clouded, the mysterious influence of the light, as the sun slowly rises higher on the meridian, sinks into the earth like a magic rain. It enters the hardest bark and the rolled-up bud, so firm that its point will prick the finger like a thorn; it stirs beneath the surface of the ground. A magnetism that is not heat, and for which there is no exact name, works out of sight in answer to the sun. Seen or unseen, clouded or not, every day the sun lifts itself an inch higher, and let the north wind shrivel as it may, this invisible potency compels the bud to swell and the flower to be ready in its calyx. Progress goes on in spite of every discouragement. The birch trees reddened all along their slender boughs, and when the sunlight struck aslant, the shining bark shone like gossamer threads wet with dew.

The wood-pigeon in the fir trees could not be silent any longer. Whoo—too—whoo—ooe! then up he flew with a clatter of his wings and down again into the trees. 'Take two cows, Taffy,' he could not be silent any longer—whoo—too—whoo—ooe! The blackthorn bloom began to faintly show the tiniest white studs, and the boys in great triumph brought in the first blue thrush's eggs. Nature would go on though under the thumb of the north wind. Poor folk came out of the towns to gather ivy leaves for sale in the streets to make button-holes. Many people think the ivy leaf has a pleasant shape; it was used of old time among the Greeks and Romans to decorate the person at joyous

festivals.   The ivy is frequently mentioned in the classic
poets.   Not so with the countrywomen in the villages
to-day, ground down in constant dread of that hateful
workhouse system of which I can find no words to express my detestation.   They tell their daughters never
to put ivy leaves in their hair or brooch, because 'they
puts it on the dead paupers in the unions and the
lunatics in the 'sylums.'   Such an association took away
all the beauty of the ivy leaf.   There is nature in their
hearts, you see, although they are under the polar
draught of poverty.   At last there came a little warmth
and the Emperor moth appeared, yellow and white
butterflies came out, flowers bloomed, buds opened—
ripened by the mystic magnetism of the sun in their
sheaths and cocoons—great humble-bees came with a
full-blown buzz, all before the swallow, the nightingale,
and cuckoo.   It was but for a day, and then down fell
the bitter polar draught again.

In a sheltered spot the cuckoo was first heard on April 29, but only for one day; then, as the wind took up its accustomed northerly drift again, he was silent. The first chimney swallows (four) appeared on April 25, and were quickly followed by a number. They might be said to be about three weeks behind time, and the cuckoo a fortnight. The chiffchaff uttered his clear yet rather sad notes on April 26. The same morning at five o'clock there had been a slight snow shower, but it was a sunny day. On May 1 a stitchwort was in flower, a plant that marks the period distinctly. A swift appeared on May 2; I should not consider this late. A whitethroat was catching insects in the garden on May 6. The cuckoo sang again on May 8; the same day a Red Admiral butterfly was seen, and the turtle-dove heard cooing. Next day, the 9th, the eave swallow appeared, and also the bank martin. With the cooing of the turtle-dove the spring migrants are generally complete; a warm summer bird, he is usually the last, and if the others had not been seen they are probably in the country somewhere. The chimney swallows had been absent five months all but five days (last seen November 30), so that reckoning the first and the last, they may be said to stay in England seven months—much longer than one would think without taking the dates. Up till April 20 the hedges seemed as bare as they were in January, a most dreary spectacle of barren branches, and the great elms gaunt against the sky. After that the hedges gradually filled with leaf, and were fully coloured when the turtle-dove began to sing, but still the elms were only just budding, and but faintly tinted with green.

Chaucer was right in singing of the ' floures ' of May notwithstanding the northern winds and early frosts and December-like character of our Mays. That the cycle of weather was warmer in his time is probably true, but still even now, under all the drawbacks of a late and wintry season, his description is perfectly accurate. If any one had gone round the fields on old May-day, the 13th, *his* May-day, they might have found the deep blue bird's-eye veronica, anemones, star-like stitchworts, cowslips, buttercups, lesser celandine, daisies, white blackthorn, and gorse in bloom—in short, a list enough to make a page bright with colour, though the wind might be bitter. In the coldest and most exposed place I ever lived in, and with a spring as cold as this, the May garlands included orchids, and the meadows were perfectly golden with marsh-marigolds. For some reason or other the flowers seem to come as near as they can to their time, let the weather be as hard as it may. They are more regular than the migrant birds, and much more so than the trees. The elm, oak, and ash appear to wait a great deal on the sun and the atmosphere, and their boughs give much better indications of what the weather has really been than birds and flowers. The migrant birds try their hardest to keep time, and some of them arrive a week or more before they are noticed. Elm, oak, and ash are the surest indicators ; the horse-chestnut is very apt to put forth its broad succulent leaves too soon ; the sycamore, too, is an early tree in spite of everything. It has been said that of late years we have not had any settled, soft, warm weather till after midsummer. There has been a steady continual cold draught from the northward till the sun reached the solstice, so that the summers, in fact, have not commenced till the end of June. There is a good deal of general truth in this observation; certainly we seem to have lost our springs. I do not think I have heard it thunder this year up to the time of writing. The absence of electrical disturbance shows a peculiar state of atmosphere unfavourable to growth, so that the corn will not hide a partridge, and in some places hardly a sparrow. Where did the painters get their green leaves from this year in time for the galleries? Not from the trees, for they had none.

A flock of rooks was waddling about in a thinly grown field of corn which scarcely hid their feet, and a number of swallows, flying very low, scarcely higher than the rooks' breasts, wound in and out among them. The day was cloudy and cold, and probably the insects had settled on the ground. The rooks' feet stirred them up, and as they rose they were taken by the swallows. All over the field there were no other swallows, nor in the adjacent fields, only in that one spot where the rooks were feeding. On another occasion swallows flying low over a closely cropped grass field alighted on the sward to try and catch their prey. There seems a scarcity of some kinds of insect life, due doubtless to the wind. Out of a dozen butterfly chrysalids collected, six were worthless; they were stiff, and when opened were stuffed full of small white larvæ, which had eaten away the coming butterfly in its shell. They were the offspring of a parasite insect, which thus provided for the sustenance of its young by eating up other young, after the cruel way of nature. Why does one robin carefully choose a thatched eave for its nest, out of reach except by a ladder, and safe from all beasts of prey, and another place its nest on a low grassy bank scarcely hidden by a plant of wild parsley, and easily taken by the smallest boy? At first it looks like a great difference in intelligence, but probably each bird acted as well as could be under the circumstances. Each robin has to fight for his locality, and he has to make the best of his territory; if he trespassed on another bird's premises he would be driven away. You must build your house where you happen to possess a plot of land. It is curious to see the male bird feeding the female, not only while on the nest, but when she comes away from it; the female perches on a branch and utters a little call, and the male brings her food. He was feeding her the other evening on the bare boughs of a fig tree some distance from the nest. The warmth of the sun, although we could not feel it, must have penetrated into the earth some time since, for a slowworm came forth on a mound for the first time on April 16. He coiled up on the eastern side every morning for some hours, but was never seen in the afternoon. His short, thick body and unfinished tail, more like a punch or the neck of a stumpy bottle, was turned in a loop, the head nearly touching the tail, like a pair of sugar-tongs. Coming out from the stitchwort and grasses, the spiders often ran over his shining dark brown surface, something the colour of glazed earthenware. A snake or an adder would have begun to move away the moment any one stopped to look at it; but the slowworm takes no notice, and hence it is often said to be blind. He seems to dislike any sharp noise, and is really fully aware of your presence. Close by the mound, which stands in a corner of the garden, there is a great bunch of blue comfrey, to which the bees and humble-bees come in such numbers as to seem to justify the idea that these insects prefer blue. Or perhaps the blue flowers secrete sweeter honey. Every kind of wild bee as yet flying visits this plant, tiny bees barely a quarter of an inch long, others as big as two filberts, some a deep amber, some striped like wasps. A little of Chaucer's May has come ; now and then a short hour or two of sunshine between the finger and thumb of the north wind. Most pleasant it is to see the eave swallow dive down from the roof and rush over the scarcely green garden—a household sign of summer. In the lane if you gather them the young leaves of the sycamore have a fragrant scent like a flower, and low down ferns are unrolling. On the low wall sits a yellow-hammer, just brightly touched afresh with colour. Happy greenfinches go by, and it is curious to note how the instant they enter the hedge they are lost now under the leaves ; so few days ago they would have been un-concealed. So near is it to summer that the first thrush begins to sing at three o'clock in the morning.

THE leaves are starting here and there from green buds on the hedge, but within doors a warm fire is still necessary, when one day there is a slight sound in the room, so peculiar, and yet so long forgotten, that though we know what it is, we have to look at the object before we can name it. It is a house-fly, woke up from his winter sleep, on his way across to the window-pane, where he will buzz feebly for a little while in the sunshine, flourishing best like a hothouse plant under glass. By-and-by he takes a turn or two under the centre-piece, and finally settles on the ceiling. Then, one or two other little flies of a different species may be seen on the sash; and in a little while the spiders begin to work, and their round silky cocoons are discovered in warm corners of the woodwork. Spiders run about the floors and spin threads by the landing windows; where there are webs it is certain the prey is about, though not perhaps noticed. Next, some one finds a moth. Poor moth! he has to suffer for being found out.

As it grows dusk the bats flitter to and fro by the house; there are moths, then, abroad for them. Upon the cucumber frame in the sunshine perhaps there may be seen an ant or two, almost the first out of the nest; the frame is warm. There are flowers open, despite the cold wind and sunless sky; and as these are fertilised by insects, it follows that there must be more winged

creatures about than we are conscious of. How strange
it seems, on a bleak spring day, to see the beautiful pink
blossom of the apricot or peach covering the grey wall
with colour—snowflakes in the air at the time! Bright
petals are so associated with bright sunshine that this
seems backward and inexplicable, till it is remembered
that the flower probably opens at the time nearest to
that which in its own country brings forth the insects
that frequent it. Now and again humble-bees go by
with a burr; and it is curious to see the largest of them
all, the big bombus, hanging to the little green goose-
berry blossom. Hive-bees, too, are abroad with every
stray gleam of sun; and perhaps now and then a drone-
fly—last seen on the blossoms of the ivy in November.
A yellow butterfly, a white one, afterwards a tortoise-
shell—then a sudden pause, and no more butterflies for
some time. The rain comes down, and the gay world
is blotted out. The wind shifts to the south, and in a
few days the first swallows are seen and welcomed, but,
as the old proverb says, they do not make a summer.
Nor do the long-drawn notes of the nightingale, nor
even the jolly cuckoo, nor the tree pipit, no, nor even
the soft coo of the turtle-dove and the smell of the
May flower. It is too silent even now: there are the
leading notes; but the undertone—the vibration of the
organ—is but just beginning. It is the hum of insects
and their ceaseless flitting that make the summer more
than the birds or the sunshine. The coming of summer
is commonly marked in the dates we note by the cuckoo
and the swallow and the oak leaves; but till the butterfly and the bee—one with its colour, and one with its
hum—fill out the fields, the picture is but an outline
sketch. The insects are the details that make the
groundwork of a summer day. Till the humble-bees

are working at the clover it is too silent ; so I think we may begin our almanack with the house-fly and the moth and the spider and the ant on the cucumber frame, and so on, till, finally, the catalogue culminates with the great yellow wasp. He is the final sign of summer ; one swallow does not make it, one wasp does. He is a connoisseur of the good things of the earth, and comes not till their season.

On the top of an old wall covered with broad masses of lichen, the patches of which grew out at their edges as if a plate had taken to spreading at its rim, the tits were much occupied in picking out minute insects ; the wagtails came too, sparrows, robins, hedge-sparrows, and occasionally a lark ; a bare blank wall to all appearance, and the bare lichen as devoid of life to our eyes. Yet there must have been something there for all these eager bills—eggs or pupæ. A jackdaw, with iron-grey patch on the back of his broad poll, dropped in my garden one morning, to the great alarm of the small birds, and made off with some large dark object in his beak—some beetle or shell probably, I could not distinguish which, and should most likely have passed the spot without seeing it. The sea-kale, which had been covered up carefully with seaweed, to blanch and to protect it from the frost, was attacked in the cold dry weather in a most furious manner by blackbirds, thrushes, and starlings. They tore away the seaweed with their strong bills, pitching it right and left behind them in as workman-like style as any miner, and so boring deep notches into the edge of the bed. When a blackbird had made a good hole he came back to visit it at various times of the day, and kept a strict watch. If he found any other blackbird or thrush infringing on his diggings, he drove him away ferociously. Never were such works carried on as at the edge of that seaweed ; they moved a bushel of it. To the eye there seemed nothing in it but here and there a small white worm ; but they found plenty, and the weather being so bitter, I let them do much as they liked ; I would rather feed than starve them.

Down at the sea-shore in the sunny hours, out from the woodwork of the groynes or bulwarks, there came a white spotted spider, which must in some way have known the height to which the tide came at that season, because he was far below high-water mark. The moles in an upland field had made in the summer a perfect network of runs. Out of curiosity we opened some, and found in them large brown pupæ. In the summer-house, under the wooden eaves, if you look, you will find the chrysalis of a butterfly, curiously slung aslant. Coming down Galley Hill, near Hastings, one day, a party was almost stopped by finding they could only walk on thousands of caterpillars, dark with bright yellow bands, which had sprung out of the grass. The great nettles—now, nothing is so common as a nettle— are sometimes festooned with a dark caterpillar, hundreds upon each plant, hanging like bunches of currants Could you find a spot the size of your watch-seal without an insect or the germ of one?

The agriculturists in some southern counties give the boys in spring threepence a dozen for the heads of young birds killed in the nest. The heads are torn off, to be produced, like the wolves' of old times, as evidence of extinction. This—apart from the cruelty of the practice—is, I think, a mistake, for, besides the insects that injure crops, there are some which may be suspected of being inimical to human life, if not directly, indirectly ; and if it were not for birds, we should run a very good chance of being literally eaten up. The difficulty is that people cannot believe what they cannot immediately see, and there are very few who have the patience or who feel sufficient interest to study minute things.

I have taken these instances haphazard; they are large instances, as it were, of big and visible things. They only give the rudest idea of the immensity and complexity of insect life in our own country. My friend the sparrow is, I believe, a friend likewise to man generally. He does a little damage, I admit; but if he were to resort to living on damage solely in his enormous numbers, we should not have a single flower or a single ear of wheat. He does not live by doing mischief alone evidently. He is the best scavenger the Londoners have got, and I counsel them to prize their sparrows, unless they would be overrun with uncomfortable creatures; and possibly he plays his part indirectly in keeping down disease. They say in some places he attacks the crocus. He does not attack mine, so I suspect there must be something wrong with the destroyed crocuses. Some tried to entice him from the flower with crumbs; they would perhaps have succeeded better if they had bought a pint of wheat at the seedsman's and scattered it. In spring, sparrows are not over-fond of crumbs; they are inordinately fond of wheat. During the months of continued dry, cold, easterly winds, which we have had to endure this season, all insect-eating birds have been almost as much starved as they are in winter when there is a deep snow. Nothing comes forth from the ground, nothing from the deep crannies which they cannot peck open; the larva remains quiescent in the solid timber. Not a speck can they find. The sparrow at such a time may therefore be driven to opening flower-buds. Looked at in a broad way, I am convinced he is a friend. I have always let them build about the house, and shall not drive them away.

If you do not know anything of insects, the fields are somewhat barren to you. The buttercups are beautiful, still they are buttercups every day. The thrush's song is lovely, still one cannot always listen to the thrush. The fields are but large open spaces after a time to many, unless they know a little of insects, when at once they become populous, and there is a link found between the birds and the flowers. It is like opening another book of endless pages, and coloured illustrations on every page.

Blessings on the man, said Sancho Panza, who first invented sleep. Blessings on the man who first invented the scarlet geranium, and thereby brought the Humming-bird moth to the window-sill; for, though seen ever so often, I can always watch it again hovering over the petals and taking the honey, and away again into the bright sunlight. Sometimes, when walking along, and thinking of everything else but it, the beautiful Peacock butterfly suddenly floats by the face like a visitor from another world, so highly coloured, and so original and unlike and unexpected. In bright painters' work like the wings of butterflies, which often have distinct hues side by side, I think nature puts very little green; the bouquet is not backed with maiden-hair fern; the red and the blue and so on have no grass or leaves as a ground colour; nor do they commonly alight on green. The bright colours are left to themselves unrelieved. None of the butterflies, I think, have green on the upper side of the wing; the Green Hairstreak has green under wings, but green is not put forward.

Something the same may be noticed in flowers themselves: the broad surface, for instance, of the peach and apricot, pink without a green leaf; the pear tree white, but the leaves come quickly; the apple, an acre of pink and white, with the merest texture of foliage. Nor are there many conspicuous green insects— the grasshopper; some green flies; the lace-fly, a green body and delicate white wings. With the wild flowers, on the contrary, there seems to come a great deal of green. There is scarcely a colour that cannot be matched in the gay world of wings. Red, blue, and yellow, and brown and purple—shaded and toned, relieved with dots and curious markings; in the butter-flies, night tints in the pattern of the under wings, as if these were shaded with the dusk of the evening, being in shadow under the vane. Gold and orange, red, bright scarlet, and ruby and bronze in the flies. Dark velvet, brown velvet, greys, amber, and gold edgings like mili-tary coats in the wild bees. If fifteen or twenty delicate plates of the thinnest possible material, each tinted differently, were placed one over the other, and all translucent, perhaps they might produce something of that singular shadow-painting seen on the wings of moths. They are the shadows of the colours, and yet they are equally distinct. The thin edges of the flies' wings catch the sunbeams, and throw them aside. Look, too, at the bees' limbs, which are sometimes yellow, and sometimes orange-red with pollen. The eyes, too, of many insects are coloured. They know your shadow from that of a cloud. If a cloud comes over, the instant the edge of the shadow reaches the Grass moths they stop, so do some of the butterflies and other insects, as the wild bees remain quiescent. As the edge of your shadow falls on them they rise and fly, so that to observe them closely it must not be allowed to overlap them.

Sometimes I think insects smell the approaching observer as the deer wind the stalker. The Gatekeeper butterfly is common ; its marking is very ingenious, may I say ? regular, and yet irregular. The pattern is complete, and yet it is incomplete ; it is finished, and yet it suggests to the mind that the lines ought to go on farther. They go out into space beyond the wing. If a carpet were copied from it, and laid down in a room, the design would want to run through the walls. Imagine the flower-bird's wing detached from some immense unseen carpet and set floating—it is a piece of something not ended in itself, and yet floating about complete. Some of their wings are neatly cut to an edge and bordered ; of some the edge is lost in colour, because no line is drawn along it. Some seem to have ragged edges naturally, and look as if they had been battered. Towards the end of their lives little bits of the wing drop out, as if punched. The markings on the under wings have a tendency to run into arches, one arch above the other. The tendency to curve may be traced everywhere in things as wide apart as a flower-bird's wing and the lines on a scallop-shell.

I own to a boyish pleasure in seeing the clouds of brown chafers in early summer clustering on the maple hedges and keeping up a continual burring. They stick to the fingers like the bud of a horse-chestnut. Now the fern owl pitches himself over the oaks in the evening as a boy might throw a ball careless whither it goes ; the next moment he comes up out of the earth under your feet. The night cuckoo might make another of his many names ; his colour, ways, and food are all cuckoo-like ; so, too, his immense gape—a cave in which endless moths end their lives ; the eggs are laid on the ground, for there is no night-feeding bird into whose nest they could be put, else, perhaps, they would be. There is no night-feeding bird to feed the fern owl's young. Does any one think the cuckoo could herself feed two young cuckoos? How many birds would it take to feed three young cuckoos? Supposing there were *five* young cuckoos in the nest, would it not take almost all the birds in a hedge to feed them? For the incredible voracity of the young cuckoo—swallow, swallow, swallow, and gape, gape, gape—cannot be computed. The two robins or the pair of hedge-sparrows in whose nest the young cuckoo is bred, work the day through, and cannot satisfy him; and the mother cuckoo is said to come and assist in feeding him at times. How, then, could the cuckoo feed two or three of its offspring and itself at the same time? Several other birds do not build nests—the plover, the fern owl. That is no evidence of lack of intelligence. The cuckoo's difficulty, or one of its difficulties, seems to be in the providing sufficient food for its ravenous young. A half-fledged cuckoo is already a large bird, and needs a bulk of soft food for its support. Three of them would wear out their mother completely, especially if—as may possibly be the case—the male cuckoo will not help in feeding. This is the simplest explanation, I think; yet, as I have often said before, we must not always judge the ways of birds or animals or insects either by strict utility, or by crediting them with semi-supernatural intelligence. They have their fancies, likes and dislikes, and caprices. There are circumstances—perhaps far back in the life-history of their race—of which we know nothing, but which may influence their conduct unconsciously still, just as the crusades have transmitted a mark to our minds to-day. Even though an explanation may satisfy us, it is by no means certain that it is the true one, for they may look at matters in an entirely different manner from what we do. The effect of the cuckoo's course is to cause an immense destruction of insects, and it is really one of the most valuable as well as the most welcome of all our birds.

The thin pipe of the gnat heard at night is often alluded to, half in jest, by our older novelists. It is now, I think, dying out a good deal, and local where it stays. It occurred to me, on seeing some such allusion the other day, that it was six years since I had heard a gnat in a bedroom—never since we left a neighbourhood where there had once been marshy ground. Gnats are, however, less common generally—exclusive, of course, of those places where there is much water. All things are local, insects particularly so. On clay soils the flies in summer are most trying ; black flies swarm on the eyes and lips, and in the deep lanes cannot be kept off without a green bough. It requires the utmost patience to stay there to observe anything. In a place where the soil was sand, with much heath, on elevated ground, there was no annoyance from flies. There were crowds of them, but they did not attack human beings. You might sit on a bank in the fields with endless insects passing without being irritated ; but everywhere out of doors you must listen for the peculiar low whir of the stoat-fly, who will fill his long grey body with your blood in a very few minutes. This is the tsetse of our woods.

STEAM ON COUNTRY ROADS.

LOSSES year after year and increasing competition indicate that the crops now grown are not sufficient to support the farmer. When he endeavours, however, to vary his method of culture, and to introduce something new, he is met at the outset by two great difficulties which crush out the possibility of enterprise. The first of these—the extraordinary tithe—has already come into prominent notice; the second is really even more important—it is the deficiency of transit. An extensive use of steam on common roads appears essential to a revival of agricultural prosperity, because without it it is almost impossible for delicate and perishable produce to be quickly and cheaply brought to market. Railways, indeed, now connect nearly every town of any size whatever throughout the country with the large cities or London; but railways are necessarily built as lines of communication between towns, and not in reference to scattered farms. Upon the map the spaces between the various rails do not look very broad, but those white bands when actually examined would be found to be six, eight, ten, or even twenty miles wide. Nor are there stations everywhere, so that a farm which may be only six miles from the metals may be ten from the nearest platform. Goods trains do not, as in the United States, stop to pick up wherever there is material or produce waiting to be loaded; the produce has to be taken where the railway chooses, and not where it would suit the farmer's convenience. When at last the farmer's waggon reaches the station he finds no particular trouble taken to meet his needs ; his horse and carters are kept hours and hours, perhaps far into the night, for a mere matter of a ton or two, nor is there any special anxiety shown to deliver his consignment early, though if it should not be moved from the companies' premises demurrage is charged. In short, the railway companies, knowing that the agriculturists until the formation of the 'Farmers' Alliance' were incapable of united action, have used them much as they liked. As for the rates charged, the evidence recently taken, and which is to be continued, shows that they are arbitrary and often excessive. The accommodation is poor in the extreme, the charges high, the speed low, and every condition against the farmer. This, in its turn, drives the farmer more into the hands of the middleman. The latter makes a study of the rail and its awkward ways, and manages to get the goods through, of course adding to their cost when they reach the public. Without the dealer, under present circumstances, the farmer would often find it practically impossible to get to markets not in his immediate neighbourhood. The rail and its awkward, inconvenient ways actually shut him off. In manufacturing districts the transit of iron and minerals and worked-up metal is managed with considerable ability. There are appointed to manage the goods traffic men who are alert to the conditions of modern requirements and quick to meet them. In agricultural districts the question often arises if there be really any responsible local goods managers at all. It seems to be left to men who are little more than labourers, and who cannot understand the patent fact that times are different now from what they were thirty years since, when they first donned their uniforms. The railways may bring their books and any number of their officers to prove that everything is perfectly satisfactory, but the feeling remains, nevertheless, that it is exactly the contrary.

Look at the map, and place the finger on any of the spaces between the lines of rail. Take, then, the case of a farmer in the midst of that space, not more than five or six miles from the metals, and able at times to hear the distant whistle of the engines, but not less than eight from a station. This present season he finds his wheat damaged by the rain after it was cut, and he comes to the conclusion that he must supplement his ordinary crops by some special culture in order to make his way. On the last occasion he was in a large city he was much struck by the quantity of fruit which he found was imported from abroad. The idea naturally occurs to him of setting aside some ten or twenty acres of his holding of four hundred or five hundred for the culture of fruit. He goes to his landlord, who is only too willing to give him every facility, provided that no injury be done to the soil. He faces the monstrous injustice of the extraordinary tithes, and expends fresh capital in the planting of various kinds of fruit.

In places at that distance from a station labour is dear relative to the low profit on the ordinary style of farming, but very cheap relative to the possible profits on an improved and specialised system. The amount of extra labour he thus employs in the preparation of the ground, the planting, cleaning, picking, and packing, is an inestimable boon to the humbler population. Not only men, but women and children can assist at times, and earn enough to add an appreciable degree of comfort to their homes. In itself this is a valuable result. But now suppose our enterprising farmer has the fortune to have a good season, and to see his twenty acres teeming with produce. He sets as many hands on as possible to get it in ; but now what is he to do with it ? Send it to London. That is easily said ; but trace the process through. The goods, perishable and delicate, must first be carted to the railway station and delivered there, eight miles from the farm, at most inconvenient hours. They must be loaded into slow goods trains, which may not reach town for four-and-twenty hours. There is not the slightest effort to accelerate the transit, and the rates are high. By the time the produce reaches the market its gloss and value are diminished, and the cost of transit has eaten away the profit. The thing has been tried over and over again and demonstrated. One need only go to the nearest greengrocer's to obtain practical proof of it. The apples he sells are American. The farmers in New York State or Massachusetts can grow apples, pack them in barrels, despatch them two thousand eight hundred miles to Liverpool, and they can then be scattered all over the country and still sold cheaper than the fruit from English orchards. This is an extraordinary fact, showing the absolute need of speedy and cheap transit to the English farmer if he is to rise again. Of what value is his proximity to the largest city in the world—of what value is it that he is only ninety miles from London, if it costs him more to send his apples about ninety miles than it does his American kinsman very nearly three thousand ?

As we have in this country no great natural waterways like the rivers and lakes of the United States, our best resource is evidently to be found in the development of the excellent common roads which traverse the

country, and may be said practically to pass every man's
door. Upon these a goods train may be run to every
farm, and loaded at the gate of the field. This assertion
is not too bold. The thing, indeed, is already done in
a manner much more difficult to accomplish than that
proposed. Traction engines, weighing many tons—so
heavy as to sometimes endanger bridges, and drawing
two trucks loaded with tons of coal, chalk, bricks, or
other materials—have already been seen on the roads,
travelling considerable distances, and in no wise impeded
by steep gradients ; so little, indeed, that they ascend
the downs and supply farms situated in the most elevated positions with fuel. What is this but a goods train,
and a goods train of the clumsiest, most awkward, and,
consequently, unprofitable description ? Yet it is run,
and it would not be run were it not to some extent useful. Anything more hideous it would be hard to conceive, yet if the world patiently submits to it for the
welfare of the agricultural community, what possible ob-
jection can there be to engines so formed as to avoid
every one of the annoyances caused by it ? It may be
asserted without the slightest fear of contradiction that
there are at least fifty engineering firms in this country
who could send forth a road locomotive very nearly
noiseless, very nearly smokeless, certainly sparkless,
capable of running up and down hill on our smooth and
capital roads, perfectly under control, not in the least
alarming to horses, and able to draw two or more trucks
or passenger cars round all their devious windings at a
speed at least equal to that of a moderate trot—say eight
miles an hour. Why, then, do we not see such useful
road trains running to and fro ? Why, indeed ? In the
first place, progress in this direction is absolutely stopped
by the Acts of Parliament regulating agricultural engines.

The Act in question was passed at a time when steam
was still imperfectly understood.   It was in itself a perfectly judicious Act, which ought to be even more
strictly enforced than it is.   But it was intended solely
and wholly for the regulation of those vast and monstrous-
looking engines which it was at once foreseen, if left to
run wild, would frighten all horse traffic off the roads.
The possibility of road locomotives in the reasonable
sense of the term was not even in the minds of the
framers.   Yet, by a singular perversity, this very Act
has shut off steam from one of its most legitimate func-
tions.

It is quite possible that the depression of agriculture
may have the effect of drawing attention to this subject,
and if so it will be but tardy justice to the rest of society
that the very calling whose engines now block the roads
should thus in the end open them.   We should then see
goods trains passing every farm and loading at the gate
of the field.   Such a road goods train would not, of
course, run regularly to and fro in the same stereotyped
direction, but would call as previously ordered, and
make three or four journeys a day, sometimes loading
entirely from one farm, sometimes making up a load
from several farms in succession.   Besides the quick
communication thus opened up with the railway station
and the larger towns, the farmer would be enabled to
work his tenancy with fewer horses.   He would get
manures, coal, and all other goods delivered for him
instead of fetching them.   He would get his produce
landed for him instead of sending his own teams, men,
and boys.   In a short time, as the railways began to
awaken to the new state of things, they would see the
advantage of accommodating their arrangements, and
open their yards and sidings to their competitor.   In

the case of long journeys, and with some kinds of goods, in order to save the cost of transhipment, it would be possible to transfer the bed of the road truck from its frame on to the frame of the railroad truck, so that the goods, with one loading, might pass direct to London. Our American cousins are quite capable of inventing a transferable truck of this kind. In return, goods loaded in London would never leave the same bottom till unloaded at the farmyard or in the midst of the village. For all long journeys the rails would probably always remain the great carriers, and the road trains serve as their most valuable feeders. When farmers found it possible to communicate with the cities at reasonable rates, and at reasonable speed, they would be encouraged to put forth fresh efforts, to plant vegetables, to grow fruit, to supplement their larger crops with every species of lesser produce. This, in its turn, would bring new traffic to the lines ; for instead of one or two crops in the year only, there would be three or four requiring carriage. There would be then speedy results of such improved communication. One would be an increased value of land ; the second, an increase in the number of small areas occupied and cultivated ; the third, an increase in the rural population. A fourth would be that the incredible amount of money which is now annually transferred to the Continent and America for the purchase of every kind of lesser produce would remain in this country to the multiplication of the accounts at Post Office savings banks. Every one who possibly could would grow or fatten something when he could just put it on a road train, and send it off to market.

Two through passenger road trains a day, one in each direction, carrying light parcels as well, and traversing say forty or fifty miles or less, would probably soon obtain sufficient support, as they ran from village to village and market town to market town. At present, those who live in villages are practically denied locomotion unless they are well enough off to keep a horse and trap and a man to look after them. A person residing in a village must either remain in the village, or walk, or go by carrier. The carrier stops at every inn, and takes a day to get over ten miles. The exposure in the carrier's cart has been the cause of serious illness to many and many a poor woman obliged to travel by it, and sit in the wind and rain for hours and hours together. Unless they ride in this vehicle, or tramp on foot, the villagers are simply shut off from the world. They have neither omnibus, tramway, nor train. Those who have not lived in a village have no idea of the isolation possible even in this nineteenth century, and with the telegraph brought to the local post office. The swift message of the electric wire, and the slow transit of the material person—the speed of the written thought, and the slowness of the bodily presence—are in strange contrast.

When people do not move about freely commerce is practically at a standstill. But if two passenger road trains, travelling at an average speed of not more than eight miles an hour, one going up and the other down, and connecting two or more market towns and lines of railway, passed through the village, how different would be the state of things ! Ease of transit multiplies business, and, besides passengers, a large amount of light material could thus be conveyed. There would be depôts at the central places, but such trains could stop to pick up travellers at any gate, door, or stile. If the route did not go through every hamlet, it would pass near enough to enable persons to walk to it and join the carriages. No one objects to walk one mile if he can afterwards ride the other ten. Besides these through trains, special trains could run on occasions when numbers of people wanted to go to one spot, such as sheep or cattle fairs and great markets. Large tracts of country look to one town as their central place, not by any means always the nearest market town ; to such places, for instance, as Gloucester and Reading, thousands resort in the course of the year from hamlets at a considerable distance. Such road trains as have been described would naturally converge on provincial towns of this kind, and bring them thrice their present trade. Country people only want facilities to travel exactly like city people. It is, indeed, quite possible that when villages thus become accessible many moderately well-to-do people will choose them for their residence, in preference to large towns, for health and cheapness. If any number of such persons took up their residence in villages, the advantage to farmers would of course be that they would have good customers for all minor produce at their doors. It is not too much to say that three parts of England are quite as much in need of opening up as the backwoods of America. When a new railroad track is pushed over prairie and through primeval woods, settlements spring up beside it. When road trains run through remote hamlets those remote hamlets will awake to a new life.

Many country towns of recent years have made superhuman efforts to get the railway to their doors. Some have succeeded, some are still trying ; in no case has it been accomplished without an immense expenditure, and for the most part these railroad branches are completely in the control of the main line with which they are connected. In one or two cases progress has been effected by means of tramways, notably one at Wantage—an excellent idea and highly to be commended.

All these are signs that by slow degrees matters are tending towards some such scheme as has been here sketched out. While local railroads are extremely expensive, slow in construction, and always dominated by main lines, and while tramways need rails, with the paraphernalia rails require, they have this drawback—they are not flexible. The engines and cars that run upon them must for ever adhere to the track : there may be goods, produce, ricks, cows, fruit, hops, and what not, wanting to be landed only a quarter of a mile distant, but the cars cannot go to the crops. The railroad is rigid, everything must be brought to it. From town to town it answers well, but it cannot suit itself and wind about from village to hamlet, from farm to farm, up hill and down dale. The projected road train is flexible and capable of coming to the crops. It can call at the farmer's door, and wait by the gate of the field for the load. We have lately seen France devote an enormous sum to the laying down of rails in agricultural districts, to the making of canals, and generally to the improvement of internal communication in provinces but thinly populated. The industrious French have recognised that old countries, whose area is limited, can only compete with America, whose area is almost unlimited, by rendering transit easy and cheap. We in England shall ultimately have to apply the same fact.

FIELD SPORTS IN ART.

THE MAMMOTH HUNTER.

THE most ancient attempt to delineate the objects of sport in existence is, I think, the celebrated engraving of a mammoth on a portion of a mammoth's tusk. I call it an engraving because the figure is marked out with incised lines such as the engraver makes with his tool, and it is perfect enough to print from. If it were inked and properly manipulated it would leave an impression—an artist's proof the most curious and extraordinary in the world, for the block was cut with flint instruments by the Cave-men an incredible number of years ago, perhaps before England was separated from the Continent by the sea, while the two were still connected, and it was dry land where now the *Calais-Douvres* steams so steadily over the waves. But it would be an artist's proof with the lights and shades reversed, the lines that sketch the form of the mammoth would be white and the body dark, yet for all that life-like, since the undulating indentations that represent the woolly hide of the immense creature would relieve the ground. This picture of a prehistoric animal, drawn by a prehistoric artist, shows that Art arose from the chase. Traced to the den of primeval man, who had no Academy to instruct him, no Ruskin to guide, and no gallery to exhibit in, it appears that Art sprang from nature, and not from science. His life was occupied with the hunt, and he represented that which filled his thoughts. Those who understand wild sports will not for a moment doubt that the mammoth was taken in pits or otherwise destroyed despite its huge strength; no matter if it had been twice as large, the cunning of man would have been equal to the difficulty. The mind is the arrow that slays the monster. The greater the danger the greater the interest, and consequently the more the imagination would dwell upon the circumstances of the chase. Afterwards resting in the cave round about the fire and thinking of the mighty work of sport which had been accomplished, the finger of the savage would involuntarily describe the outline of the creature so laboriously captured. His finger might describe it upon the scattered ashes whitening the ground beside him. Or it might describe the outline simply in the air. Speech in its inception was as much expressed by the finger as the tongue; perhaps the fingers talked before the mouth, and in a sense writing preceded language. Uttering the unpolished sound which in their primitive society indicated the mammoth, the savage drew rapidly a figure with his finger, and his companions read his meaning written in the air. To this day it is common for the Italian peasantry to talk with their fingers; a few syllables suffice, illustrated and emphasised by those dexterous hands. A more subtle meaning is thus conveyed than could be put in words. Some of the most ancient languages seem bald and incomplete, too rigid; they need intonation, as it were, to express passion or changes of emotion, and when written the letters are too far apart to indicate what is meant. Not too far apart upon the page, but far apart in their sense, which has to be supplied as you supply the vowels.

In actual use such languages must have required much gesture and finger-sketching in the air. The letters of the Egyptians largely consist of animals and birds, which represent both sounds and ideas. Dreaming over the embers of his fire, the Cave-man saw pass before his mental vision all the circumstances of the chase, ending with the crash when the mammoth crushed into the pit, at which he would start and partially awake. Intentness of mind upon a pursuit causes an equivalent intentness of dream, and thus wild races believe their dreams to be real and substantial things, and not mere shadows of the night. To those who do not read or write much, even in our days, dreams are much more real than to those who are continuously exercising the imagination. If you use your imagination all day you will not fear it at night. Since I have been occupied with literature my dreams have lost all vividness and are less real than the shadows of trees, they do not deceive me even in my sleep. At every hour of the day I am accustomed to call up figures at will before my eyes, which stand out well defined and coloured to the very hue of their faces. If I see these or have disturbed visions during the night they do not affect me in the least. The less literary a people the more they believe in dreams ; the disappearance of superstition is not due to the cultivation of reason or the spread of knowledge, but purely to the mechanical effect of reading, which so perpetually puts figures and aërial shapes before the mental gaze that in time those that occur naturally are thought no more of than those conjured into existence by a book. It is in far-away country places, where people read very little, that they see phantoms and consult the oracles of fate. Their dreams are real.

The mammoth came through his cave before the

embers of his fire—the sleeping savage could touch it with his flint-headed spear—there was the crash as it fell into the prepared pit; he awakes, the dying embers cast shadows on the walls, and in these he traces the shape of the vast creature hastening away. The passing spirit has puffed the charred brands into a second's flame, and thus shadowed itself in the hollow of the cavern.

Deeper than the excitement of the chase lies that inner consciousness which dwells upon and questions itself—the soul of the Cave-man pondered upon itself; the question came to him, as he crouched in the semi-darkness, over the fire which he had stirred, 'Will my form and aërial shadow live on after my death like that which passed but now? Shall I, too, be a living dream?' The reply was, 'Yes, I shall continue to be; I shall start forth from my burial-mound upon the chase in the shadow-land just as now I start forth from my cave. I shall entrap the giant woolly elephant—I shall rejoice at his capture; we shall triumph yet again and again. Let then my spear and knife be buried with me, but chip them first—kill them—that I may use their spirit likenesses in the dream-chase.'

With a keen-edged splinter of flint in the daylight he incised the outlines of the mammoth upon a smooth portion of its tusk—its image was associated with his thoughts of a future life, and thus Art in its earliest inception represented the highest aspirations of man.

But could the ignorant savage of that long-lost day have been capable of such work? The lowest race of savages in Southern Africa—the Bushmen—go about with festoons of entrails wound around their loins. After a successful hunt—with the pit or poisoned arrows —they remove the entrails of the slain animal and wear them like coronals for present ornament and future regalement. These creatures are nevertheless artists. On the walls of caves they have painted the antelope and the lion in bright colours; they have not only caught the shape and hue of the animals about them, but their action and movement. The figures are in motion, skilfully drawn and full of spirit.

If any one asks, Is the application of Art to the chase really so old, so very very old, as this? I refer them to the stars. How long ago is it since the constellations received their names? At what date were they first arranged in groups? Upon the most ancient monuments and in the most ancient writings they have the same forms assigned to them as at this day, and that too in countries remote from each other. The signs of the Zodiac are almost as old as the stars themselves; that is, as old as the time when the stars were first beheld of human eyes. Amongst them there is the Archer— Sagittarius—the chase in the shape of man; greatest and grandest of all the constellations is Orion, the mighty hunter, the giant who slew the wild beasts by strength. There is no assemblage of stars so brilliant as those which compose the outline of Orion; the Hunter takes the first place in the heavens. Art exists in the imagination— imagination drew lines from star to star, and repeated its life on earth in the sky.

So it is true that the first picture—whether drawn by the imagination alone in the constellations, on the walls of the cave with ochre and similar materials, or engraved with keen splinters of flint on the mammoth's tusk—the first picture was of the chase. Animals are earliest, the human form next, flowers and designs and stories in drawings next, and landscape last of all. Landscape is peculiarly the art of the moderns—it is the art of *our* civilisation ; no other civilisation seems to have cared for it. Towers and castles are indeed seen on the bas-reliefs of Assyria, and waving lines indicate rivers, but these are merely subsidiary, and to give place and locality to the victories the king is achieving. The battle is the interest, the landscape merely the stage. Till the latter days of European life the artist took no notice of landscape.

The painting of hills and rocks and rivers, woods and fields, is of recent date, and even in these scenes the artist finds it necessary to place some animals or birds. Even now he cannot ignore the strong love of human beings for these creatures ; if they are omitted the picture loses its interest to the majority of eyes. Every one knows how wonderfully popular the works of Landseer have been, and he was an animal painter, and his subjects chiefly suggested by sport. The same spirit that inspired the Cave-dweller to engrave the mammoth on the slab of ivory still lives in the hearts of men.

There is a beautiful etching of " The Poacher " (to which I shall have to recur); he is in the wood, and his dog is watching his upraised finger. From that finger the dog learns everything. He knows by its motion when to start, which way to go, what to do, whether to be quick or slow, to return or to remain away. He understands his master quite as well as if they conversed in human speech. He enters into the spirit of the enterprise. ' If you want your business done, go ; if not, send,' is true only of men. The poacher wants his business done, and he sends his agent—his dog —certain that it will be done for him better than he could do it himself. The dog is conscientious, he will omit nothing, he will act as if his master's eye was on him the whole time. Now this attitude of the dog's mind is so exquisitely rendered in the picture that he seems verily to speak with intelligence. I love that dog though he does but exist in ink ; he is the true image of a real dog, and his mind shines through his body. This effect upon me as the spectator is produced by a clever arrangement of lines upon the plate from which the etching was printed, thin lines cut into the copper with curious sharp tools, behind a screen of tissue-paper to shield the eyes from the light, done in the calm of the studio, thoughtfully, with artistic skill. Given the original genius to conceive such a dog, the knowledge how to express the ideas, and the tools to work with, and we see how it became possible to execute the etching. But suppose the artist supplied with a piece of smooth ivory for his plate, and a sharp penknife for his etching needle, and set behind a boulder to watch the mammoth and sketch it by incision on the ivory, and there would be produced very much the same kind of picture as the Cave-man made. It could not have the delicate shading, the fine edge, the completion and finish of the dog ; it could not visibly think as that dog thinks. It would consist of a few quick strong dashes, conveying the weight and force and image of the elephant in as few strokes as possible. It would be a charcoal sketch ; broad and powerful lines that do not themselves delineate, but compel your imagination to do the picture in your mind, so that you see a great deal more than is drawn. So that the Cave-man was really a great artist—his intense interest in the chase supplied the lack of academies and scientific knowledge and galleries to copy from. This primeval picture thus tells you that the highly educated artist of the present day, removed from his accessories, away from his liquid colours, easels, canvas, prepared paper, and so forth, can only do what the Cave-man did. But still further, he can only do that if he possesses great natural genius—only a man who could draw the poacher's dog could do it. Those who depend altogether on the prepared paper and liquid colours, patent easel and sketching stool, could simply do nothing.

It is nearly certain that if the primeval man sketched the mammoth he likewise carved his spear-shaft, the haft of his knife, the handle of his 'celt,' that chisel-like weapon whose shape so closely resembles the front teeth. The 'celt' is a front tooth in flint or bronze, enlarged and fitted to a handle for chipping, splitting, and general work. In museums celts are sometimes fitted to a handle to show how they were used, but the modern adapter has always overlooked the carving. Wild races whose time is spent in sport or war—very nearly synonymous terms—always carve or ornament their weapons, their canoes, the lintels of their doors, the posts of their huts. There is in this the most singular difference from the ways of landscape civilisation. Things that we use are seldom ornamented—our tables, our chairs, our houses, our carriages, our everything is as plain as plain can be. Or if ornamented, it is ornamented in a manner that seems to bear no kind of relation to the article or its uses, and to rouse no sympathies whatever. For instance, our plates—some have the willow pattern, some designs of blackberry bushes, and I really cannot see what possible connection the bushes or the Chinese summerhouses have with the roast beef of old England or the *côtelette* of France. The last relic of Art carving is visible round about a bread platter, here and there wreaths of wheatears ; very suitable these to a platter bearing bread formed of corn. Alas! I touched one of these platters one day to feel the grain of the wood, and it was cold earthenware—cold, ungenial, repellent crockery, a mockery, sham! Now the original wooden platter was, I think, true Art, and the crockery copy is not Art. The primeval savage, without doubt, laboriously cut out a design, or at least gave some curve and shape to the handle of his celt or the shaft of his spear, and the savages at this day as laboriously carve their canoes. The English sportsman, however, does not cut, or carve, or in any way shape his gun-stock to his imagination. The stock is as smooth and as plain as polished wood can be. There is a sort of speckling on the barrels, and there is a conventional design on the lock-plate; conventional, indeed, in the most *blasé* sense of the word—quite *blasé* and worn out, this scratch of intertwisted lines, not so much as a pheasant even engraved on the lock-plate; it is a mere killing machine, this gun, and there is no Art, thought or love of nature about it. Sometimes the hammers are filed, little notches crossing, and there imagination stops. The workman can get no farther than his file will go, and you know how that acts to and fro in a straight groove. A pheasant or hare at full speed, a few trees—firs as most characteristic—could be put on the plate, and something else on the trigger guard; firs are easily drawn, and make most appearance for a few touches; pheasants roost in them. Even a coat of arms, if it were the genuine coat-of-arms of the owner's family, would look well. Men have their book-plates and stamp their library volumes, why not a gun design? As many sportsmen scarcely see their guns for three-fourths of the year, it is possible to understand that the gun becomes a killing machine merely to them, to be snatched up and thrown aside the instant its office is over. But the gamekeeper carries his gun the year through, and sits in the room with it when indoors, still he never even so much as scratches an outline of his favourite dog on it. In these landscape days we put our pictures on the walls only, and no imagination into the things we handle and use. A good deal of etching might be done on a gun, most of it being metal, while more metal could be easily inlaid for the purpose. Etching, I suppose, is the right word ; at all events, designs, records of actual sporting feats, or outlines of favourite sporting places— nooks in the woods, falls of the stream, deep combes of the hills—could be cut in with aquafortis. So many draw or paint nowadays, and in this manner they could make some use of their skill, drawing perhaps for those who only understand the use of cartridge-paper when it has gunpowder inside it. Sportsmen see the very best of scenery, and come across old hollow trunks and curious trees, effects, and 'bits' of every kind, from a twisted hawthorn to an antlered stag ; if they could get an artistic friend to see these, there would be some good gun-etchings done.

'PERFECTLY lovely!' 'Such pretty colours!' 'So neat; isn't it wonderful how the little things do it with their beaks?' 'The colours are so arranged as to conceal it; the instinct is marvellous;' and so on. These comments were passed on a picture of a bird's nest—rather a favourite subject with amateur painters. The nest was represented among grass, and was tilted aside so as to exhibit the eggs, which would have rolled out had they been real. It was composed of bright-green moss with flowers intertwined, and tall bluebells, rising out of the grass, overhung it. Nothing could be more poetical. In reality, the flowers—if ever actually used by a bird—would have faded in a day, and the moss would never have had so brilliant and metallic a tint. The painter had selected the loveliest colours of the mead and gathered them into a bouquet, with the nest in the centre. This is not exactly like nature: a robin's nest for instance, the other day was discovered in an old shoe, discarded by a tramp and thrown over the wall into the shrubbery. Nests are not always made where flowers grow thickest, and birds have the oddest way of placing them—a way which quite defeats rational search. After looking into every nook, and places where if built a nest would be hidden from passers-by, suddenly it is found right in front of you and open to view. You have attributed so much cunning to the bird that you have deceived youself. In fact, it sometimes happens that the biggest fool is the best bird's-nester, and luck in eggs falls to those who have no theory. But December throws doubt even on the fool's capacity, for as the leaves fall there appear nests by the dozen in places never suspected, and close to people's faces. For one that has been taken ten have escaped.

The defect of nest-building lies in the absence of protection for the young birds. When they grow large and feel strong they bubble, as it were, over the edge of the cup-shaped nest. Their wings, though not yet fullgrown, save them from injury in descent by spreading out like a parachute, but are powerless to assist them after reaching the ground. In the grass they are the prey of rooks, crows, magpies, jackdaws, snakes, rats, and cats. They have no means of escape whatever: they cannot fly nor run—the tall grass stops running —and are frequently killed for amusement by their enemies, who do not care to eat them. Numbers die from exposure in the wet grass, or during rain, for they are not able to fly up and perch on a branch. The nest requires a structure round it like a cage, so that the fledglings might be prevented from leaving it till better able to save themselves. Those who go to South Kensington to look at the bird's-nest collection there should think of this if they hear any one discoursing on infallible instinct on the one hand, or evolution on the other. These two theories, the infallible instinct and that of evolution, practically represent the great opposing lines of thought—the traditional and the scientific. An examination of birds' nests, if conducted free of prejudice, will convince any independent person neither that the one nor the other explains these common hedge difficulties. Infallible instinct has not supplied protection for the young birds, nor has the experience of hundreds of years of nest-building taught the chaffinch or the missel-thrush to give its offspring a fair start in the famous ' struggle for existence.' Boys who want linnets or goldfinches watch till the young are almost ready to bubble over, and then place them in a cage where the old birds come and feed them. There is, then, no reason why the nest itself should not be designed for the safety of the fledgling as well as of the egg. Birds that nest in holes are frequently very prolific, notably the starling, which rears its brood by thousands in the hollow trees of forests. Though not altogether, in part their vast numbers appear due to the fact that their fledglings escape decimation.

Country boys set some value on the eggs of the nettle-creeper or whitethroat because the nest is difficult to find, and the eggs curiously marked. They want the eggs as soon as laid, when they blow well ; and it is just at this stage that the nest is most difficult to discover, as the bird gives little evidence of its presence. The nest is placed among the thick grasses and plants that grow at the verge or down the sides of dry ditches, and is frequently overshadowed by nettles. But there does not appear to be any conscious effort at concealment. The bird spends the day searching for food in such places—hence its name nettle-creeper—creeping along the hedges, under brambles and thorns, and builds its nest in the locality to which it is accustomed. It may appear to be cunning to a superficial human observer, but it is certain that the bird does not think itself cunning. Men who live by fishing build their houses near the sea ; those who cultivate wheat, in open plains; artisans, by factories. The whitethroat frequents the hedge and ditch, and there weaves its slender nest. So much has been attributed to birds of which they are

really quite unconscious. It has even been put forward
that the colours of their eggs are intended to deceive;
and those of the dotterel, laid on the open beach, are
often mentioned as an instance. The resemblance of
the dotterel's egg to a pebble is no greater than the
resemblance between many eggs laid in nests and pebbles. If the whitethroat eggs were taken from the nest
and placed among particoloured pebbles such as are
common on some shores, it would need care to distinguish them. If the dotterel's eggs were put down
among grass, or even among the clods of ploughed land,
they would be equally difficult to find. You might as
well suppose that the whitethroat is aware that nettles
will sting the human hand approaching its nest as that
eggs are especially adjusted in colour to deceive human
eyes. As for deceiving the eyes of those birds that are
fond of eating eggs, the thing is impossible; the size of
the egg is alone sufficient: how conceal an object of
that size from an eye that can distinguish insects?
The egg takes its chance, coloured or not. Sportsmen
would be very glad if pheasants would kindly learn by
experience, and lay eggs of a hue invisible to the poaching rook or crow. Nor is this nest, that seems so slender
and so delicately made, really so slender to the bird itself. To a man or woman, so many times larger than
the nest, its construction appears intricate. Suppose a
lady stands five feet four inches high, and the nest
placed in her hand measures two inches across: the
difference is immense. The bird who built it is smaller
than the nest. The thing is reversed, and it does not
look tiny to the bird. The horsehair or fibre, which to
us is an inch or two long, to the bird is a bamboo or
cane three or four feet in length. No one would consider it difficult to weave cane or willow wands as tall as
himself. The girls at Luton perform much more difficult

feats in weaving straw-plait for bonnets than any bird accomplishes. A rook's nest looked at in the same way is about as large to the bird as a small breakfast-parlour, and is composed of poles. To understand birds you must try and see things as they see them, not as you see them. They are quite oblivious of your sentiments or ideas, and their actions have no relation to yours. A whole system of sentiment and conduct has been invented for birds and animals based entirely upon the singular method of attributing to them plans which might occur to a human being. The long-tailed tit often builds its nest in the midst of blackthorn thickets (which afford it the lichen it uses), or in deep hawthorn bushes. A man comes along, sees the nest, and after considerable exertion—having to thrust himself into the hedge—and after some pain, being pricked by the thorns, succeeds, with bleeding hands, in obtaining possession of it. ' Ah,' he moralises, ' what wonderful instinct on the part of this little creature to surround itself with a zareba like the troops after Osman Digma! Just look at my hands.' Proof positive to him ; but not to any one who considers that through the winter, up till nesting-time, these little creatures have been creeping about such thorns and thickets, and that they had no expectation whatever of a hand being thrust into the bushes. The spot which is so difficult of access to a man is to them easy of entrance. They look at the matter from the very opposite point of view. The more thoroughly the artificial system of natural history ethics is dismissed from the mind the more interesting wild creatures will be found, because while it is adhered to a veil is held before the eyes, and nothing useful can ever be discovered. Put it aside, and there is always something new and as interesting as a fresh nest to a boy.

NATURE IN THE LOUVRE.

TURNING to the left on entering the Louvre, I found myself at once among the sculpture, which is on the ground-floor. Except that the Venus of Milo was in the collection, I had no knowledge of what I was about to see, but stepped into an unknown world of statuary. Somewhat indifferently I glanced up and then down, and instantly my coolness was succeeded by delight, for there, in the centre of the gallery, was a statue in the sense in which I understand the word—the beautiful made tangible in human form. I said at once, 'That is *my* statue. There lies all Paris for me; I shall find nothing further.' I was then at least thirty yards distant, with the view partly broken, but it was impossible to doubt or question lines such as those. On a gradual approach the limbs become more defined, and the torso grows, and becomes more and more human—this is one of the remarkable circumstances connected with the statue. There is life in the wide hips, chest, and shoulders; so marvellous is the illusion that not only the parts that remain appear animated, but the imagination restores the missing and mutilated pieces, and the statue seems entire. I did not see that the hand was missing and the arms gone; the idea of form suggested by the existing portions was carried on over these, and filled the vacant places.

Going nearer, the large hips grow from stone to life,

the deep folds of the lower torso have but this moment been formed as she stooped, and the impulse is to extend the hands to welcome this beautiful embodiment of lovingkindness. There, in full existence, visible, tangible, seems to be all that the heart has imagined of the deepest and highest emotions. She stoops to please the children, that they may climb her back ; the whole of her body speaks the dearest, the purest love. To extend the hands towards her is so natural, it is difficult to avoid actually doing so. Hers is not the polished beauty of the Venus de Medici, whose very fingers have no joints. The typical Venus is fined down from the full growth of human shape to fit the artist's conception of what beauty should be. Her frame is rounded ; her limbs are rounded ; her neck is rounded ; the least possible appearance of fulness is removed ; any line that is not in exact accordance with a strict canon is worked out—in short, an ideal is produced, but humanity is obliterated. Something of the too rounded is found in it—a figure so polished has an air of the bath and of the mirror, of luxury ; it is *too* feminine ; it obviously has a price payable in gold. But here is a woman perfect as a woman, with the love of children in her breast, her back bent for their delight. An ideal indeed, but real and human. Her form has its full growth of wide hips, deep torso, broad shoulders. Nothing has been repressed or fined down to a canon of art or luxury. A heart beats within her bosom ; she is love ; with her neither gold nor applause has anything to do ; she thinks of the children. In that length of back and width of chest, in that strong torso, there is just the least trace of manliness. She is not all, not too feminine ; with all her tenderness, she can think and act as nobly as a man.

Absorbed in the contemplation of her beauty, I did

not for some time think of inquiring into material particulars. But there is a tablet on the pedestal which tells all that is known. This statue is called the ' Venus Accroupie,' or Stooping Venus, and was found at Vienne, France. The term ' Venus ' is conventional, merely to indicate a female form of remarkable beauty, for there is nothing in the figure to answer to what one usually understands as the attributes of the goddess. It is simply a woman stooping to take a child pick-a-back, the child's little hand remaining upon the back, just as it was placed, in the act of clinging. Both arms are missing, and there appears to be some dispute as to the exact way in which they were bent across the body. The right arm looks as if it had passed partly under the left breast, the fingers resting on the left knee, which is raised ; while the left arm was uplifted to maintain the balance. The shoulders are massive rather than broad, and do not overshadow the width of the hips. The right knee is rounded, because it is bent ; the left knee less so, because raised. Bending the right knee has the effect of slightly widening the right thigh. The right knee is very noble, bold in its slow curve, strong and beautiful.

Known of course to students, this wonderful work seems quite overlooked by the mass of visitors to the Louvre, and its fame has not spread. Few have even heard its name, for it has not been written and lectured into the popular mind like the Venus de Medici. While I was studying it several hundred visitors went straight past, without so much as a casual glance, on their way direct to the Venus of Milo, of which they had read in their guide-books, and of which they had seen splendid photographs in every window. One came along, on the contrary, very slowly, carefully examining the inscriptions upon the altars and various figures; he appeared to understand the Latin and Greek, and it might have been expected that he would stay to look at the Accroupie. He did not; he worked all round the statue, reading every word legible on the base of the insignificant figures against the wall, and so onwards down the *salon.* One of the most complete of the guide-books dismisses the Accroupie in a single line, so it is not surprising that people do not seek it. But what is surprising is that in a city so artistic as Paris there should be so few photographs of this statue. I could get but two—these were duplicates, and were all the proprietor of the shop possessed; there was some trouble to find them. I was told that, as they were so seldom asked for, copies were not kept, and that there was only this one particular view—a very bad one. Other shops had none. The Venus of Milo is in every shop—in every size, and from every point of view; of the Accroupie these two poor representations were hunted out from the bottom of a portfolio. Of course, these remarks apply only to Paris as the public know it; doubtless the studios have the Accroupie, and could supply representations of every kind: casts, too, can be obtained at the Louvre. But to those who, like myself, wander in the outer darkness of common barbarian life, the Accroupie is unknown till we happily chance upon it. Possibly the reason may be that this statue infinitely surpasses those fixed ideals of art which the studios have for so many centuries resolutely forced upon the world. It seems that after a certain length of art study the natural eyesight is lost. But I hope and believe there are thousands of people in the world in full possession of their natural eyesight, and capable of appreciating the Accroupie when once their attention is called to it.

I knew it was useless to search further among the galleries of the Louvre, for there could not be two such works in existence anywhere, much less in one collection. Therefore I did not go a step beyond, but sat down to enjoy it, and when I had gazed enough for one morning I turned to leave the place. There are never two works of equal beauty of any kind, just as there are never two moments of equal pleasure : seize the one you have, and make much of it, for such a moment will never return. In walking away I frequently looked back—first at three or four yards', then at ten yards' distance ; gradually the proportions diminished, but the great sweep of outline retained its power. At about thirty yards it is remarkable how this noble work entirely overshadows the numerous figures close to it. Upon each side of the gallery the wall is lined with ranks of statuary, but they are quite lost as statuary, and seem nothing more than wall decorations, merely curious castings put there to conceal the monotony of the surface. Cleverly executed they may be, but there is no other merit, and they appear commonplace. They have no meaning ; the eye glances along them without emotion. It always returns to, and rests upon, the Accroupie—the living and the beautiful. Here is the difference between genius and talent. Talent has lined the walls with a hundred clever things, and could line miles of surface ; genius gives us but one example, and the clever things are silenced. Here is the difference between that which expresses a noble idea, and that which is dexterously conventional. The one single idea dominates the whole. Here is the difference, again, between the secret of the heart, the aspiration of the soul, and that which is only the workmanship of a studio ancient or modern. The Accroupie is human, loving tender; how poor are goddesses beside her! At forty, fifty, sixty yards, still looking back, though the details now disappeared, the wonderful outline of the torso and hips was as powerful as ever. Ascending the steps which lead from the gallery I paused once more, standing close against the wall, for other figures interfere with a distant view, and even at that distance (eighty yards or more) the same beauty was recognisable. Yet there is no extended arm, no attitude to force attention—nothing but the torso is visible; there is no artificial background (as with the Venus of Milo) to throw it into relief; the figure crouches, and the love expressed in the action is conveyed by the marvel of the work as far as it can be seen.

Returning next morning I took the passage on the left (not as before on the right), and so came at once to the top of the steps, and to a spot whence a view can with little trouble be obtained. Perhaps it is more than eighty yards away, but the effect is the same despite the distance. The very best place to view the statue is exactly in front of it, two or three yards away, or as close as you like, but precisely in front. It requires no careful choice of position so as to give a limb more prominence, or render the light more effective (the light just there is bad, though it is near a window). The sculptor did not rely upon 'artistic' and selected attitudes—something made up for the occasion. No meretricious aid whatever has been called in—no trick, no illusion of the eye, nothing theatrical. He relied solely and simply upon a true representation of the human body—the torso, the body itself—as he really saw it in life. When we consider that the lines of the body seen in front are gentle, and in no way prominent, it is apparent how beautiful the original must have been, and how wonderfully the form has been rendered in marble for this to be the best position to view it.

Three large folds, marked by deep lines, cross the lower part of the torso, and it is these creases that give the work its life. They are but just made in stooping, and will disappear as she rises from that position. These three grooves cross the entire front of the torso; the centre one is forked at its extremity near the right hip, and the fork of this groove encloses a smaller crease. Immediately under the right breast there is a short separate groove caused by the body leaning to the right; this is a fold of the side, not of the front. Under these folds there must be breath, there must be blood; they indicate a glowing life. The immense vitality of the form appears in them, and even as an athlete's muscles are exhibited in relief at his exercises, so exceeding strength of life is evident in these grooves. A heart throbbing steadily and strong, veins full of rich, pure blood, a warm touch, an eager wish to be affectionate, and self lost in the desire to love—this is the expression of the folds. Full of the energy of exceptional vitality, she gladly gives that energy for the delight of the little one.

There are no grooves on the torso of the Venus de Medici or of the Venus of Cnidus; they are sculptured in attitudes chosen to allow of the body and the limbs presenting an unbroken smoothness. They have the roundness of the polished column. They are ideals, but do not live. Here the deep grooves and the large folds are life.

As we move slowly around the statue from left to right, after observing it in front, the right breast gradually advances, and its outline appears. The act of

stooping and leaning to one side causes the right breast
to be lower than the left.   By degrees the right breast
recedes and the left advances, and, standing at the full
left of the figure, there are three chief lines to notice—
that of the back seen in profile, of the torso, and of the
left thigh.   The thigh is raised, and, so stretched, seems
slightly compressed near the knee.   It is more rotund
than thick or heavy; it is not so much size as roundness; it is not mere plumpness, but form.

A step farther and the back begins to appear, and
the outline of its right edge.   Standing exactly at the
back, there is a remarkable flatness at the lower end of
the mesial groove.   This flatness is somewhat in the
shape of an elongated diamond; it is rather below the
loins, and is, I think, caused by the commencement or
upper part of the pelvis.   In stooping and at the same
time leaning to one side, the flesh at this spot is drawn
tightly against the firm structure under the skin, so that
the flatness is almost, if not quite, hollow.   Had the
sculptor been representing a goddess he would have
concealed this flatness in some way or other, or selected
a position which did not cause it, for the conventional
art-beauty must be equally rounded everywhere.   Had
he been poorer in conception he would have slurred it
over, or not even observed it.   The presence of this flatness or slightly hollow surface demonstrates how true
the work is to reality.   The statue is a personality, a
living thing.   As the line of the horizon recedes at sea,
and that which now appears the edge or boundary is
presently sailed over, so the edge or outline of the body
recedes as you move around it.   Another step, and the
right thigh and the right breast are in sight, with the
ends of the grooves.   Lines that look almost straight
are changed, as you approach, into curves.   The action

of the limbs is most apparent when viewed from the right side of the statue ; but its most beautiful aspect is exactly in front. In moving round, it is very striking to observe how the least change of position—if you do but move an inch—alters the outline and curve of the work ; the breast, not visible before, is now apparent as the bust rises ; another inch and it becomes a demi-lune, till it swells to its full undulation. At every step the figure alters, but no matter at how many angles it is looked at, it always has beautiful curves. They adapt themselves, these curves, to the position of the eye, and wherever the eye is placed they satisfy its demands for beauty. Examine any part, and it is found perfect ; for instance, the inside of the right knee (visible from the left of the statue) slightly bulges, being pressed out by the stooping position.

At a third visit it seemed to me that the statue had grown much more beautiful in the few days which had elapsed since I first saw it. Pondering upon the causes of this increasing interest, I began to see that one reason was because it recalled to my memory the loveliness of nature. Old days which I had spent wandering among deep meadows and by green woods came back to me. In such days the fancy had often occurred to me that, besides the loveliness of leaves and flowers, there must be some secret influence drawing me on as a hand might beckon. The light and colour suspended in the summer atmosphere, as colour is in stained but translucent glass, were to me always on the point of becoming tangible in some beautiful form. The hovering lines and shape never became sufficiently defined for me to know what form it could be, yet the colours and the light meant something which I was not able to fix. I was now sitting in a gallery of stone, with cold marbles, cold floors, cold light from the windows. Without there were only houses, the city of Paris—a city above all other cities farthest from woods and meads. Here, nevertheless, there came back to me this old thought born in the midst of flowers and wind-rustled leaves, and I saw that with it the statue before me was in concord. The living original of this work was the human impersonation of the secret influence which had beckoned me on in the forest and by running streams. She expressed in loveliness of form the colour and light of sunny days; she expressed the deep aspiring desire of the soul for the perfection of the frame in which it is encased, for the perfection of its own existence.

The sun rolls on in the far dome of heaven, and now day and now night sweeps with alternate bands over the surface of hill, and wood, and sea ; the sea beats in endless waves, which first began to undulate a thousand thousand years ago, starting from the other rim of Time ; the green leaves repeat the beauty that gladdened man in ancient days. But for themselves they are, and not for us. Their glory fills the mind with rapture but for a while, and it learns that they are, like carven idols, wholly careless and indifferent to our fate. Then is the valley incomplete, and the void sad ! Its hills speak of death as well as of life, and we know that for man there is nothing on earth really but man ; the human species owns and possesses nothing but its species. When I saw this I turned with threefold concentration of desire and love towards that expression of hope which is called beauty, such as is worked in marble here. For I think beauty is truthfully an expression of hope, and that is why it is so enthralling—because while the heart is absorbed in its contemplation, unconscious but powerful hope is filling the breast. So powerful is it as to banish for the time all care, and to make this life seem the life of the immortals.

Returning the next morning, my thoughts went on, and found that this ideal of nature required of us something beyond good. The conception of moral good did not satisfy one while contemplating it. The highest form known to us at present is pure unselfishness, the doing of good, not for any reward, now or hereafter, nor for the completion of an imaginary scheme. This is the best we know. But how unsatisfactory! Filled with the aspirations called forth by the ideal before me, it appeared as if even the saving of life is a little work compared to what the heart would like to do. An outlet is needed more fully satisfying to its inmost desires than is afforded by any labour of self-abnegation. It must be something in accord with the perception of beauty and of an ideal. Personal virtue is not enough. The works called good are dry and jejune, soon consummated, often of questionable value, and leaving behind them when finished a sense of vacuity. You give a sum of money to a good object and walk away, but it does not satisfy the craving of the heart. You deny yourself pleasure to sit by the bedside of an invalid—a good deed; but when it is done there remains an emptiness of the soul. It is not enough—it is casuistry to say that it is. I often think the reason the world is so cold and selfish, so stolid and indifferent, is because it has never yet been shown how to be anything else. Listening to the prophets of all times and climes, it has heard them proclaim their ordinances, and has seen these observances punctually obeyed for hundreds of years, and nothing has come of it all. To-day it listens to the prophets of humanity, and it sees much real benevolence actually carried out. But the result is infinitesimal. Nothing comes of it; it does not satisfy the individual heart. The world at large continues untouched and indifferent—first because its common sense is not convinced, and secondly because its secret aspirations are in no degree satisfied. So that it is not altogether the world's fault if it is stolid. Everything has been tried and found wanting. Men rushed in crowds to the gold-diggings of California, to the Australian 'finds;' and in like manner, if any real spiritual or ideal good were proffered, crowds would rush to participate in it. Nothing yet has been given but empty words, and these so-called 'goods' have proved as tasteless, and as much Dead Sea apples, as the apples of vice; perhaps even more bitter than the regrets of vice. Though I cannot name the ideal good, it seems to me that it will be in some way closely associated with the ideal beauty of nature.

THE brown Barle River running over red rocks aslant
its course is pushed aside, and races round curving
slopes. The first shoot of the rapid is smooth and
polished like a gem by the lapidary's art, rounded and
smooth as a fragment of torso, and this convex undulation maintains a solid outline. Then the following
scoop under is furrowed as if ploughed across, and the
ridge of each furrow, where the particles move a little
less swiftly than in the hollow of the groove, falls backwards as foam blown from a wave. At the foot of the
furrowed decline the current rises over a rock in a broad
white sheet—white because as it is dashed to pieces the
air mingles with it. After this furious haste the stream
does but just overtake those bubbles which have been
carried along on another division of the water flowing
steadily but straight. Sometimes there are two streams
like this between the same banks, sometimes three or
even more, each running at a different rate, and each
gliding above a floor differently inclined. The surface
of each of these streams slopes in a separate direction,
and though under the same light they reflect it at vary-
ing angles. The river is animated and alive, rushing
here, gliding there, foaming yonder ; its separate and
yet component parallels striving together, and talking
loudly in incomplete sentences. Those rivers that move

through midland meads present a broad, calm surface, at the same level from side to side ; they flow without sound, and if you stood behind a thick hedge you would not know that a river was near. They dream along the meads, toying with their forget-me-nots, too idle even to make love to their flowers vigorously. The brown Barle enjoys his life, and splashes in the sunshine like boys bathing—like them he is sunburnt and brown. He throws the wanton spray over the ferns that bow and bend as the cool breeze his current brings sways them in the shade. He laughs and talks, and sings louder than the wind in his woods.

Here is a pool by the bank under an ash—a deep green pool inclosed by massive rocks, which the stream has to brim over. The water is green—or is it the ferns, and the moss, and the oaks, and the pale ash reflected ? This rock has a purple tint, dotted with moss spots almost black ; the green water laps at the purple stone, and there is one place where a thin line of scarlet is visible, though I do not know what causes it. Another stone the spray does not touch has been dried to a bright white by the sun. Inclosed, the green water slowly swirls round till it finds crevices, and slips through. A few paces farther up there is a red rapid— reddened stones, and reddened growths beneath the water, a light that lets the red hues overcome the others—a wild rush of crowded waters rotating as they go, shrill voices calling. This next bend upwards dazzles the eyes, for every inclined surface and striving parallel, every swirl, and bubble, and eddy, and rush around a rock chances to reflect the sunlight. Not one long pathway of quiet sheen, such as stretches across a rippled lake, each wavelet throwing back its ray in just proportion, but a hundred separate mirrors vibrating, each inclined at a different angle, each casting a tremulous flash into the face. The eyelids involuntarily droop to shield the gaze from a hundred arrows; they are too strong—nothing can be distinguished but a woven surface of brilliance, a mesh of light, under which the water runs, itself invisible. I will go back to the deep green pool, and walking now with the sun behind, how the river has changed!

Soft, cool shadows reach over it, which I did not see before; green surfaces are calm under trees; the rocks are less hard; the stream runs more gently, and the oaks come down nearer; the delicious sound of the rushing water almost quenches my thirst. My eyes have less work to do to meet the changing features of the current which now seems smooth as my glance accompanies its movement. The sky, which was not noticed before, now appears reaching in rich azure across the deep hollow, from the oaks on one side to the oaks on the other. These woods, which cover the steep and rocky walls of the gorge from river to summit, are filled with the June colour of oak. It is not green, nor russet, nor yellow; I think it may be called a glow of yellow under green. It is warmer than green; the glow is not on the outer leaves, but comes up beneath from the depth of the branches. The rush of the river soothes the mind, the broad descending surfaces of yellow-green oak carry the glance downwards from the blue over to the stream in the hollow. Rush! rush!— it is the river, like a mighty wind in the wood. A pheasant crows, and once and again falls the tap, tap of woodmen's axes—scarce heard, for they are high above. They strip the young oaks of their bark as far as they can while the saplings stand, then fell them, and as they all lie downhill there are parallel streaks of buff (where the sap has dried) **drawn** between the yellow-green masses of living leaf. The pathway winds in among the trees at the base of the rocky hill; light green whortleberries fill every interstice, bearing tiny red globes of flower — flower-lamps — open at the top. Wood-sorrel lifts its delicate veined petals; the leaf is rounded like the shadow of a bubble on a stone under clear water. I like to stay by the wood-sorrel a little while—it is so chastely beautiful; like the purest verse, it speaks to the inmost heart. Staying, I hear unconsciously — listen! Rush! rush! like a mighty wind in the wood.

It draws me on to the deep green pool inclosed about by rocks—a pool to stand near and think into. The purple rock, dotted with black moss; the white rock; the thin scarlet line; the green water; the overhanging tree; the verdant moss upon the bank; the lady fern—are there still. But I see also now a little pink somewhere in the water, much brown too, and shades I know no name for. The water is not green, but holds in solution three separate sets of colours. The confervæ on the stones, the growths beneath at the bottom waving a little as the water swirls like minute seaweeds—these are brown and green and somewhat reddish too. Under water the red rock is toned and paler, but has deep black cavities. Next, the surface, continually changing as it rotates, throws back a different light, and thirdly, the oaks' yellow-green high up, the pale ash, the tender ferns drooping over low down confer their tints on the stream. So from the floor of the pool, from the surface, and from the adjacent bank, three sets of colours mingle. Washed together by the slow swirl, they produce a shade—the brown of the Barle—lost in darkness where the bank overhangs.

Following the current downwards at last the river
for a while flows in quietness, broad and smooth. A
trout leaps for a fly with his tail curved in the air, full a
foot out of water. Trout watch behind sunken stones,
and shoot to and fro as insects droop in their flight and
appear about to fall. So clear is the water and so
brightly illuminated that the fish are not easily seen—
for vision depends on contrast—but in a minute I find a
way to discover them by their shadows. The black
shadow of a trout is distinct upon the bottom of the
river, and guides the eye to the spot; then looking higher
in the transparent water there is the fish. It was curious
to see these black shadows darting to and fro as if themselves animated and without bodies, for if the trout
darted before being observed the light concealed him in
motion. Some of the trout came up from under Torre-
steps, a singular structure which here connects the
shores of the stream. Every one has seen a row of
stepping-stones across a shallow brook ; now pile other
stones on each of these, forming buttresses, and lay flat
stones like unhewn planks from buttress to buttress, and
you have the plan of this primitive bridge. It has a
megalithic appearance, as if associated with the age of
rude stone monuments. They say its origin is doubtful;
there can be no doubt of the loveliness of the spot. The
Barle comes with his natural rush and fierceness under
the unhewn stone planking, then deepens, and there
overhanging a black pool—for the shadow was so deep
as to be black—grew a large bunch of marsh-marigolds
in fullest flower, the broad golden cups almost resting
on the black water. The bridge is not intended for
wheels, and though it is as firm as the rock, foot passengers have to look at their steps, as the great planks,
flecked with lichen at the edges, are not all level. The

horned sheep and lambs go over it—where do they not go? Like goats they wander everywhere.

In a cottage some way up the hill we ate clotted cream and whortleberry jam. Through the open door came the ceaseless rush! rush! like a wind in the wood. The floor was of concrete, lime and sand; on the open hearth—pronounced 'airth'—sods of turf cut from the moor and oak branches were smouldering under the chimney crook. Turf smoke from the piled-up fires of winter had darkened the beams of the ceiling, but from that rude room there was a view of the river, and the hill, and the oaks in full June colour, which the rich would envy. Sometimes in early morning the wild red deer are seen feeding on the slope opposite. As we drove away in reckless Somerset style, along precipices above the river, with nothing but a fringe of fern for parapet, the oak woods on the hills under us were shading down into evening coolness of tint, the yellow less warm, the green more to the surface. Upon the branches of the trees moss grows, forming a level green top to the round bough like a narrow cushion along it, with frayed edges drooping over each side. Though moss is common on branches, it does not often make a raised cushion, thick, as if green velvet pile were laid for the birds to run on. There were rooks' nests in some tall ash trees; the scanty foliage left the nests exposed, they were still occupied by late broods. Rooks' nests are not often seen in ashes as in elms.

By a mossy bank a little girl—a miniature Audrey —stout, rosy, and ragged, stood with a yellow straw hat aslant on her yellow hair, eating the leaves from a spray of beech in her hand. Audrey looked at us, eating the beech leaves steadily, but would not answer, not even 'Where's your father to?' For in Somerset the 'to' is put last, and must never be omitted; thus, instead of saying 'I bought this at Taunton,' it is correct to say 'I bought this to Taunton.' There are models under glass cases in places of entertainment with a notice to say that if a penny be inserted the machine will go. Audrey the Little would not speak, but when a penny was put in her hand she began to move, and made off for home with the treasure. The road turned and turned, but whichever way the Barle was always under us, and the red rock rose high at the side. This rock fractures aslant if worked, vast flakes come out, and the cleavage is so natural that until closely approached a quarry appears a cliff. Stone got out in squares, or cut down straight, leaves an artificial wall; these rocks cannot be made to look artificial, and if painted a quarry would be certainly quite indistinguishable from a natural precipice. Entering a little town (Dulverton) the road is jammed tight between cottages: so narrow is the lane that foot passengers huddle up in doorways to avoid the touch of the wheels, and the windows of the houses are protected by iron bars like cages lest the splash-boards should crack the glass. Nowhere in closest-built London is there such a lane—one would imagine land to be dear indeed. The farm labourers, filing homewards after their day's work, each carry poles of oak or fagots on their shoulders for their hearths, generally oak branches; it is their perquisite. The oak somehow takes root among the interstices of the stones of this rocky land. Past the houses the rush! rush! of the brown Barle rises again in the still evening air.

From the Devon border I drifted like a leaf detached from a tree, across to a deep coombe in the Quantock Hills. The vast hollow is made for repose and lotus-eating; its very shape, like a hammock, indicates idleness. There

the days go over noiselessly and without effort, like
white summer clouds. Ridges each side rise high and
heroically steep—it would be proper to set out and climb
them, but not to-day, not now : some time presently.
To the left massive Will's Neck stands out in black
shadow defined and distinct, like a fragment of night in
the bright light of the day. The wild red deer lie there,
but the mountain is afar ; a sigh is all I can give to it
for the Somerset sun is warm and the lotus sweet.
Yonder, if the misty heat moves on, the dim line of
Dunkery winds along the sky, not unlike the curved back
of a crouching hare. The weight of the mountains is too
great—what is the use of attempting to move ? It is
enough to look at them. The day goes over like a white
cloud ; as the sun declines it is pleasant to go into the
orchard—the vineyard of Somerset, and then perhaps
westward may be seen a light in the sky by the horizon
as if thrown up from an immense mirror under. The
mirror is the Severn sea, itself invisible at this depth,
but casting a white glow up against the vapour in the
air. By it you may recognise the nearness of the sea.
The thumb-nail ridges of the Quantocks begin to grow
harder, they carry the eye along on soft curves like those
of the South Downs in Sussex, but suddenly end in a
flourish and point as if cut out with the thumb-nail.
Draw your thumb-nail firmly along soft wood, and it will,
by its natural slip, form such a curve. Blackbird and
thrush commence to sing as the heavy heat decreases ;
the bloom on the apple trees is loose now, and the blackbird as he springs from the bough shakes down flakes of
blossom.

Towards even a wind moves among the lengthening
shadows, and my footsteps involuntarily seek the glen,
where a streamlet trickles down over red flat stones which

resound musically as the water strikes them. Ferns are growing so thickly in the hedge that soon it will seem composed of their fronds ; the first June rose hangs above their green tips. A water-ousel with white breast rises and flies on ; again disturbed, he makes a circle, and returns to the stream behind. On the moist earth there is the print of a hare's pad ; here is a foxglove out in flower ; and now as the incline rises heather thickens on the slope. Sometimes we wander beside the streamlet which goes a mile into the coombe—the shadow is deep and cool in the vast groove of the hill, the shadow accumulates there, and is pressed by its own weight— up slowly as far as the 'sog,' or peaty place where the spring rises, and where the sundew grows. Sometimes climbing steep and rocky walls—scarce sprinkled with grass—we pause every other minute to look down on the great valley which reaches across to Dunkery. The horned sheep, which are practically wild, like wild creatures, have worn out holes for themselves to lie in beside the hill. If resolution is strong, we move through the dark heather (soon to be purple), startling the heath-poults, or black game, till at last the Channel opens, and the far-distant Flat and Steep Holms lie, as it looks, afloat on the dim sea. This is labour enough ; stern indeed must be the mind that could work at summer's noon in Somerset, when the apple vineyards slumber ; when the tall foxgloves stand in the heavy heat and the soft air warms the deepest day-shadow so that nothing is cool to the touch but the ferns. Is there anything so good as to do nothing ?

Fame travels slowly up these breathless hills, and pauses overcome in the heated hollow lanes. A famous wit of European reputation, when living, resided in Somerset. A traveller one day chancing to pass through the very next parish inquired of a local man if somebody called Sydney Smith did not once live in that neighbourhood. 'Yes,' was the reply, 'I've heard all about Sydney Smith ; I can tell you. He was a highwayman, and was hung on that hill there.' He would have shown the very stump of the gallows-tree as proof positive, like Jack Cade's bricks, alive in the chimney to this day.

There really was a highwayman, however, whose adventures are said to have suggested one of the characters in the romance of 'Lorna Doone.' This desperate fellow had of course his houses of call, where he could get refreshment safely, on the moors. One bitter winter's day the robber sat down to a hearty dinner in an inn at Exford. Placing his pistols before him, he made himself comfortable, and ate and drank his fill. By-and-by an old woman entered, and humbly took a seat in a corner far from the fire. In time the highwayman observed the wretched, shivering creature, and of his princely generosity told her to come and sit by the hearth. The old woman gladly obeyed, and crouched beside him. Presently, as he sat absorbed in his meal, his arms were suddenly pinioned from behind. The old woman had him tight, so that he could not use his weapons, while at a call constables, who had been posted about, rushed in and secured him. The old woman was in fact a man in disguise. A relation of the thief-taker still lives and tells the tale. The highwayman's mare, mentioned in the novel, had been trained to come at his call, and was so ungovernable that they shot her.

Such tracts of open country, moors, and unenclosed hills were the haunts of highwaymen till a late period, and memories of the gallows, and of escapes from them,

are common. A well-to-do farmer who used to attend
Bristol market, and dispose there of large quantities
of stock and produce, dared not bring home the money
himself lest he should be robbed. He entrusted the
cash to his drover ; the farmer rode along the roads, the
drover made short cuts on foot, and arrived safely with
the money. This went on for years, in which time the
honest fellow—a mere labourer—carried some thousands of pounds for his master, faithfully delivering every
shilling. He had, however, a little failing—a dangerous
one in those days, when the gallows was the punishment
for sheep-stealing. He was known to be a sheep-stealer,
and actually after bringing home a hundred pounds would
go and put his neck in danger the very same night by
taking a sheep. This went on for some time, people
shut their eyes, but at last patience was exhausted, and
efforts were made to catch him in the act, without
success.

One night he came home in the usual manner from
market, delivered the cash, and went to his cottage.
Next day a little girl was sent on an innocent errand to
the cottage, with orders while she was there to look
sharply round and observe if there were any ashes on
the floor. She came back with the news that there was
a heap of wood ashes. Immediately a posse set out, and
the drover was arrested. The use of the ashes by sheep-
stealers was to suck up and remove stains of blood,
which were certain to be left in cutting up the animal.
Sufficient proof was found in the cottage to condemn
the honest thief to be hung ; great exertions were, however, made in his behalf ; and principally, it is supposed,
on account of his character for carrying large sums of
money untouched, he was saved. There is a story of the
smugglers—once notorious folk on these hills—teaching

their horses to understand the usual words of command backwards. If they were driving pack-horses along at night with a load of brandy landed from a lugger, and were met by the revenue men, who ordered them to stop that the packs might be searched, the smugglers, like good and loyal subjects, called 'Whoa! whoa!' Instantly the horses set off at a tearing gallop, for they understood 'Whoa!' as 'Gee-up!'

By a farmer's door I found a tall branch of oak lying against the porch. The bark was dry, and the leaves were shrivelled, but the bough had been originally taken green from the tree. These boughs are discovered against the door on the morning of the 29th of May, and are in memory of the escape of King Charles from his enemies by hiding in an oak. The village ringers leave them, and then go to the church and ring a peal, for which they expect cider or small coin from each loyal person honoured with an oak branch. Another custom, infinitely more ancient, is that of singing to the apple trees in early spring, so that the orchards may be induced to bear a good crop. The singers come round and visit each orchard; they have a rhyme specially for the purpose, part of the refrain of which is that a cup of good cider cannot do any one harm—a hint which brings out a canful. In strange contrast to these genial customs, which accord so well with flowery fields, I heard an instance of the coldest indifference. An old couple lived for many years in a cottage; at last the wife died, and the husband, while the body was in the house, had his meals on the coffin as a table.

A hundred years since, before steam, the corn was threshed out by the flail—a slow, and consequently expensive process. Many efforts were made to thresh quicker. Among others, wooden machines were put up in some of the villages, something resembling a water-wheel placed horizontally. This was moved by horses walking round and round, and drove machinery in the barn by belt or shafting. The labourers, greatly incensed—for they regarded threshing by the flail as their right—tried to burn them, but the structures were guarded and still exist. Under the modern conditions of farming they are still found useful to cut chaff, crack corn, and so on. The ancient sickle is yet in use for reaping in Somerset; the reapers sharpen it by drawing the edge through an apple, when the acid bites and cleans the steel. While we were sauntering through a village one morning, out rushed the boys from school, and instantly their tongues began to wag of those things on which their hearts were set. 'I know a jay's nest,' said one; 'I know an owl's nest,' cried a second; a third hastened to claim knowledge of a pigeon's nest. It will be long before education drives the natural love of the woods out of the children's hearts. Of old time a village school used to be held in an ancient building, the lower part of which was occupied as almshouses. Underneath the ancient folk lived as best they might, while the young folk learned and gave their class responses, or romped on the floor overhead. The upper part of the building belonged to one owner, the lower part to another landlord. It came about that the roof decayed and the upper owner suggested to the lower owner that they should agree in bearing the cost of repairs. Upon which the owner of the basement remarked that he contemplated *pulling his part down.*

In these hamlets along the foot of the hills ancient stone crosses are often found. One of them has retained its top perfect, and really is a cross, not a shaft only. This is, I think, rare. Sometimes in the village street, the slender column grey against the green trees, sometimes in the churchyard, these crosses come on the mind like a sudden enigma. It requires an effort to grasp their meaning, so long have the ideas passed away which led to their erection. They almost startle modern thought. How many years since the peasant women knelt at their steps ! On the base of one which has a sculptured shaft the wall-rue fern was growing. A young starling was perched on the yew by it ; he could but just fly, and fluttered across to the sill of the church window. Young birds called pettishly for food from the bushes. Upon the banks hart's-tongue was coming up fresh and green, and the early orchis was in flower. Fern and flower and fledglings had come again as they have come every year since the oldest of these ancient shafts was erected, for life is older, life is greyer, than the weather-beaten mouldings. But life, too, is fresh and young ; the stern thought in the stone becomes more cold and grim as the centuries pass away. In the crevices at the foot of another cross wallflowers blossomed, and plants of evening primrose, not yet in flower, were growing. Under a great yew lay the last decaying beam of the stocks. A little yew tree grew on the top of the church tower, its highest branch just above the parapet. A thrush perhaps planted it—thrushes are fond of the viscous yew berries. Through green fields, in which the grass was rising high and sweet, a footpath took me by a solitary mill with an undershot wheel. The sheds about here are often supported on round columns of stone. Beyond the mill is a pleasant meadow, quiet, still, and sunlit ; buttercup, sorrel, and daisy flowered among the grasses down to the streamlet, where comfrey, with white and pink-lined bells, stood at the water's edge. A renowned painter, Walker, who died early, used to work in this meadow : the original scene from which he took his picture of *The Plough* is not far distant. The painter is gone ; the grasses and the flowers are renewed with the summer. As I stood by the brook a water-rat came swimming, drawing a large dock-leaf in his mouth ; seeing me, he dived, and took the leaf with him under water.

Everywhere wild strawberries were flowering on the banks—wild strawberries have been found ripe in January here ; everywhere ferns were thickening and extending, foxgloves opening their bells. Another deep coombe led me into the mountainous Quantocks, far below the heather, deep beside another trickling stream. In this land the sound of running water is perpetual, the red flat stones are resonant, and the speed of the stream draws forth music like quick fingers on the keys ; the sound of running water and the pleading voice of the willow-wren are always heard in summer. Among the oaks growing on the steep hill-side the willow-wrens repeated their sweet prayer ; the water as it ran now rose and now fell ; there was a louder note as a little stone was carried over a fall. The shadow came slowly out from the oak-grown side of the coombe, it reached to the margin of the brook. Under the oaks there appears nothing but red stones, as if the trees were rooted in them ; under the boughs probably the grass does not cover the rock as it does on the opposite side. There mountain-ashes flowered in loose order on the green slope. Redstarts perched on them, darting out to seize passing insects. Still deeper in the coombe the oaks stood on either side of the stream ; it was the beginning of woods which reach for miles, in which occasionally the wild red deer wander, and drink at the clear waters. By now the shadow of the western hill-top had crossed

the brooklet, and the still coombe became yet more
silent. There was an alder, ivy-grown, beside the stream
—a tree with those lines which take an artist's fancy.
Under the roots of alders the water-ousel often creeps
by day, and the tall heron stalks past at night. Receding up the eastern slope of the coombe the sunlight
left the dark alder's foliage in the deep shadow of the
hollow. I went up the slope till I could see the sun,
and waited ; in a few minutes the shadow reached me,
and it was sunset ; I went still higher, and presently the
sun set again. A cool wind was drawing up the coombe,
it was dusky in the recesses of the oaks, and the water
of the stream had become dark when we emerged from
the great hollow, and yet without the summer's evening
had but just commenced, and the banks were still heated
by the sun.

In contrast to the hills and moors which are so open
and wild, the broad vales beneath are closely shut in
with hedges. The fields are all of moderate size, unlike
the great pastures elsewhere, so that the constant succession of hedges, one after the other, for ten, twenty, or
more miles, encloses the country as it were fivefold.
Most of the fields are square, or at all events right-
angled, unlike the irregular outline and corners of fields
in other counties. The number of meadows make it
appear as if the land was chiefly grass, though there is
really a fair proportion of arable. Over every green
hedge there seems a grassy mead ; in every hedge trees
are numerous, and their thick June foliage, green too,
gives a sense of green colour everywhere. But this is
relieved with red—the soil is red, and where the plough
has been the red furrows stand out so brightly as to
seem lifted a little from the level. These red squares
when on the side of rising ground show for many miles.

The stones are red that lie about, the road dust has a reddish tint, so have the walls of the cottages and mills. Where the banks of the hedges can be seen (or where rabbits have thrown out the earth) they are red, and the water in the ditches and streamlets looks red—it is in fact clear, and the colour is that of the sand and stones. The footpath winds a red band through the grass of the meads, and if it passes under a cliff the rock too rises aslant in red lines. Along the cropped hedges red campions flower so thickly as to take the place of green leaves, and by every gateway red foxgloves grow. Red trifolium is a favourite crop; it is not much redder than the land which bears it. The hues of the red ploughed squares, seen through the trees, vary as the sun dries or the rain moistens the colour. Then, again, the ferns as the summer advances bring forward their green to the aid of the leaves and grass, so that red and green constantly strive together.

There is a fly-rod in every house, almost every felt hat has gut and flies wound round it, and every one talks trout. Every one, too, complained that the rivers were so low it was difficult to angle. This circumstance, however, rendered the hues of the rocky banks more distinct. Sitting down to dinner by chance with two farmers, one began to tell me how he had beguiled three trout the previous evening; and the other described how, as he was walking in a field of his by the river, he had seen an otter. These creatures, which are becoming sadly scarce, if not indeed extinct in many counties, are still fairly numerous in the waters here. I hope they will long remain so, for although they certainly do destroy great numbers of fish, yet it must be remembered that in this country our list of wild animals has been gradually decreasing for centuries, and especially wild animals that show sport. The otter, I fear, is going; I hope the sportsmen of Somerset will see that it remains in their county, at all events, when it has become a tradition elsewhere. Otter hounds frequently visit the rivers, and first-rate sport is obtained. In these villages, two hundred miles from London, and often far from the rail, some of the conditions resemble those in the United States, where, instead of shops, 'stores' supply every article from one counter. So here you buy everything in one shop; it is really a 'store' in the American sense. A house which seems amid fields is called 'The Dragon;' you would suppose it an inn, but it is a shop, and has been so ever since the olden times when every trader put out a sign. The sign has gone, but the name remains.

Somewhere in a wood there is a stone, supposed to be a tombstone of the prophetess Mother Shipton, and bearing an undecipherable inscription. One of her rhymes is well remembered in the neighbourhood :—

> When Watchet is all washed down
> Williton shall be a seaport town.

This is founded on the gradual encroachment of the sea, which is a fact, but it will be some time yet before masts are seen at Williton.

At Dunster there is a curious mill which has two wheels, overshot, one in front of the other, and both driven by the same sluice. It was very hot as we stood by the wheels; the mill dust came forth and sprinkled the foliage so that the leaves seemed scarce able to breathe; it drifted almost to the stream hard by, where trout were watching under a cloud of midges dancing over the ripples. They look as if entangled in an inextricable maze, but if you let your eye travel, say to the right, as you would follow the flight of a bird, you find that one side of the current of insects flies up that way, and the other side returns. They go to and fro in regular order, exactly like the fashionable folk in Rotten Row, but the two ranks pass so quickly that looked at both together the vision cannot separate them, they are faster than the impression on the retina.

At Selworthy a footpath leads up through a wood on Selworthy Hill, and as it ascends, always at the side of the slope, gradually opens out what is perhaps the finest view of Dunkery Beacon, the Dunkery range, and that edge of Exmoor on to the shore of the sea. Across the deep vale the Exmoor mountains rise and reach on either hand, immense breadths of dark heather, deep coombes filled with black shadow, and rounded masses that look dry and heated. To the right is the gleaming sea, and the distant sound of the surge comes up to the wood. The headland and its three curves boldly project into the sunlit waters; from its foot many a gallant stag hard pressed by the hounds has swum out into the track of passing vessels. Selworthy Woods were still in the afternoon heat; except for the occasional rustle of a rabbit or of a pheasant, there was no evidence of life; the sound of the sea was faint and soon lost among the ferns. Slowly, very slowly, great Dunkery grew less hard of aspect, shadows drew along at the base, while again the declining sun from time to time sent his beams into valleys till now dark. The thatched house at Holnicote by the foot of Selworthy much interested me; it is one of the last of thatched houses inhabited by a gentleman and landed proprietor. Sir Thomas Acland, who resides here, is a very large owner. Thatch prevails on his estates; thatched cottages, thatched farmhouses, and his thatched mansion. In the coolness of the evening the birds began to sing and squirrels played across the lawn in front of Holnicote House. Humble-bees hummed in the grass and visited the flowers of the holly bushes. Thrushes sang, and chaffinches, and, sweetest of all, if simplest in notes, the greenfinches talked and courted in the trees. Two cuckoos called in different directions, wood-pigeons raised their voices in Selworthy Wood, and rooks went over cawing in their deliberate way. In the level meadow from among the tall grasses and white-flowering wild parsley a landrail called 'crake, crake,' ceaselessly. There was a sense of rest and quiet, and with it a joyousness of bird-life, such as should be about an English homestead.

AN ENGLISH DEER-PARK.

THERE is an old park wall which follows the highway
in all its turns with such fidelity of curve that for some
two miles it seems as if the road had been fitted to the
wall. Against it hawthorn bushes have grown up at
intervals, and in the course of years their trunks have
become almost timber. Ivy has risen round some of
these, and, connecting them with the wall, gives them
at a distance the appearance of green bastions. Large
stems of ivy, too, have flattened themselves upon the
wall, as if with arched back they were striving like athletes
to overthrow it. Mosses, brown in summer, soft green
in winter, cover it where there is shadow, and if pulled
up take with them some of the substance of the stone or
mortar like a crust. A dry, dusty fern may perhaps be
found now and then on the low bank at the foot—a fern
that would rather be within the park than thus open to
the heated south with the wall reflecting the sunshine
behind. On the other side of the road, over the thin
hedge, there is a broad plain of corn-fields. Coming
from these the labourers have found out, or made, notches
in the wall ; so that, by putting the iron-plated toes of
their boots in, and holding to the ivy, they can scale it
and shorten their long trudge home to the village. In
the spring the larks, passing from the green corn to the
pasture within, fluttering over with gently vibrating
wings and singing as they daintily go, sometimes settle

on the top. There too the yellowhammers stay. In the crevices blue tits build deep inside passages that abruptly turn, and baffle egg-stealers. Partridges come over with a whir, but just clearing the top, gliding on extended wings, which to the eye look like a slight brown crescent. The waggoners who go by know that the great hawthorn bastions are favourite resorts of wood-pigeons and missel-thrushes. The haws are ripe in autumn and the ivy berries in spring, so that the bastions yield a double crop. A mallow, the mauve petals of which even the dust of the road cannot impair, flowers here and there on the dry bank below, and broad moon-daisies among the ripe and almost sapless grass of midsummer.

If any one climbed the wall from the park and looked across at the plain of corn-fields in early spring, everywhere there would be seen brown dots in the air—above the first slender green blades ; above the freshly turned dark furrows ; above the distant plough, the share of which, polished like a silver mirror by friction with the clods, reflects the sunshine, flashing a heliograph message of plenty from the earth ; everywhere brown dots, and each a breathing creature—larks ceaselessly singing, and all unable to set forth their joy. Swift as is the vibration of their throats, they cannot pour the notes fast enough to express their eager welcome. As a shower falls from the sky, so falls the song of the larks. There is no end to them : they are everywhere ; over every acre away across the plain to the downs, and up on the highest hill. Every crust of English bread has been sung over at its birth in the green blade by a lark.

If one looked again in June, the clover itself, a treasure of beauty and sweetness, would be out, and the south wind would come over acres of flower—acres of clover, beans, tares, purple trifolium, far-away crimson sainfoin (brightest of all on the hills), scarlet poppies, pink convolvulus, yellow charlock, and green wheat coming into ear. In August, already squares would be cut into the wheat, and the sheaves rising, bound about the middle, hour-glass fashion ; some breadths of wheat yellow, some golden-bronze ; besides these, white barley and oats, and beans blackening. Turtle-doves would be in the stubble, for they love to be near the sheaves. The hills after or during rain look green and near ; on sunny days, a far and faint blue. Sometimes the sunset is caught in the haze on them and lingers, like a purple veil about the ridges. In the dusk hares come heedlessly along ; the elder-bushes gleam white with creamy petals through the night.

Sparrows and partridges alike dust themselves in the white dust, an inch deep, of midsummer, in the road between the wall and the corn—a pitiless Sahara road to traverse at noonday in July, when the air is still and you walk in a hollow way, the yellow wheat on one side and the wall on the other. There is shade in the park within, but a furnace of sunlight without—weariness to the eyes and feet from glare and dust. The wall winds with the highway and cannot be escaped. It goes up the slight elevations and down the slopes ; it has become settled down and bound with time. But presently there is a steeper dip, and at the bottom, in a narrow valley, a streamlet flows out from the wheat into the park. A spring rises at the foot of the down a mile away, and the channel it has formed winds across the plain. It is narrow and shallow ; nothing but a larger furrow, filled in winter by the rains rushing off the fields, and in summer a rill scarce half an inch deep. The wheat hides the channel completely, and as the wind blows, the tall ears bend over it. At the edge of the bank pink convolvulus twines round the stalks and the green-flowered buckwheat gathers several together. The sunlight cannot reach the stream, which runs in shadow, deep down below the wheat-ears, over which butterflies wander. Forget-me-nots flower under the banks; grasses lean on the surface; willow-herbs, tall and stiff, stand up; but out from the tangled and inter-laced fibres the water flows as clear as it rose by the hill. There is a culvert under the road, and on the opposite side the wall admits the stream by an arch jealously guarded by bars. In this valley the wall is lower and thicker and less covered at the top with ivy, so that where the road rises over the culvert you can see into the park. The stream goes rounding away through the sward, bending somewhat to the right, where the ground gradually descends. On the left side, at some distance, stands a row of full-grown limes, and through these there is a glimpse of the old manor-house. It is called the old house because the requirements of modern days have rendered it unsuitable for an establishment. A much larger mansion has been erected in another part of the park nearer the village, with a façade visible from the highway. The old manor-house is occupied by the land-steward, or, as he prefers to be called, the deputy-forester, who is also the oldest and largest tenant on the estate. It is he who rules the park. The labourers and keepers call him the 'squire.'

Now the old squire's favourite resort is the window-seat in the gun-room, because thence he can see a section of the highway, which, where it crosses the streamlet, comes within half a mile of the house. There the hollow and the lower wall permit any one at this window to obtain a view of the road on one of the sides of the valley. At this declivity it almost faces the house, and whether the passers-by are going to the market town, or returning to the village, they cannot escape observation. If they come from the town, the steep descent compels them to walk their horses down it; if from the village, they have a hard pull up. So the oaken window-seat in the gun-room is as polished and smooth as an old saddle; for if the squire is indoors, he is certain to be there. He often rests there after half an hour's work on one or other of the guns in the rack; for, though he seldom uses but one, he likes to take the locks to pieces upon a little bench which he has fitted up, and where he has a vice, tools, a cartridge-loading apparatus, and so forth, from which the room acquired its name. With the naked eye, however, as the road is half a mile distant, it is not possible to distinguish persons, except in cases of very pronounced individuality. Nevertheless old 'Ettles,' the keeper, always declared that he could see a hare run up the down from the park, say a mile and a half. This may be true; but in the gun-room there is a field-glass, said to have been used at the siege of Seringapatam, which the squire can bring to bear upon the road in an instant, for from constant use at the same focus there is a rim round the tarnished brass. No time, therefore, need be lost in trials; it can be drawn out to the well-known mark at once. The window itself is large, but there is a casement in it,—a lesser window,—which can be thrown open with a mere twist of the thumb on the button, and as it swings open it catches itself on a hasp. Then the field-glass examines the distant wayfarer.

When people have dwelt for generations in one place they come to know the history of their immediate world. There was not a waggon that went by without a meaning to the squire. One perhaps brought a load of wool

from the downs : it was old Hobbes's, whose affairs he
had known these forty years.   Another, with wheat, was
Lambourne's team : he lost heavily in 1879, the wet
year.   The family and business concerns of every man
of any substance were as well known to the squire as if
they had been written in a chronicle.   So, too, he knew
the family tendency, as it were, of the cottagers.   So
and So's lads were always tall, another's girls always
tidy.   If you employed a member of this family, you
were sure to be well served ; if of another, you were sure
to be cheated in some way.   Men vary like trees : an
ash sapling is always straight, the bough of an oak
crooked, a fir full of knots.   A man, said the squire,
should be straight like a gun.   This section of the highway gave him the daily news of the village as the daily
papers give us the news of the world.   About two
hundred yards from the window the row of limes began,
each tree as tall and large as an elm, having grown to
its full natural size.   The last of the row came very near
obstructing the squire's line of sight, and it once chanced
that some projecting branches by degrees stretched out
across his field of view.   This circumstance caused him
much mental trouble ; for, having all his life consistently
opposed any thinning out or trimming of trees, he did
not care to issue an order which would almost confess
a mistake.   Besides which, why only these particular
branches ?—the object would be so apparent.   The
squire, while conversing with Ettles, twice, as if unconsciously, directed his steps beneath these limes, and,
striking the offending boughs with his stick, remarked
that they grew extremely fast.   But the keeper, usually
so keen to take a hint, only answered that the lime was
the quickest wood to grow of which he knew.   In his
heart he enjoyed the squire's difficulty.   Finally the

squire, legalising his foible by recognising it, fetched a
ladder and a hatchet, and chopped off the boughs with
his own hands.

It was from the gun-room window that the squire
observed the change of the seasons and the flow of time.
The larger view he often had on horseback of miles of
country did not bring it home to him. The old familiar
trees, the sward, the birds, these told him of the advan-
cing or receding sun. As he reclined in the corner of
the broad window-seat, his feet up, and drowsy, of a
summer afternoon, he heard the languid cawing of an
occasional rook, for rooks are idle in the heated hours
of the day. He was aware, without conscious observation, of the swift, straight line drawn across the sky by
a wood-pigeon. The pigeons were continually to and
fro the cornfields outside the wall to the south and the
woods to the north, and their shortest route passed
directly over the limes. To the limes the bees went
when their pale yellow flowers appeared. Not many
butterflies floated over the short sward, which was fed
too close for flowers. The butterflies went to the old
garden, rising over the high wall as if they knew beforehand of the flowers that were within. Under the sun
the short grass dried as it stood, and with the sap went
its green. There came a golden tint on that part of the
wheat-fields which could be seen over the road. A few
more days—how few they seemed!—and there was a
spot of orange on the beech in a little copse near the
limes. The bucks were bellowing in the forest: as the
leaves turned colour their loves began and the battles
for the fair. Again a few days and the snow came, and
rendered visible the slope of the ground in the copse
between the trunks of the trees: the ground there was
at other times indistinct under brambles and withered

fern. The squire left the window for his arm-chair by
the fire; but if presently, as often happens when frost
quickly follows a snow-storm, the sun shone out and a
beam fell on the wall, he would get up and look out.
Every footstep in the snow contained a shadow cast by
the side, and the dazzling white above and the dark
within produced a blue tint. Yonder by the limes the
rabbits ventured out for a stray bunch of grass not quite
covered by the drift, tired, no doubt, of the bitter bark
of the ash-rods that they had nibbled in the night. As
they scampered, each threw up a white cloud of snow-
dust behind him. Yet a few days and the sward grew
greener. The pale winter hue, departing as the spring
mist came trailing over, caught for a while in the copse,
and, lingering there, the ruddy buds and twigs of the
limes were refreshed. The larks rose a little way to sing
in the moist air. A rook, too, perching on the top of a
low tree, attempted other notes than his monotonous
caw. So absorbed was he in his song that you might
have walked under him unnoticed. He uttered four or
five distinct sounds that would have formed a chant, but
he paused between each as if uncertain of his throat.
Then, as the sun shone, with a long-drawn 'ca-awk'
he flew to find his mate, for it would soon be time to
repair the nest in the limes. The butterflies came again
and the year was completed, yet it seemed but a few
days to the squire. Perhaps if he lived for a thousand
years, after a while he would wonder at the rapidity
with which the centuries slipped by.

By the limes there was a hollow—the little circular
copse was on the slope—and jays came to it as they
worked from tree to tree across the park. Their screech-
ing often echoed through the open casement of the gun-
room. A faint mark on the sward trended towards this

hollow ; it was a trail made by the squire, one of whose favourite strolls was in this direction. This summer morning, taking his gun, he followed the trail once more.

The grass was longer and coarser under the shadow of the limes, and upborne on the branches were numerous little sticks which had dropped from the rookery above. Sometimes there was an overthrown nest like a sack of twigs turned out on the turf, such as the hedgers rake together after fagoting. Looking up into the trees on a summer's day not a bird could be seen, till suddenly there was a quick 'jack-jack' above, as a daw started from his hole or from where the great boughs joined the trunk. The squire's path went down the hollow till it deepened into a thinly wooded coomb, through which ran the streamlet coming from the wheat-fields under the road. As the coomb opened, the squire went along a hedge near but not quite to the top. Years ago the coomb had been quarried for chalk, and the pits were only partly concealed by the bushes: the yellow spikes of wild mignonette flourished on the very hedge, and even half way down the precipices. From the ledge above, the eye could see into these and into the recesses between the brushwood. The squire's son, Mr. Martin, used to come here with his rook-rifle, for he could always get a shot at a rabbit in the hollow. They could not see him approach ; and the ball, if it missed, did no damage, being caught as in a bowl. Rifles in England, even when their range is but a hundred yards or so, are not to be used without caution. Some one may be in the hedge nutting, or a labourer may be eating his luncheon in the shelter ; it is never possible to tell who may be behind the screen of brambles through which the bullet slips so easily. Into these hollows Martin could shoot with safety. As for the squire, he did not approve of rifles. He adhered to his double-barrel ; and if a buck had to be killed, he depended on his smooth-bore to carry a heavy ball forty yards with fair accuracy. The fawns were knocked over with a wire cartridge unless Mr. Martin was in the way—he liked to try a rifle. Even in summer the old squire generally had his double-barrel with him—perhaps he might come across a weasel, or a stoat, or a crow. That was his excuse ; but, in fact, without a gun the woods lost half their meaning to him. With it he could stand and watch the buck grazing in the glade, or a troop of fawns— sweet little creatures—so demurely feeding down the grassy slope from the beeches. Already at midsummer the nuts were full formed on the beeches ; the green figs, too, he remembered were on the old fig-tree trained against the warm garden wall. The horse-chestnuts showed the little green knobs which would soon enlarge and hang all prickly, like the spiked balls of a holy-water sprinkle, such as was once used in the wars. Of old the folk, having no books, watched every living thing, from the moss to the oak, from the mouse to the deer ; and all that we know now of animals and plants is really founded upon their acute and patient observa-tion. How many years it took even to find out a good salad may be seen from ancient writings, wherein half the plants about the hedges are recommended as salad herbs : dire indeed would be our consternation if we had to eat them As the beech-nuts appear, and the horse-chestnuts enlarge, and the fig swells, the apples turn red and become visible in the leafy branches of the apple-trees. Like horses, deer are fond of apples, and in former times, when deer-stealing was possible, they were often decoyed with them.

There is no tree so much of the forest as the beech. On the verge of woods the oaks are far apart, the ashes thin ; the verge is like a wilderness and scrubby, so that the forest does not seem to begin till you have penetrated some distance. Under the beeches the forest begins at once. They stand at the edge of the slope, huge round boles rising from the mossy ground, wide fans of branches —a shadow under them, a greeny darkness beyond There is depth there—depth to be explored, depth to hide in. If there is a path, it is arched over like a tunnel with boughs ; you know not whither it goes. The fawns are sweetest in the sunlight, moving down from the shadow ; the doe best partly in shadow, partly in sun, when the branch of a tree casts its interlaced work, fine as Algerian silverwork, upon the back ; the buck best when he stands among the fern, alert, yet not quite alarmed—for he knows the length of his leap—his horns up, his neck high, his dark eye bent on you, and every sinew strung to spring away. One spot of sunlight, bright and white, falls through the branches upon his neck, a fatal place, or near it : a guide, that bright white spot, to the deadly bullet, as in old days to the cross-bow bolt. It was needful even then to be careful of the aim, for the herd, as Shakespeare tells us, at once recognised the sound of a cross-bow : the jar of the string, tight-strained to the notch by the goat's-foot lever, the slight whiz of the missile, were enough to startle them and to cause the rest to swerve and pass out of range. Yet the cross-bow was quiet indeed compared with the gun which took its place. The cross-bow was the beginning of shooting proper, as we now understand it ; that is, of taking an aim by the bringing of one point into a line with another. With the long-bow aim indeed was taken, but quite differently, for if the arrow were kept waiting with the string drawn, the eye and the hand would not go true together. The quicker the arrow left the bow the moment that it was full drawn, the better the result. On the other hand, the arblast was in no haste, but was adjusted deliberately—so deliberately that it gave rise to a proverb, 'A fool's bolt is soon shot.' This could not apply to the long-bow, with which the arrow was discharged swiftly, while an arblast was slowly brought to the level like a rifle. As it was hard to draw again, that added strength to the saying ; but it arose from the deliberation with which a good cross-bowman aimed. To the long-bow the cross-bow was the express rifle. The express delivers its bullet accurately point-blank— the bullet flies straight to its mark up to a certain distance. So the cross-bow bolt flew point-blank, and thus its application to hunting when the deer were really killed for their venison. The hunter stole through the fern, or crept about the thickets—thickets and fern exactly like those here to-day—or waited Indian-like in ambush behind an oak as the herd fed that way, and, choosing the finest buck, aimed his bolt so as either to slay at once or to break the fore-leg. Like the hare, if the fore-leg is injured, deer cannot progress ; if only the hind-quarter is hit, there is no telling how far they may go. Therefore the cross-bow, as enabling the hunter to choose the exact spot where his bolt should strike, became the weapon of the chase, and by its very perfection began the extermination of the deer. Instead of the hounds and the noisy hunt, any man who could use the cross-bow could kill a buck. The long-bow, of all weapons, requires the most practice, and practice begun in early youth. Some of the extraordinary feats attributed to the outlaws in the woods and to the archers of the ancient English army are quite possible, but must have necessitated the constant use of a bow from child-hood, so that it became second nature. But almost any man who has strength to set a cross-bow, with moderate practice, and any idea at all of shooting, could become a fairly good shot with it. From the cross-bow to a gun was a comparatively easy step, and it was the knowledge of the power of the one that led to the quick introduction of the other. For gunpowder was hardly discovered before hand-guns were thought of, and no discovery ever spread so swiftly. Then the arquebuse swept away the old English chase.

These deer exist by permission. They are pro-tected with jealous care; or rather they have been protected so long that by custom they have grown semi-consecrated, and it is rare for anyone to think of touch-ing them. The fawns wander, and a man, if he choose, might often knock one over with his axe as he comes home from his work. The deer browse up to the very skirts of the farmhouse below, sometimes even enter the rick-yard, and once now and then, if a gate be left open, walk in and eat the pease in the garden. The bucks are still a little wilder, a little more nervous for their liberty, but there is no difficulty in stalking them to within forty or fifty yards. They have either lost their original delicacy of scent, or else do not respond to it, as the approach of a man does not alarm them, else it would be necessary to study the wind; but you may get thus near them without any thought of the breeze—no nearer; then, bounding twice or thrice, lifting himself each time as high as the fern, the buck turns half towards you to see whether his retreat should or should not be continued.

The fawns have come out from the beeches, because there is more grass on the slope and in the hollow, where trees are few. Under the trees in the forest proper there is little food for them. Deer, indeed, seem fonder of half-open places than of the wood itself. Thickets, with fern at the foot and spaces of sward between, are their favourite haunts. Heavily timbered land and impenetrable underwood are not so much resorted to. The deer here like to get away from the retreats which shelter them, to wander in the half-open grounds on that part of the park free to them, or, if possible, if they see a chance, out into the fields. Once now and then a buck escapes, and is found eight or ten miles away. If the pale were removed how quickly the deer would leave the close forest which in imagination is so associated with them! It is not their ideal. They would rather wander over the hills and along the river valleys. The forest is, indeed, and always would be their cover, and its shadows their defence; but for enjoyment they would of choice seek the sweet herbage, which does not flourish where the roots of trees and underwood absorb all the richness of the soil. The farther the trees are apart the better the forest pleases them. Those great instinctive migrations of wild animals which take place annually in America are not possible in England. The deer here cannot escape—solitary individuals getting free of course, now and then; they cannot move in a body, and it is not easy to know whether any such desire remains among them. So far as I am aware, there is no mention of such migrations in the most ancient times; but the omission proves nothing, for before the Normans, before the game laws and parks together came into existence, no one who could write thought enough of the deer to notice their motions. The monks were engaged in chronicling the inroads of the pagans, or writing chronologies of the Roman Empire. On ana logical grounds it would seem quite possible that in their original state the English deer did move from part to part of the country with the seasons. Almost all the birds, the only really free things in this country now, move, even those that do not quit the island; and why not the deer in the old time when all the woods were open to them? England is not a large country, but there are considerable differences in the climate and the time at which vegetation appears, quite sufficient of themselves to induce animals to move from place to place. We have no narrowing buffalo zone to lament, for our buffalo zone disappeared long ago. These parks and woods are islets of the olden time, dotted here and there in the midst of the most modern agricultural scenery. These deer and their ancestors have been confined within the pale for hundreds of years, and though in a sense free, they are in no sense wild. But the old power remains still. See the buck as he starts away, and jumps at every leap as high as the fern. He would give the hounds a long chase yet.

The fern is fully four feet tall, hiding a boy entirely, and only showing a man's head. The deer do not go through it unless startled; they prefer to follow a track already made, one of their own trails. It is their natural cover, and when the buckhounds meet near London the buck often takes refuge in one or other of the fern-grown commons of which there are many on the southern side. But fern is inimical to grass, and, while it gives them cover, occupies the place of much more pleasant herbage. As their range is limited, though they have here a forest of some extent as well as the park to roam over, they cannot always obtain enough in winter. In frost, when the grass will not grow, or when snow is on the ground, that which they can find is supplemented with hay. They are, in fact, foddered exactly the same as cattle. In some of the smaller parks they are driven into inclosures and fed altogether. This is not the case here. Perhaps it was through the foggers, as the labourers are called who fodder cattle and carry out the hay in the morning and evening, that deer poachers of old discovered that they could approach the deer by carrying a bundle of sweet-smelling hay, which overcame the scent of the body and baffled the buck's keen nostrils till the thief was within shot. The foggers, being about so very early in the morning,—they are out at the dawn,—have found out a good many game secrets in their time. If the deer were outside the forest at any hour it was sure to be when the dew was on the grass, and thus they noticed that with the hay truss on their heads they could walk up quite close occasionally. Foggers know all the game on the places where they work; there is not a hare or a rabbit, a pheasant or a partridge, whose ways are not plain to them. There are no stories now of stags a century old (three would go back to Queen Elizabeth); they have gone, like other traditions of the forest, before steam and breechloader. Deer lore is all but extinct, the terms of venery known but to a few; few, indeed, could correctly name the parts of a buck if one were sent them. The deer are a picture only—a picture that lives and moves and is beautiful to look at, but must not be rudely handled. Still, they linger while the marten has disappeared, the polecat is practically gone, and the badger becoming rare. It is curious that the badger has lived on through sufferance for three centuries. Nearly three centuries ago, a chronicler observed that the badger would have been rooted out before his time had it not been for the parks. There was no great store of badgers then; there is no great store now. Sketches remain in old country-houses of the chase of the marten; you see the hounds all yelping round the foot of a tree, the marten up in it, and in the middle of the hounds the huntsman in top-boots and breeches. You can but smile at it. To Americans it must forcibly recall the treeing of a 'coon. The deer need keep no watch, there are no wolves to pull them down; and it is quite probable that the absence of any danger of that kind is the reason of their tameness even more than the fact that they are not chased by man. Nothing comes creeping stealthily through the fern, or hunts them through the night. They can slumber in peace. There is no larger beast of prey than a stoat, or a stray cat. But they retain their dislike of dogs, a dislike shared by cattle, as if they too dimly remembered a time when they had been hunted. The list of animals still living within the pale and still wild is short indeed. Besides the deer, which are not wild, there are hares, rabbits, squirrels, two kinds of rat,—the land and the water rat,—stoat, weasel, mole, and mouse. There are more varieties of mouse than of any other animal: these, the weakest of all, have escaped best, though exposed to so many enemies. A few foxes, and still fewer badgers, complete the list, for there are no other animals here. Modern times are fatal to all creatures of prey, whether furred or feathered; and so even the owls are less numerous, both in actual numbers and in variety of species, than they were even fifty years ago.

But the forest is not vacant. It is indeed full of happy life. Every hollow tree—and there are many hollow trees where none are felled—has its nest of starlings, or titmice, or woodpeckers. Woodpeckers are numerous, and amusing to watch. Wood-pigeons and turtle-doves abound, the former in hundreds nesting here. Rooks, of course, and jackdaws,—daws love hollow trees,—jays, and some magpies. The magpie is one of the birds which have partly disappeared from the fields of England. There are broad lands where not one is to be seen. Once looking from the road at two in a field, a gentleman who was riding by stopped his horse and asked, quite interested, 'Are those magpies?' I replied that they were. 'I have not seen any since I was a boy till now,' he said. Magpies are still plentiful in some places, as in old parks in Somersetshire, but they have greatly diminished in the majority of instances. There are some here, and many jays. These are handsome birds, and with the green woodpeckers give colour to the trees. Night-jars or fernowls fly round the outskirts and through the open glades in the summer twilight. These are some of the forest birds. The rest visit the forest or live in it, but are equally common to hedgerow and copse. Woodpeckers, jays, magpies, owls, night-jars, are all distinctly forest and park birds, and are continually with the deer. The lesser birds are the happier that there are fewer hawks and crows. The deer are not torn with the cruel tooth of hound or wolf, nor does the sharp arrow sting them. It is a little piece of olden England without its terror and bloodshed.

The fawns fed away down the slope and presently into one of the broad green open paths or drives, where the underwood on each side is lined with bramble and with trailing white rose, which loves to cling to bushes scarcely higher than itself. Their runners stretch out at the edges of the drive, so that from the underwood the mound of green falls aslant to the sward. This gradual descent from the trees and ash to the bushes of hawthorn,

from the hawthorn to the bramble, thence to the rose
and the grass, gives to the vista of the broad path a soft,
graceful aspect.

After the fawns had disappeared, the squire went on and
entered under the beeches from which they had emerged.
He had not gone far before he struck and followed a
path which wound between the beech trunks and was
entirely arched over by their branches. Squirrels raced
away at the sound of his footsteps, darting over the
ground and up the stems of the trees in an instant. A
slight rustling now and then showed that a rabbit had
been startled. Pheasants ran too, but noiselessly, and
pigeons rose from the boughs above. The wood-
pigeons rose indeed, but they were not much frightened,
and quickly settled again. So little shot at, they felt
safe, and only moved from habit.

He crossed several paths leading in various directions,
but went on, gradually descending till the gable end of
a farmhouse became visible through the foliage. The
old red tiles were but a few yards distant from the
boughs of the last beech, and there was nothing between the house and the forest but a shallow trench
almost filled with dead brown leaves and edged with
fern. Out from that trench, sometimes stealthily slipping
between the flattened fern-stalks, came a weasel, and,
running through the plantains and fringe-like mayweed
or stray pimpernel which covered the neglected ground,
made for the straw-rick. Searching about for mice, he
was certain to come across a hen's egg in some corner,
perhaps in a hay-crib, which the cattle, now being in
the meadow, did not use. Or a stronger stoat crept out
and attacked anything that he fancied. Very often
there was a rabbit sitting in the long grass which grows
round under an old hay-rick. He would sit still and let

anyone pass who did not know of his presence, but those who were aware used to give the grass a kick if they went that way, when he would carry his white tail swiftly round the corner of the rick. In winter hares came nibbling at everything in the garden, and occasionally in summer, if they fancied an herb: they would have spoiled it altogether if free to stay there without fear of some one suddenly appearing.

Dogs there were in plenty, but all chained, except a few mere puppies which practically lived indoors. It was not safe to have them loose so near the wood, the temptation to wander being so very strong. So that, though there was a continual barking and long, mournful whines for liberty, the wild creatures came in time to understand that there was little danger, and the rabbit actually sat under the hay-rick.

Pheasants mingled with the fowls, and, like the fowls, only ran aside out of the way of people. In early summer there were tiny partridge chicks about, which rushed under the coop. The pheasants sometimes came down to the kitchen door, so greedy were they. With the dogs and ponies, the pheasants and rabbits, the weasels and the stoats, and the ferrets in their hutches, the place seemed really to belong more to the animals than to the tenant.

The forest strayed indoors. Bucks' horns, feathers picked up, strange birds shot and stuffed, fossils from the sand-pits, coins and pottery from the line of the ancient Roman road, all the odds and ends of the forest, were scattered about within. To the yard came the cows, which, with bells about their necks, wandered into the fern, and the swine, which searched and rooted about for acorns and beech-mast in autumn. The men who dug in the sand-pits or for gravel came this way in

and out to their labour, and so did those who split up
the fallen trunks into logs. Now and then a woodpecker
came with a rush up from the meadows, where he had
been visiting the hedgerows, and went into the forest
with a yell as he entered the trees. The deer fed up to
the precincts, and at intervals a buck at the dawn got
into the garden. But the flies from the forest teased
and terrified the horses, which would have run away
with the heavily loaded waggon behind them if not pro-
tected with fine netting as if in armour. They did run
away sometimes at harrow, tearing across the field like
mad things. You could not keep the birds out of the
garden, try how you would. They had most of the
sowings up. The blackbirds pecked every apple in the
orchard. How the dead leaves in autumn came whirling
in thousands through rick-yard and court in showers
upon the tiles! Nor was it of much avail to sweep them
away; they were there again to-morrow, and until the
wind changed. The swallows were now very busy
building; there were not many houses for them, and
therefore they flocked here. Up from over the meadows
came the breeze, drawing into the hollow recesses of the
forest behind. It came over the grass and farther away
over corn just yellowing, the shadows of the clouds racing
with it and instantly lost in the trees. It drew through
the pillars of the forest, and away to the hills beyond.

The squire's ale was duly put for him, the particular
gossip he liked was ready for him; and having taken
both, he looked at his old watch and went on. His
path now led for a while just inside the pale, which here
divided the forest from the meadows. In the olden
time it would have been made of oak, for they built all
things then with an eye to endurance; but it was now
of fir, pitched, sawn from firs thrown in the copses. For

the purpose of keeping the deer in, it was as useful as the pale of oak. Oak is not so plentiful nowadays. The high spars were the especial vaunting-places of the little brown wrens which perched there and sang, in defiance of all that the forest might hold. Rabbits crept under, but the hares waited till evening and went round by the gates. Presently the path turned and the squire passed a pond partly dried up, from the margin of which several pigeons rose up, clattering their wings. They are fond of the neighbourhood of water, and are sure to be there some time during the day. The path went upwards, but the ascent was scarcely perceptible through hazel bushes, which became farther apart and thinner as the elevation increased, and the soil was less rich. Some hawthorn bushes succeeded, and from among these he stepped out into the open park. Nothing could be seen of the manor-house here. It was hidden by the roll of the ground and the groups of trees. The close sward was already a little brown—the trampling of hoofs as well as the heat causes the brownish hue of fed sward, as if it were bruised. He went out into the park, bearing somewhat to the right and passing many hawthorns, round the trunks of which the grass was cut away in a ring by the hoofs of animals seeking shadow. Far away on a rising knoll a herd of deer were lying under some elms. In front were the downs, a mile or so distant; to the right, meadows and corn-fields, towards which he went. There was no house nor any habitation in view; in the early part of the year, the lambing-time, there was a shepherd's hut on wheels in the fields, but it had been drawn away.

According to tradition, there is no forest in England in which a king has not hunted. A king, they say, hunted here in the old days of the cross-bow; but

happily the place escaped notice in that artificial era
when half the parks and woods were spoiled to make
the engraver's ideal landscape of straight vistas, broad
in the foreground and narrowing up to nothing. Wide,
straight roads—you can call them nothing else—were
cut through the finest woods, so that upon looking from
a certain window, or standing at a certain spot in the
grounds, you might see a church tower at the end of
the cutting, In some parks there are half a dozen such
horrors shown to you as a great curiosity ; some have a
monument or pillar at the end. These hideous dis-
figurements of beautiful scenery should surely be wiped
out in our day. The stiff, straight cutting could soon
be filled up by planting, and after a time the woods
would resume their natural condition. Many common
highway roads are really delightful, winding through
trees and hedgerows, with glimpses of hills and distant
villages. But these planned, straight vistas, radiating
from a central spot as if done with ruler and pen, at
once destroy the pleasant illusion of primeval forest.
You may be dreaming under the oaks of the chase or
of Rosalind : the moment you enter such a vista all
becomes commonplace. Happily this park escaped,
and it is beautiful. Our English landscape wants no
gardening : it *cannot* be gardened. The least interference kills it. The beauty of English woodland and
country is in its detail. There is nothing empty and
unclothed. If the clods are left a little while undis-
turbed in the fields, weeds spring up and wild-flowers
bloom upon them. Is the hedge cut and trimmed, lo !
the bluebells flower the more and a yet fresher green
buds forth upon the twigs. Never was there a garden
like the meadow : there is not an inch of the meadow
in early summer without a flower. Old walls, as we

saw just now, are not left without a fringe; on the top of the hardest brick wall, on the sapless tiles, on slates, stonecrop takes hold and becomes a cushion of yellow bloom. Nature is a miniature painter and handles a delicate brush, the tip of which touches the tiniest spot and leaves something living. The park has indeed its larger lines, its broad open sweep, and gradual slope, to which the eye accustomed to small inclosures requires time to adjust itself. These left to themselves are beautiful; they are the surface of the earth, which is always true to itself and needs no banks nor artificial hollows. The earth is right and the tree is right: trim either and all is wrong. The deer will not fit to them then.

The squire came near enough to the corn-field to see that the wheat-ears were beginning to turn yellow and that the barley had the silky appearance caused by the beard, the delicate lines of which divide the light and reflect it like gossamer. At some distance a man was approaching; he saw him, and sat down on the grass under an oak to await the coming of Ettles the keeper. Ettles had been his rounds and had visited the outlying copses, which are the especial haunts of pheasants. Like the deer, pheasants, if they can, will get away from the main wood. He was now returning, and the squire, well knowing that he would pass this way, had purposely crossed his path to meet him. The dogs ran to the squire and at once made friends with him. Ettles, whose cheek was the colour of the oak-apples in spring, was more respectful: he stood till the squire motioned him to sit down. The dogs rolled on the sward, but, though in the shadow, they could not extend themselves sufficiently nor pant fast enough. Yonder the breeze that came up over the forest on its way to the downs blew through the group of trees on the knoll, cooling the deer as it passed.

MY OLD VILLAGE.

'JOHN BROWN is dead,' said an aged friend and visitor in answer to my inquiry for the strong labourer.

'Is he really dead?' I asked, for it seemed impossible.

'He is. He came home from his work in the evening as usual, and seemed to catch his foot in the threshold and fell forward on the floor. When they picked him up he was dead.'

I remember the doorway; a raised piece of wood ran across it, as is commonly the case in country cottages, such as one might easily catch one's foot against if one did not notice it; but he knew that bit of wood well. The floor was of brick, hard to fall on and die. He must have come down over the crown of the hill, with his long slouching stride, as if his legs had been half pulled away from his body by his heavy boots in the furrows when a ploughboy. He must have turned up the steps in the bank to his cottage, and so, touching the threshold, ended. He is gone through the great doorway, and one pencil-mark is rubbed out. There used to be a large hearth in that room, a larger room than in most cottages; and when the fire was lit, and the light shone on the yellowish red brick beneath and the large rafters overhead, it was homely and pleasant. In summer the door was always wide open. Close by on the high bank there was a spot where the first wild violets came. You might look along miles of hedgerow, but there were never any until they had shown by John Brown's.

If a man's work that he has done all the days of his life could be collected and piled up around him in visible shape, what a vast mound there would be beside some ! If each act or stroke was represented, say by a brick, John Brown would have stood the day before his ending by the side of a monument as high as a pyramid. Then if in front of him could be placed the sum and product of his labour, the profit to himself, he could have held it in his clenched hand like a nut, and no one would have seen it. Our modern people think they train their sons to strength by football and rowing and jumping, and what are called athletic exercises ; all of which it is the fashion now to preach as very noble, and likely to lead to the goodness of the race. Certainly feats are accomplished and records are beaten, but there is no real strength gained, no hardihood built up. Without hardihood it is of little avail to be able to jump an inch farther than somebody else. Hardihood is the true test, hardihood is the ideal, and not these caperings or ten minutes' spurts.

Now, the way they made the boy John Brown hardy was to let him roll about on the ground with naked legs and bare head from morn till night, from June till December, from January till June. The rain fell on his head, and he played in wet grass to his knees. Dry bread and a little lard was his chief food. He went to work while he was still a child. At half-past three in the morning he was on his way to the farm stables, there to help feed the cart-horses, which used to be done with great care very early in the morning. The carter's whip used to sting his legs, and sometimes he felt the butt. At fifteen he was no taller than the sons of well-to-do people at eleven ; he scarcely seemed to grow at all till he was eighteen or twenty, and even then very slowly, but at last became a tall big man. That slouching walk, with knees always bent, diminished his height to appearance ; he really was the full size, and every inch of his frame had been slowly welded together by this ceaseless work, continual life in the open air, and coarse hard food. This is what makes a man hardy. This is what makes a man able to stand almost anything, and gives a power of endurance that can never be obtained by any amount of gymnastic training.

I used to watch him mowing with amazement. Sometimes he would begin at half-past two in the morning, and continue till night. About eleven o'clock, which used to be the mowers' noon, he took a rest on a couch of half-dried grass in the shade of the hedge. For the rest, it was mow, mow, mow for the long summer day.

John Brown was dead : died in an instant at his cottage door. I could hardly credit it, so vivid was the memory of his strength. The gap of time since I had seen him last had made no impression on me ; to me he was still in my mind the John Brown of the hayfield ; there was nothing between then and his death.

He used to catch us boys the bats in the stable, and tell us fearful tales of the ghosts he had seen ; and bring the bread from the town in an old-fashioned wallet, half in front and half behind, long before the bakers' carts began to come round in country places. One evening he came into the dairy carrying a yoke of milk, staggering, with tipsy gravity ; he was quite sure he did not want any assistance, he could pour the milk into the pans. He tried, and fell at full length and bathed himself from head to foot. Of later days they say he worked in the town a good deal, and did not look so well or so happy as on the farm. In this cottage opposite the violet bank they had small-pox once, the only case I recollect in the hamlet—the old men used to say everybody had it when they were young ; this was the only case in my time, and they recovered quickly without any loss, nor did the disease spread. A roomy well-built cottage like that, on dry ground, isolated, is the only hospital worthy of the name. People have a chance to get well in such places ; they have very great difficulty in the huge buildings that are put up expressly for them. I have a Convalescent Home in my mind at the moment, a vast building. In these great blocks what they call ventilation is a steady draught, and there is no ' home ' about it. It is all walls and regulations and draughts, and altogether miserable. I would infinitely rather see any friend of mine in John Brown's cottage. That terrible disease, however, seemed to quite spoil the violet bank opposite, and I never picked one there afterwards. There is something in disease so destructive, as it were, to flowers.

The hundreds of times I saw the tall chimney of that cottage rise out of the hill-side as I came home at all hours of the day and night ! the first chimney after a long journey, always comfortable to see, especially so in earlier days, when we had a kind of halting belief in John Brown's ghosts, several of which were dotted along that road according to him. The ghosts die as we grow older, they die and their places are taken by real ghosts. I wish I had sent John Brown a pound or two when I was in good health ; but one is selfish then, and puts off things till it is too late—a lame excuse verily. I can scarcely believe now that he is really dead, gone as you might casually pluck a hawthorn leaf from the hedge.

The next cottage was a very marked one, for houses grow to their owners. The low thatched roof had rounded itself and stooped down to fit itself to Job's shoulders ; the walls had got short and thick to suit him, and they had a yellowish colour, like his complexion, as if chewing tobacco had stained his cheeks right through. Tobacco juice had likewise penetrated and tinted the wall. It was cut off as it seemed by a party-wall into one room, instead of which there were more rooms beyond which no one would have suspected. Job had a way of shaking hands with you with his right hand, while his left hand was casually doing something else in a detached sort of way. 'Yes, sir,' and 'No, sir,' and nodding to everything you said all so complaisant, but at the end of the bargain you generally found yourself a few shillings in some roundabout manner on the wrong side. Job had a lot of shut-up rooms in his house and in his character, which never seemed to be opened to daylight. The eaves hung over and beetled like his brows, and he had a forelock, a regular antique forelock, which he used to touch with the greatest humility. There was a long bough of an elm hanging over one gable just like the forelock. His face was a blank, like the broad end wall of the cottage, which had no window—at least you might think so until you looked up and discovered one little arrow slit, one narrow pane, and woke with a start to the idea that Job was always up there watching and listening. That was how he looked out of his one eye so intensely cunning, the other being a wall eye—that is, the world supposed so, as he kept it half shut, always between the lights ; but whether it was really blind or not I cannot say. Job caught rats and rabbits and moles, and bought fagots or potatoes, or fruit or rabbit-skins, or rusty iron : wonderful how he seemed to have command of money. It was done probably by buying and selling almost simultaneously, so that the cash passed really from one customer to another, and was never his at all. Also he worked as a labourer, chiefly piecework; also Mrs. Job had a shop window about two feet square: snuff and tobacco, bread and cheese, immense big round jumbles and sugar, kept on the floor above, and reached down by hand, when wanted, through the opening for the ladder stairs. The front door—Job's right hand—was always open in summer, and the flagstones of the floor chalked round their edges; a clean table, clean chairs, decent crockery, an old clock about an hour slow, a large hearth with a minute fire to boil the kettle without heating the room. Tea was usually at half-past three, and it is a fact that many well-to-do persons, as they came along the road hot and dusty, used to drop in and rest and take a cup—very little milk and much gossip. Two paths met just there, and people used to step in out of a storm of rain, a sort of thatched house club. Job was somehow on fair terms with nearly everybody, and that is a wonderful thing in a village, where everybody knows everybody's business, and petty interests continually cross. The strangest fellow and the strangest way of life, and yet I do not believe a black mark was ever put against him; the shiftiness was all for nothing. It arose, no doubt, out of the constant and eager straining to gain a little advantage and make an extra penny. Had Job been a Jew he would have been rich. He was the exact counterpart of the London Jew dealer, set down in the midst of the country. Job should have been rich. Such immense dark brown jumbles, such cheek-distenders— never any French sweetmeats or chocolate or bonbons to equal these. I really think I could eat one now. The pennies and fourpenny bits—there were fourpenny bits in those days—that went behind that two-foot window, goodness! there was no end. Job used to chink them in a pint pot sometimes before the company, to give them an idea of his great hoards. He always tried to impress people with his wealth, and would talk of a fifty-pound contract as if it was nothing to him. Jumbles are eternal, if nothing else is. I thought then there was not such another shop as Job's in the universe. I have found since that there is a Job shop in every village, and in every street in every town—that is to say, a window for jumbles and rubbish; and if you don't know it, you may be quite sure your children do, and spend many a sly penny there. Be as rich as you may, and give them gilded sweetmeats at home, still they will slip round to the Job shop.

It was a pretty cottage, well backed with trees and bushes, with a south-east mixture of sunlight and shade, and little touches that cannot be suggested by writing. Job had not got the Semitic instinct of keeping. The art of acquisition he possessed to some extent, that was his right hand; but somehow the half-crowns slipped away through his unstable left hand, and fortune was a greasy pole to him. His left hand was too cunning for him, it wanted to manage things too cleverly. If it had only had the Semitic grip, digging the nails into the flesh to hold tight each separate coin, he would have been village rich. The great secret is the keeping. Finding is by no means keeping. Job did not flourish in his old days; the people changed round about. Job is gone, and I think every one of that cottage is either dead or moved. Empty.

The next cottage was the water-bailiff's, who looked after the great pond or 'broad.' There were one or two old boats, and he used to leave the oars leaning against

a wall at the side of the house. These oars looked like
fragments of a wreck, broken and irregular. The right-
hand scull was heavy, as if made of ironwood, the blade
broad and spoon-shaped, so as to have a most powerful
grip of the water. The left-hand scull was light and
slender, with a narrow blade like a marrow scoop; so
when you had the punt, you had to pull very hard with
your left hand and gently with the right to get the
forces equal. The punt had a list of its own, and no
matter how you rowed, it would still make leeway.
Those who did not know its character were perpetually
trying to get this crooked wake straight, and consequently went round and round exactly like the whirligig
beetle. Those who knew used to let the leeway proceed
a good way and then alter it, so as to act in the other
direction like an elongated zigzag. These sculls the old
fellow would bring you as if they were great treasures,
and watch you off in the punt as if he was parting with
his dearest. At that date it was no little matter to coax
him round to unchain his vessel. You had to take an
interest in the garden, in the baits, and the weather, and
be very humble; then perhaps he would tell you he did
not want it for the trimmers, or the withy, or the flags,
and you might have it for an hour as far as he could
see; 'did not think my lord's steward would come over
that morning; of course, if he did you must come in,'
and so on; and if the stars were propitious, by-and-by
the punt was got afloat. These sculls were tilted up
against the wall, and as you innocently went to take
one, Wauw!—a dirty little ill-tempered mongrel poodle
rolled himself like a ball to your heels and snapped his
teeth—Wauw! At the bark, out rushed the old lady,
his housekeeper, shouting in the shrillest key to the dog
to lie still, and to you that the bailiff would be there in

a minute. At the sound of her shrewish 'yang-yang' down came the old man from the bank, and so one dog fetched out the lot. The three were exactly alike somehow. Beside these diamond sculls he had a big gun, with which he used to shoot the kingfishers that came for the little fish ; the number he slaughtered was very great ; he persecuted them as Domitian did the flies : he declared that a kingfisher would carry off a fish heavier than itself. Also he shot rooks, once now and then strange wild fowl with this monstrous iron pipe, and something happened with this gun one evening which was witnessed, and after that the old fellow was very benevolent, and the punt was free to one or two who knew all about it. There is an old story about the stick that would not beat the dog, and the dog would not bite the pig, and so on ; and so I am quite sure that ill-natured cur could never have lived with that 'yang-yang' shrew, nor could any one else but he have turned the gear of the hatch, nor have endured the dog and the woman, and the constant miasma from the stagnant waters. No one else could have shot anything with that cumbrous weapon, and no one else could row that punt straight. He used to row it quite straight, to the amazement of a wondering world, and somehow supplied the motive force—the stick—which kept all these things going. He is gone, and, I think, the housekeeper too, and the house has had several occupants since, who have stamped down the old ghosts and thrust them out of doors.

After this the cottages and houses came in little groups, some up crooked lanes, hidden away by elms as if out of sight in a cupboard, and some dotted along the brooks, scattered so that, unless you had connected them all with a very long rope, no stranger could have told which belonged to the village and which did not. They drifted into various tithings, and yet it was all the same place. They were all thatched. It was a thatched village. This is strictly accurate and strictly inaccurate, for I think there were one or two tiled and one 'slated,' and perhaps a modern one slated. Nothing is ever quite rigid or complete that is of man ; all rules have a chip in them. The way they builded the older thatched farmhouses was to put up a very high wall in front and a very low one behind, and then the roof in a general way sloped down from the high wall to the low wall, an acre broad of thatch. These old thatched houses seemed to be very healthy so long as the old folk lived in them in the old-fashioned way. Thatch is believed to give an equable temperature. The air blew all round them, and it might be said all through them ; for the front door was always open three parts of the year, and at the back the dairies were in a continual blow. Upstairs the houses were only one room thick, so that each wall was an outside wall, or rather it was a wall one side and thatched the other, so that the wind went through if a window was open. Modern houses are often built two rooms thick, so that the air does not circulate from one side to the other. No one seemed to be ill, unless he brought it home with him from some place where he had been visiting. The diseases they used to have were long-lived, such as rheumatism, which may keep a man comfortably in aches and pains forty years. My dear old friend, however, taking them one by one, went through the lot and told me of the ghosts. The forefathers I knew are all gone—the stout man, the lame man, the paralysed man, the gruff old stick : not one left. There is not one left of the old farmers, not a single one. The fathers, too, of our own generation have been dropping away. The strong young man who used to fill us with such astonishment at the feats he would achieve without a thought, no gymnastic training, to whom a sack of wheat was a toy. The strong young man went one day into the harvest-field, as he had done so many times before. Suddenly he felt a little dizzy. By-and-by he went home and became very ill with sunstroke; he recovered, but he was never strong again; he gradually declined for twelve months, and next harvest-time he was under the daisies. Just one little touch of the sun, and the strength of man faded as a leaf. The hardy dark young man, built of iron, broad, thick, and short, who looked as if frost, snow, and heat were all the same to him, had something go wrong in his lung: one twelvemonth, and there was an end. This was a very unhappy affair. The pickaxe and the spade have made almost a full round to every door; I do not want to think any more about this. Family changes and the pressure of these hard times have driven out most of the rest; some seem to have quite gone out of sight; some have crossed the sea; some have abandoned the land as a livelihood. Of the few, the very few that still remain, still fewer abide in their original homes. Time has shuffled them about from house to house like a pack of cards. Of them all, I verily believe there is but one soul living in the same old house. If the French had landed in the mediæval way to harry with fire and sword, they could not have swept the place more clean.

Almost the first thing I did with pen and ink as a boy was to draw a map of the hamlet with the roads and lanes and paths, and I think some of the ponds, and with each of the houses marked and the occupier's name, Of course it was very roughly done, and not to any scale, yet it was perfectly accurate and full of detail. I wish I could find it, but the confusion of time has scattered and mixed these early papers. A map by Ptolemy would bear as much resemblance to the same country in a modern atlas as mine to the present state of that locality. It is all gone—rubbed out. The names against the whole of those houses have been altered, one only excepted, and changes have taken place there. Nothing remains. This is not in a century, half a century, or even in a quarter of a century, but in a few ticks of the clock.

I think I have heard that the oaks are down. They may be standing or down, it matters nothing to me; the leaves I last saw upon them are gone for evermore, nor shall I ever see them come there again ruddy in spring. I would not see them again even if I could; they could never look again as they used to do. There are too many memories there. The happiest days become the saddest afterwards; let us never go back, lest we too die. There are no such oaks anywhere else, none so tall and straight, and with such massive heads, on which the sun used to shine as if on the globe of the earth, one side in shadow, the other in bright light. How often I have looked at oaks since, and yet have never been able to get the same effect from them! Like an old author printed in another type, the words are the same, but the sentiment is different. The brooks have ceased to run. There is no music now at the old hatch where we used to sit in danger of our lives, happy as kings, on the narrow bar over the deep water. The barred pike that used to come up in such numbers are no more among the flags. The perch used to drift down the stream, and then bring up again. The sun shone there for a very long time, and the water rippled and sang, and it always seemed to me that I could feel the rippling and the singing and the sparkling back through the centuries. The brook is dead, for when man goes nature ends. I dare say there is water there still, but it is not the brook; the brook is gone like John Brown's soul. There used to be clouds over the fields, white clouds in blue summer skies. I have lived a good deal on clouds; they have been meat to me often; they bring something to the spirit which even the trees do not. I see clouds now sometimes when the iron grip of hell permits for a minute or two; they are very different clouds, and speak differently. I long for some of the old clouds that had no memories. There were nights in those times over those fields, not darkness, but Night, full of glowing suns and glowing richness of life that sprang up to meet them. The nights are there still; they are everywhere, nothing local in the night; but it is not the Night to me seen through the window.

There used to be footpaths. Following one of them the first field always had a good crop of grass; over the next stile there was a great oak standing alone in the centre of the field, generally a great cart-horse under it, and a few rushes scattered about the furrows; the fourth was always full of the finest clover; in the fifth you could scent the beans on the hill, and there was a hedge like a wood, and a nest of the long-tailed tit; the sixth had a runnel and blue forget-me-nots; the seventh had a brooklet and scattered trees along it; from the eighth you looked back on the slope and saw the thatched houses you had left behind under passing shadows, and rounded white clouds going straight for the distant hills, each cloud visibly bulging and bowed down like a bag. I cannot think how the distant thatched houses came to stand out with such clear definition and etched outline and bluish shadows ; and beyond these was the uncertain vale that had no individuality, but the trees put their arms together and became one.   All these were meadows, every step was among grass, beautiful grass, and the cuckoos sang as if they had found paradise.   A hundred years ago a little old man with silver buckles on his shoes used to walk along this footpath once a week in summer, taking his children over to drink milk at the farm ; but though he set them every time to note the number of fields, so busy were they with the nests and the flowers, they could never be sure at the end of the journey whether there were eight or nine.   To make quite sure at last, he took with them a pocket full of apples, one of which was eaten in each field, and so they came to know for certain that the number of meadows was either eight or nine, I forget which ; and so you see this great experiment did not fix the faith of mankind. Like other great truths, it has grown dim, but it seems strange to think how this little incident could have been borne in mind for a century.   There was another footpath that led through the peewit field, where the green plovers for evermore circle round in spring ; then past the nightingale field, by the largest maple trees that grew in that country ; this too was all grass.   Another led along the water to bluebell land ; another into the coombs of the hills ; all meadows, which was the beauty of it ; for though you could find wheat in plenty if you liked, you always walked in grass.   All round the compass you could still step on sward.   This is rare.   Of one other path I have a faded memory, like a silk marker in an old book ; in truth, I don't want to remember it except the end of it where it came down to the railway. So full was the mind of romance in those days, that I used to get there specially in time to see the express go

up, the magnificent engine of the broad gauge that swept
along with such ease and power to London. I wish I
could feel like that now. The feeling is not quite gone
even now, and I have often since seen these great broad-
gauge creatures moving alive to and fro like Ezekiel's
wheel dream beside the platforms of Babylon with much
of the same old delight. Still I never went back with
them to the faded footpath. They are all faded now,
these footpaths.

The walnut trees are dead at home. They gave such
a thick shade when the fruit was juicy ripe, and the hoods
cracked as they fell; they peeled as easy as taking off a
glove; the sweetest and nuttiest of fruit. It was delicious
to sit there with a great volume of Sir Walter Scott,
half in sunshine, half in shade, dreaming of 'Kenilworth'
and Wayland Smith's cave; only the difficulty was to
balance the luxuries, when to peel the walnuts and when
to read the book, and how to adjust oneself to perfection
so as to get the exact amount of sunshine and shadow.
Too much luxury. There was a story, too, told by one Abu-
Kaka ibn Ja'is, of the caravan that set forth in 1483 to
cross the desert, and being overwhelmed by a sandstorm,
lost their way. They wandered for some time till hunger and thirst began to consume them, and then suddenly
lit on an oasis unknown to the oldest merchant of
Bagdad. There they found refreshing waters and palms
and a caravanserai; and, what was most pleasant, the
people at the bazaar and the prince hastened to fill them
with hospitality; sheep were killed, and kids were roasted,
and all was joy. They were not permitted to depart
till they had feasted, when they set out again on their
journey, and each at leaving was presented with strings
of pearls and bags of rubies, so that at last they came
home with all the magnificence of kings. They found,

however, that instead of having been absent only a month or two they had been gone twenty years, so swiftly had time sped. As they grew old, and their beards grey, and their frames withered, and the pearls were gone, and the rubies spent, they said, 'We will go back to the city of the oasis.' They set out, each on his camel, one lame, the other paralytic, and the third blind, but still the way was plain, for had they not trodden it before? and they had with them the astrolabe of the astronomer that fixes the track by the stars. Time wore on, and presently the camels' feet brought them nearer and nearer the wished-for spot. One saw the water, and another the palms, but when they came near, it was the mirage, and deep sand covered the place. Then they separated, and each hastened home; but the blind had no leader, and the lame fell from his camel, and the paralytic had no more dates, and their whited bones have disappeared.[1] Many another tale, too, I read under the trees that are gone like human beings. Sometimes I went forth to the nooks in the deep meadows by the hazel mounds, and sometimes I parted the ash-tree wands. In my waistcoat pocket I had a little red book, made square; I never read it out of doors, but I always carried it in my pocket till it was frayed and the binding broken; the smallest of red books, but very much therein—the poems and sonnets of Mr. William Shakespeare. Some

---

[1] The Arabian commentator thinks this story a myth: the oasis in the desert is the time of youth, which passes so quickly, and is not recognised till it is gone; the pearls and rubies, the joys of love, which make the fortunate lover as a king. In old age every man is afflicted with disease or infirmity, every one is paralytic, lame, or blind. They set out to find a second youth—the dream of immortality—with the astrolabe, which is the creed or Koran all take as their guide. And death separated the company. This is only his pragmatic way; the circumstance is doubtless historic.

books are alive. The book I have still, it cannot die; the ash copses are cut, and the hazel mounds destroyed.

Was every one, then, so pleasant to me in those days? were the people all so beneficent and kindly that I must needs look back; all welcoming with open hand and open door? No, the reverse; there was not a single one friendly to me. Still that has nothing to do with it; I never thought about them, and I am quite certain they never thought about me. They are all gone, and there is an end. Incompatibility would describe our connection best. Nothing to do with them at all; it was me. I planted myself everywhere—in all the fields and under all the trees. The curious part of it is that though they are all dead, and 'worms have eaten them, but not for love,' we continually meet them in other shapes. We say, 'Holloa, here is old So-and-so coming; that is exactly his jaw, that's his Flemish face;' or, 'By Jove, yonder is So-and-so; that's his very walk:' one almost expects them to speak as one meets them in the street. There seem to be certain set types which continually crop up again whithersoever you go, and even certain tricks of speech and curves of the head—a set of family portraits walking about the world. It was not the people, neither for good, for evil, nor indifference.

I planted myself everywhere under the trees in the fields and footpaths, by day and by night, and that is why I have never put myself into the charge of the many wheeled creatures that move on the rails and gone back thither, lest I might find the trees look small, and the elms mere switches, and the fields shrunken, and the brooks dry, and no voice anywhere. Nothing but my own ghost to meet me by every hedge. I fear lest I should find myself more dead than all the rest. And verily I wish, could it be without injury to others, that the sand of the desert would rise and roll over and obliterate the place for ever and ever.

I need not wish, for I have been conversing again with learned folk about this place, and they begin to draw my view to certain considerations. These very learned men point out to me a number of objections, for the question they sceptically put is this : are you quite certain that such a village ever existed ? In the first place, they say, you have only got one other witness beside yourself, and she is aged, and has defective sight ; and really we don't know what to say to accepting such evidence unsupported. Secondly, John Brown cannot be found to bear testimony. Thirdly, there are no ghosts there ; that can be demonstrated. It renders a case unsubstantial to introduce these flimsy spirits. Fourthly, the map is lost, and it might be asked was there ever such a map ? Fifthly, the people are all gone. Sixthly, no one ever saw any particular sparkle on the brook there, and the clouds appear to be of the same commonplace order that go about everywhere. Seventhly, no one can find these footpaths, which probably led nowhere ; and as for the little old man with silver buckles on his shoes, it is a story only fit for some one in his dotage. You can't expect grave and considerate men to take your story as it stands ; they must consult the Ordnance Survey and Domesday Book ; and the fact is, you have not got the shadow of a foundation on which to carry your case into court. I may resent this, but I cannot deny that the argument is very black against me, and I begin to think that my senses have deceived me. It is as they say. No one else seems to have seen the sparkle on the brook, or heard the music at the hatch, or to have felt back through the centuries ; and when I try to describe these things to them they look at me with stolid incredulity. No one seems to understand how I got food from the clouds, nor what there was in the night, nor why it is not so good to look at it out of window. They turn their faces away from me, so that perhaps after all I was mistaken, and there never was any such place or any such meadows, and I was never there. And perhaps in course of time I shall find out also, when I pass away physically, that as a matter of fact there never was any earth.